D1600176

Poverty, Migration, and Settlement
in the Industrial Revolution

Thomas Rowlandson, "Rural Landscape with a Church on a Hill," detail, early nineteenth century (Henry E. Huntington Library and Art Gallery)

Poverty, Migration, and Settlement in the Industrial Revolution
Sojourners' Narratives

JAMES STEPHEN TAYLOR

The Society for the Promotion of
Science and Scholarship
Palo Alto, California
1989

The Society for the Promotion of
Science and Scholarship, Inc.
Palo Alto, California
© 1989 by James Stephen Taylor
Printed in the United States of America

The Society for the Promotion of Science and Scholarship is a
nonprofit corporation established for the purposes of scholarly
publishing; it has special interests in British and European studies.

Library of Congress Cataloging-in-Publication Data

Taylor, James Stephen.
Poverty, migration, and settlement in the Industrial Revolution.
Bibliography: p.
Includes index.
1. Poor laws—Great Britain—History.   2. Domicile in
public welfare—Great Britain—History.   3. Poor—Great
Britain—History.   4. Migration, Internal—Great Britain
—History.   I. Title.
KD3311.T39   1989   344.42'0325   89-60546
ISBN 0-930664-09-4   344.204325

To Marie

Acknowledgments

I AM GRATEFUL to many archivists and librarians for courtesy, assistance, and commentary, especially Michael Dickinson, Senior Assistant Archivist of the Devon Record Office, Sheila MacPherson, Cumbria County Archivist, Joan Sinar, Derbyshire County Archivist, and Margaret Cash, former County Archivist of Hampshire, all of whom I first met during the historically cold winter of 1962–63 at The Castle, Exeter, where the county record office was then located. I also thank Margery Rowe, current Devon County Archivist, who was Archivist of the Exeter City Library when I first explored Devon records in 1962, and Peter Kennedy, former Devon County Archivist.

I benefited from the opportunity to develop my understanding of pauper settlement under the pre-1834 poor law, first through a paper the late Dr. A. H. John invited me to give at the Institute of Historical Research, London, in 1972, then through a much-revised essay for *Past & Present* in 1976, and finally through a paper given for the Pacific Coast Conference on British Studies at Asilomar in 1984. Dr. Michael E. Rose, Professor Richard N. Chapman, Professor Roger Manning, and Mr. Brett Harrison offered encouragement and counsel at crucial stages. To Dr. Richard Lyman, my doctoral dissertation advisor, I owe a special debt for his interest in my work over many years.

The American Philosophical Society gave me a grant-in-aid in 1977 for study of the settlement papers of Kenton in Devon and Kirkby Lonsdale in Westmorland. This book is not exactly along the lines of my original grant proposal, but I hope they will accept this modification and my warmest thanks. I am also indebted to Wells College for summer grants, to Cornell University's Society for the Humanities for a summer fellowship in

1984, and to the National Endowment for the Humanities for a summer stipend in 1987.

For permission to quote from documents, I am grateful to the London Borough of Camden, Local History Library, and the Liberty of Saffron Hill; the Rev. Graham W. Bettridge, Rector of Kirkby Lonsdale; the Cumbria County Council, Archives Department; Lady Margaret Fortescue; the Devon Record Office, and the parishes of Bishops Tawton, Blackawton, Cheriton Bishop, East Budleigh, Kenton, Membury, Modbury, Sampford Courtenay, Sampford Peverell, Shebbear, Sidmouth, South Molton, Totnes, Ugborough, Warkleigh, and West Alvington; the Greater London Record Office, and the parishes of St. George, Southwark, St. Leonard, Shoreditch, St. Luke, Chelsea (London Records), Friern Barnet, Great Stanmore, and Harrow-on-the-Hill (Middlesex Records); the Guildhall Library of the City of London, and the parishes of St. Ethelburga, Bishopsgate, St. Faith, under St. Paul's, St. Helen, Bishopsgate, St. Martin, Ludgate, St. Martin, Vintry, St. Mary, Aldermary, and St. Mildred, Poultry; and the Westminster City Library, Archives Section, and the parishes of St. Mary-le-Strand and St. Martin-in-the-Fields. I thank the Devon parishes of Ilsington and Marystow for the use of their records, without quotations.

I am also grateful to the trustees of the British Museum for permission to reproduce the watercolor painting by Samuel Bough, "View of a Manufacturing Town," and to the Henry E. Huntington Library and Art Gallery for permission to reproduce Thomas Rowlandson's watercolor painting entitled "Rural Landscape with a Church on a Hill." I am particularly grateful to Mrs. Claire R. Morehouse for preparing the five sketch maps for the book. The librarians of Wells College deserve, as ever, my heartfelt thanks.

No words can express my debt to Laura, Mark, and Amy, my three children, and to Marie, my wife, to whom this book is rightfully dedicated. She transcribed, proofread, and provided that measure of criticism and support beyond the capacity of a printed acknowledgment to express.

I recall a moment in the office of Dr. John in Houghton Street one early evening shortly after Michaelmas, 1956, when he suggested that my first tutorial paper might focus on the social im-

pact of the Industrial Revolution as revealed in local records at
the Guildhall Library, London. I do not recall the precise references he gave me, but remember how the warmth of his interest
in the topic, and in a new L.S.E. student, stayed with me on my
return through amber light and mist to Torrington Square.

Wells College   J.S.T.
Aurora, New York
May 1989

Contents

Poverty, Migration, and Settlement
in the Industrial Revolution

Introduction

NINETY-SEVEN ENCOUNTERS with the poor law are used here to illustrate the human condition and the ways in which settlement laws influenced social welfare, regulated migration, and enhanced industrial development. The aim is to use case histories, in themselves interesting, as a vehicle for analyzing an institution and thus to contribute a new perspective on poverty, migration, and settlement in the Industrial Revolution.

Although close examination of specific events in the lives of ordinary people as a means of addressing large questions is an approach that owes much to the *Annales* school and to work emanating from such universities as Cambridge and Princeton, my approach is not quantitative or anthropological, for the evidence is fragmentary and geographically diffused and the nature of the settlement laws is so ill-understood that another approach seemed in order. My greatest debt is to the pre-1834 casebooks that parish officers and magistrates used to apply settlement laws and to the documents themselves, from which much may be inferred.

The Law of Settlement, as the relevant laws and judicial decisions are sometimes called, was arguably the most important branch of pre-1834 English law, if judged by the number of lives directly affected and of lawyers' hours expended. Richard Burn, author of the standard manual on local government of the time, *The Justice of the Peace and Parish Officer*, wrote that more cases had been adjudged under the 1662 Settlement Act "than upon any other act in the statute book." In fact, it was not just the one act but a corpus having to do with settlement that occupied the lawyers.

Remarkably, there is no modern exposition of the pre-1834

settlement laws; nor does any book consider their significance. Only K.D.M. Snell, in *Annals of the Labouring Poor: Social Change and Agrarian England, 1660–1900* (London, 1985), makes effective use of settlement records, but he does not focus on the laws or their impact on British (not simply English) society. Pervasive ignorance, examples of which appear in the conclusion, has led to general neglect and a consequent misreading of key aspects of the poor law and of Britain's path to industrial development.

On one level this is a "documents" book and may be used with profit on that level alone; none of the documents have hitherto been published, and they derive from collections not readily accessible. But the larger purpose is to use the documents as the clearest and most effective vehicle for interpreting the operation and significance of a complex and important branch of law.

The records on which the book are based are drawn from three locations: greater London, Devon, and the southeastern Westmorland township of Kirkby Lonsdale.

London attracted migrants—the sojourners—from all over the British Isles and beyond; metropolitan parishes did what they could to send the least welcome of them home. The resulting letters, petitions, examinations, and depositions are often extremely illuminating in their detail, although for most London parishes little or nothing has survived fires, bombs, and housecleanings. Destruction of settlement records inhibits statistical analysis, for London as elsewhere, but enough documents survive to indicate the sorts of people who found their way to London and, with the help of parish officers, their way home again. The evidence is most valuable for St. Martin, Vintry, which deserves, and receives, a separate chapter.

Devon, the largest of English counties for administrative purposes, had a diverse community and economic structure. Arable and pastoral farming, fishing, weaving, mining, shipping, supplying the Navy, tourism, and all manner of entrepreneurial activities went on there. But no county is a microcosm of England. Devon, for all its diversity, belonged in the main to an older England that suffered a diminution of its economic importance during the Industrial Revolution because of developments elsewhere. Paternal attitudes toward the poor prevailed in many parts of Devon well into the nineteenth century, and a less

Sojourners' Routes

professional thoroughness in cleaning house has led to the survival of more settlement papers in this county than perhaps in any other. Devon, like London, attracted migrants, drawn by its relative wealth and warmth and by employment opportunities, especially in and around Plymouth and the Exe Estuary.

Kirkby Lonsdale provides an element missing from London and Devon, through an exceptional collection of extant letters from paupers, their friends, and parish officers, written between 1809 and 1836, by or about persons legally settled in the township, yet sojourning elsewhere, many of them in the industrial areas of the West Riding and Lancashire. Historians do well to avoid the word *unique*, yet I know of no comparable collection, and I have looked for them.

Altogether, I have selected nearly a hundred cases, ranging in time from 1709 to 1857. About a third date from before Waterloo, another third are from the decade after, and the final third concentrate mainly on the years just before the 1834 Poor Law Amendment Act. In editing the documents I omitted preliminary and concluding legal phraseology, and modernized paragraphing, spelling, capitalization, and punctuation. Occasionally a document has been pruned of repetitive passages and details irrelevant to both the law and the experiences of examinees and petitioners. However, the choice of words and the syntax are unaltered. Proper names, underlined words, and abbreviations are also given without change, except in the case of St. Martin, Vintry, where the parish clerk abbreviated beyond what a twentieth-century reader could be expected to endure. I have not attempted to eliminate all errors and inconsistencies where clarity was not in question, for that would sacrifice color for a marginal gain in form. Of course, there are bound to be errors of my own in attempting to interpret something as complex as the Law of Settlement, and I hope that readers will charitably bring these to my attention. The Notes are intended primarily for the student of the period, but the text may be taken without the qualifications and details provided there.

History never speaks for itself. Behind every decision to select, order, edit, and comment is the historian, with his or her judgment of significance. There are few topics on which it is more difficult to achieve impartiality than the social history of the Industrial Revolution. Yet I have tried to present as clearly and objectively as possible the varieties of human experience found among the records of the sojourners, while showing how a particular settlement case, however unusual the specific circumstances may be, can generally illuminate the lives and settlements of the poor in the eighteenth and early nineteenth centuries. A few cases concern the settled poor, but these are designed to highlight the contrasts between the settled and the sojourning poor; indeed, most individuals inevitably knew both conditions at one time or another in their life.

The chapter organization reflects those topics best covered in the records of settlement; some overlap was unavoidable, since a poor person's life, though especially enlightening for one topic, may cut across others. At bottom, I have tried to defer to my source material, which, as Emmanuel Le Roy Ladurie found, imposes "its own rhythms, its own chronology, and its own particular truth." Within each chapter, the ordering is usually chronological. Chapter One, the major exception to that ordering, is, I fear, burdened with extensive commentary to explain the principal features of the Law of Settlement, necessary to a better understanding of what follows.

Grains of sand occasionally adhere to a settlement document, grains scattered long ago to dry the ink. Here, on a table of a modern county record office, lies a document containing part of the story of an individual who may seem to have been of little historical consequence. Yet the document contains part of the record of a single life that once had immeasurable importance to a few, and may still, in and by itself, have significance to the historian. Grains of sand—there are so many of them—yet each with its own integrity, none without meaning.

ONE

The Law

We are not to argue from the letter of the
law, but from the practice under it.
—William Bodkin, 1821 [1]

FROM THE LAST YEARS of the sixteenth century, English and
Welsh paupers were legally entitled to a basic maintenance under
the provisions of the poor law. "For there is no man so indigent
or wretched, but he may demand a supply sufficient for all the
necessities of life, from the more opulent part of the community," William Blackstone wrote, expressing the legal right of the
poor if not always the actual treatment they received.[2] National
in scope, secular in administration, comprehensive in needs addressed, and supported by compulsory rates, the Elizabethan
poor law's other fundamental characteristic until 1834 was that
relief was parochially funded and administered.[3] Each parish
was responsible for its own poor, even though it was exceptional
for a person to live a life entirely within the bounds of a single
parish.

Sojourner was the word used in documents to define the person living away from his parish of settlement, meaning that place
in which he or she had a right to receive continuous assistance in
time of unemployment, sickness, disability, and age. This home
parish was determined by a variety of related factors, such as
parentage and employment experience, until well into Victoria's
reign. These factors were spelled out by a complex set of statutes
and judicial decisions collectively known as the Law of Settlement. Modifying the law were the paternalistic values of the
administrators, as well as the initiatives of the sojourners themselves.

The approach of this book is remarkably simple, yet hitherto
untried—to present case histories of sojourners during the Industrial Revolution from original documents in parish collections, with sufficient commentary to explain how the poor law

worked. To be sure, this method was employed in the legal treatises of the time to help parish officers and magistrates apply
settlement laws to particular circumstances, but a selective use of
the microscope may also have value for the social historian wishing to understand the intricate relationship between the poor
and the poor law and the influence of that relationship on migration and much else. We start, then, with the individual, but
interpret each case in order to address the large questions. There
is human interest in the stories that follow—they are worth reading for that reason alone—but this collection of cases provides
a means to understand hitherto neglected or misunderstood aspects of the world's first industrial revolution.

We begin with four settlement examinations from Devon parishes. Together they serve to introduce the principal features of
the Law of Settlement.

* * *

2 May 1829

Harriet Williams, the widow of James Williams, was born in the
parish of St. Thomas, Exeter, where her father resided as a dairyman.
She married James Williams, a servantman, in the parish church of
St. Thomas. He was a native of South Bedder [South Petherwin], near
Launceston in Cornwall. Her husband went to live as a servant with
Colonel Parker of the Artillery and was killed in June of 1815 at the
Battle of Waterloo.

After the death of her husband she went to live with Mrs. Parker,
the wife of her late husband's master, and lived with her as a yearly
servant eleven years, and then left on account of her mistress dying.
Mrs. Parker, during the time she served her, lived in Grosvenor Square
in the parish of St. George, Hanover Square, London. When she quitted
Mrs. Parker's service, she took two rooms in the same parish near the
White Horse Cellars at 6/6 a week, and lived in them two years. And
left them about a week since on account of ill health, and came to Exeter
by Russell's Wagon, for the purpose of visiting her uncle, Mr. Joseph
Smith, a dairyman residing at Exmouth.

She applied to Mr. Bidwill, Exeter, for relief, but did not receive any.
He put her into a car and ordered her to be put down when out of the
parish. She was put down by the side of a hedge, very ill. Farmer Pooke
of Exminster came to her, took her by the arm, and helped her to walk
past the arch, and then left her in Powderham parish. A gentleman in

a gig passing by took her up, and brought her on some way, and put her down when she fainted, and was found by two laboring men, who borrowed a chair and brought her to the Dolphin Inn, Kenton.

Harriet Williams
Kenton, Devon[4]

There she told her story to an unknown clerk, presumably employed by the parish, but no magistrate was summoned, no formal settlement examination was taken, and no resort was made to Kenton's legal rights when Kenton was suddenly confronted with a sick sojourner. She may have been given food and drink at the Dolphin Inn by those who heard her story, and perhaps arrangements were made to ferry her across the Exe Estuary to her uncle at Exmouth, but all that is known is that Kenton gave her 5/6. Thereafter she disappears from record.

Her case is an interesting illustration of the Law of Settlement. A Devonian born and bred in a parish on the western edge of Exeter, she married a Cornishman, and by so doing lost her settlement in St. Thomas, assuming she was a legitimate child of parents who were settled there. She became instead a potential charge to a Cornish parish she most probably had never seen, for wives assumed their husbands' settlements. But South Petherwin was spared the welfare obligation, for after her husband died at Waterloo, Williams was taken into yearly service by Mrs. Parker; a full year's service to the same employer by an unmarried or widowed person without dependents (at the time of the contract) entitled a servant to a settlement in the parish where he or she had completed that service. Williams had still another claim on St. George, Hanover Square, for she had paid a good rent for her rooms near the White Horse Cellars, and a weekly rental that over the course of a year would total £10 or more also brought settlement at the time her story was recorded, if occupancy had been for at least one year, and Williams had lived there for two. But a large and populous urban parish was likely to offer cold comfort to a sick widow living in rented rooms. She therefore decided to visit her uncle in Exmouth, perhaps thinking that the sea air would do her good.

There is much left unsaid in the record taken down at the Dolphin Inn: Harriet Williams's age, the nature of her illness, the

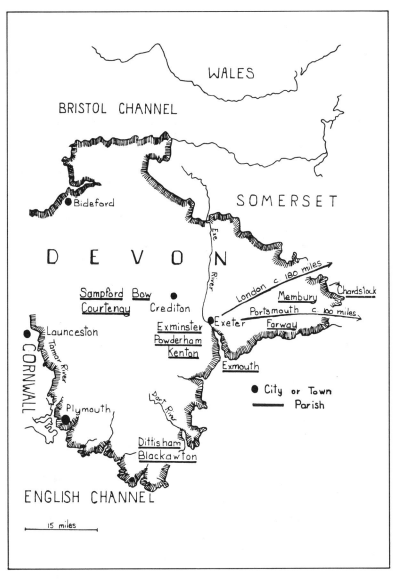

Devon: Places Named in Chapter One

extent of her material resources (if any), whether she had been inveigled into taking Russell's Wagon by a parish officer of St. George, who may have funded the trip in the hope of saving his parish the necessity of pensioning her—a common tactic among London officers. Whatever the reason, she lumbered some 200 miles through southern England, enduring a week of uncomfortable travel, to arrive in Exeter in need of immediate attention.

Unfortunately for her, welfare in St. Thomas, the parish of her birth, was then managed by Joseph Bidwill, an efficient and thoroughly professional man. Only the previous year a pamphlet had extolled St. Thomas as a model in its provision for the poor (with a workhouse regimen that foreshadowed the reforms of 1834).[5] Yet Williams's settlement was no longer in St. Thomas. Bidwill had to do something about her, if not for her, for himself, because if she had died in his parish after being denied relief it would have been legally troublesome to him. Since invoking settlement law would cost time and money, he had her carted into an adjoining parish.

There Farmer Pooke found her, took her by the arm, and helped her walk the two miles across Exminster parish to Powderham. Perhaps he was motivated by the thought that he was sending her in the direction of Exmouth, which was where she wished to go, but he must surely have thought he was "saving his parish harmless" by getting her out of Exminster. Once in Powderham she must have recovered enough to have a gentleman offer her a ride in his gig, given that it was the sort of gentleman who would choose to abandon a fainting woman by the roadside. And so it was left to two laboring men to bring her to the Dolphin Inn.

There is one unassailable generalization about the local operation of the pre-1834 poor law, and that is that parish authorities conformed to no one model. On the last page of the Poor Book of Gamlingay, Cambridgeshire, dated 1701, are the following lines: "I said in my hast all men are lyers / I was naked and ye clothed me not / The poor you have with you allways." Humane scriptural reminders, and there was probably even more humanity in Harriet Williams's day than when those lines were transcribed,[6] but there were also the likes of Mr. Bidwill and Farmer Pooke. Kenton represented no extreme of charity. A relatively populous and prosperous parish, bordering the Exe Estuary and traversed by a well-traveled road from Exeter to Teignmouth and the south Devon coast, Kenton had more than its share of sojourners.

Kenton's parish officers had three options in the treatment of Williams. First, they could have followed the Bidwill-Pooke precedents and had her dumped in Dawlish, the next parish on her way to Exmouth. Yet even a parish officer devoid of humane impulses might shrink from Bidwill's solution, if only to avoid retaliation from neighboring parishes. Bidwill had, in fact, committed an indictable offense; if Williams had died at that stage in her journey, Bidwill could have faced a charge of murder. The possibility of an indictment was, however, too remote to inhibit parish officers in such matters; retaliation in kind was a much more tangible constraint, reinforced no doubt in many cases by moral constraints as well.

Second, Kenton could have invoked the Law of Settlement. This required that the magistrates hear her sworn testimony in order to determine her parish of settlement. Meanwhile, Kenton would have been obliged to pay for all her immediate expenses. After the examination, a removal order would have been prepared so that she could be transported legally to her parish of settlement, presumably St. George, Hanover Square, if her story at the inn were true and complete. However, she was ill, and since 1795 the law had required that the removal order must be suspended in such circumstances. Kenton could then have written to St. George, demanding support for Williams during her illness, but recovery of full costs was unlikely. Moreover, there was always the risk that St. George would deny responsibility for Williams, which would have thrown the case into litigation, thus opening the door to incalculable expense. At best, Kenton would have had the trouble of her care and some portion of her costs, including the expensive business of helping her return to London when she had recovered. Sarah Charlton and her son were conveyed from Farway in eastern Devon to Crondall in Hampshire in 1827, about half the distance of a Kenton–London removal, at a cost to Farway of £6.12.2.[7] Whatever the outcome, if Kenton had invoked the law, trouble and cost would surely have followed.

There was a third option, a middle ground, both humane in a

limited sense, and economical: to give Williams casual relief in
the form of immediate care, a few shillings, and perhaps transportation across the Exe Estuary to Exmouth. Only the likelihood
of her long-term dependency in Kenton would have financially
justified recourse to the Law of Settlement. This third option
was far and away the least troublesome way to deal with a sojourner in need, and Kenton regularly resorted to it, as did other
parishes, as the safe, cheap, conscience-salving option; yet it
is rare to find it recorded, for it entailed no formal examination, no removal order, no litigation, and few costs. Williams's
story survives because Kenton's records, even the most ephemeral scraps of paper on settlement problems, have survived,
an exceptional circumstance. They constitute perhaps the full-
est record of settlement of any parish in England. Without that
anonymous account of her travels and travails, the only evidence
in Kenton of this sojourner would have been the uninterpretable
entry in the overseers' account book: "Harriet Williams 5/6."

There was nothing unusual about her trip from London to
Devon. Migration was, in Peter Clark's words, "the social and
demographic norm," with London functioning "as an enormous
pair of revolving doors, pulling migrants in one side and pushing
those that survived its disease-stricken world out on the other."[8]
On a still broader canvas, Charles Tilly wrote: "The history of
European migration is the history of European social life."[9] Sojourners were in fact the great majority of the poor, and the
"poor" were the great majority of the population. Not many sojourners traveled frequently or far, and not all the poor ever
received poor relief, but at some time in most lives that were
vulnerable to need migration occurred. Usually no record marks
the passage. Like soft-bodied creatures of the Paleozoic era that
left little trace in the fossil record, the poor who did not come to
the formal attention of the law left little or no evidence of their
time on earth.

Settlement records contain excellent evidence of migration, yet
only fragments remain, and generally the more formal and least
informative ones at that, such as removal orders. No quantitative
study of extant settlement records could begin to measure the
extent of migration or the impact of the Law of Settlement on the
movements of the poor, for the law ignored the poor who moved
without triggering its cumbersome machinery. Yet the poor who

moved, as well as those who stayed home, must be assumed to have possessed some interest in guarding a favored settlement or finding a favorable parish in which to establish one, and in avoiding painful removal. All that is required for that assumption is the belief that most of the poor had at least an elementary instinct for self-preservation. A second key assumption is that parish officers usually opted for the least expensive and least troublesome option open to them. This was as true then as it is now—always allowing for the unusual official who takes satisfaction in doing good or being perverse or promoting a cause. Certainly the stories that follow support these assumptions. Harriet Williams's movements, like the movements of others near the poverty line, were moderated by the Law of Settlement, whether the law was formally invoked or influenced mental calculations —hers and those of parish officers. If each parish had been responsible for granting her relief, or if none had, her story would have been different.

*   *   *

27 November 1822

About twenty years since at Crediton [Devon] this deponent, James Fewings, became acquainted with Sally Golsworth, who traveled the country selling handkerchiefs—that this deponent at that time was accustomed to travel the country purchasing skins and rags and selling them to manufacturers—that this deponent and the said Sally Golsworth agreed to travel together, and from that period they did so until the death of the said Sally Golsworth, cohabiting as man and wife.

About eighteen months or two years after their first acquaintance Sally was delivered at Bow [Devon] of William Golsworth, alias Fewings, and that this deponent considered himself to be father of the said child, and acknowledged him as such. About two years afterwards Sally was delivered of another child in the town of Bideford [Devon], James Golsworth, alias Fewings. This deponent considered and acknowledged it to be his child—but Sally and he were never married. She died at Bow about two years ago. She was a native of Wales. James continued to travel with his mother, and this deponent until his mother's death, but William left them when he was about eleven years old, and ran the country with a blind fiddler.

James Fewings
Sampford Courtenay, Devon

A Devon peddler during the Napoleonic wars, Fewings had managed to establish a settlement in the parish of Sampford Courtenay, which is why in this story there is nothing about his history before he met Sally Golsworth. It was the settlements of his sons that concerned the authorities. The father's deposition established that they were both illegitimate. Since a bastard usually took the parish of his birth for a first settlement,[10] it appears the older boy, William, belonged to Bow, a few miles east of Sampford Courtenay, whereas the younger boy, James, belonged to Bideford, twenty miles to the northeast. If the boys had been under the age of seven, they could not have been removed from their mother, but William and James were then motherless, and in any case old enough to be removed or threatened with the prospect.

Sampford Courtenay was fortunate to have such a clear account of things, for a grown bastard's settlement could be difficult to identify, since illegitimate births often occurred in mean streets among inhabitants who did not necessarily seek to have the event recorded in the parish register of baptisms. There might thus be opportunity for the presumed parish of birth to foreswear settlement of a child others claimed was theirs. When a parish did accept responsibility, the circumstances were likely to result in harsh care, grudgingly given. Even before delivery of the child, the woman might be hustled out of one parish into another in the manner of Bidwill's treatment of Williams. The Law of Settlement was cruel to unmarried pregnant women sojourning out of their home parish; by attaching settlement to birth, parishes had an incentive to move such women on. Moreover, the shame associated with illegitimacy ensured that many women would leave their parish of settlement, becoming unwelcome sojourners wherever they went. These were the cases in which a prudent parish *would* conduct a formal examination to acquire a removal order, which is why the examinations give a distorted view of the number of unmarried pregnant sojourners.

The Fewings case, in short, is a common one with regard to what was at issue in determining the children's settlements, but what was less usual was the parents' occupation. There were peddlers aplenty in England at that time, but they were more likely to fall under the vagrancy laws, which were harsher than the Law of Settlement. The masterless stranger who was poor and intentionally traveling, and who was not apparently on his way to or from service, was held in deep suspicion, especially if he were far from home. It had always been so.[11] It still is.

* * *

27 February 1709

This examinant saith that he was born within the parish of Chardstock, Dorset, and there lived until he attained the age of about ten years, at which time, his father dying, he went to Membury, Devon, where he lived with his uncle, Thomas Pennington, a farmer, for about four years, and received of him meat, drink, clothes and washing, lodging, and other necessaries, but no wages in money. Then this examinant's said uncle left off renting, so he had no more employment for this examinant.

Then he went to William Smith of Membury, with whom he continued about five years, receiving meat, drink, washing and lodging, and wages to the value of about 50/ per annum. Toward the end of the five years he received wages to the value of £4.7 per annum, but he did not receive his wages yearly or quarterly, but had them at any time when he had occasion for the same. He made no covenant by the year with Smith, for Smith was unwilling to make him an inhabitant of Membury.

He left Smith's service about six years ago, and married Elizabeth, by whom he has two children, John and Mary, and he has remained in Chardstock ever since his marriage, but never rented any estate nor served in any public and annual office, nor paid any public tax or otherwise acquired a legal settlement there. He has a single cottage on the waste in Chardstock, built by his father about twenty-five years since, but he has no copy loan or other assurance.

John Keate
Chardstock, Dorset

This examination was taken in 1709, which makes it an extremely early one, for the full flowering of the Law of Settlement occurred in the late eighteenth and early nineteenth centuries. Otherwise, the story has representative elements to it. John Keate's life was chiefly remarkable for its uneventfulness, which is the norm among settlement examinees (*examinant* is the word employed in local records; the word has a double meaning, the examiner or the examinee, but the second meaning applies for all cases quoted in this book). He had migrated between two counties, to be sure, but the parishes border one another, and Chardstock has since been joined to Devon. The presiding magistrate, John Tucker, knew the right questions to ask this agricultural laborer, but posed them with a thoroughness suggesting conscientiousness rather than familiarity with the Law of Settlement. William Smith, the farmer who Keate had served for five years, was aware of the law, for he did not wish Keate to earn his settlement in Membury, but he had imperfect knowledge. Smith believed he was denying Keate a settlement by not hiring him for a full year, but Smith had erred, for Keate had what was called a general hiring, which the law assumed meant a yearly contract. For this there was no need for a formal agreement, so long as the arrangement was indefinite and lasted more than one year. In consequence, this family of four squatters on the Chardstock waste, and very likely unwelcome for that reason, had to find a new home in the adjoining parish of Membury, their lives disrupted by an ambiguous hiring in Membury six years before. It was later to be held that long occupancy of such a cottage as the Keates had in Chardstock could in itself bring a settlement,[12] but this case most likely would have involved risky litigation on Membury's part at any time in the eighteenth century.

The Law of Settlement, in its glorious detail, has a fascination all its own. Although most people of the time—the poor and payers of the poor rate alike—had some knowledge of how the law worked, many, like Farmer Smith, had imperfect knowledge. There were guides, such as Richard Burn's ever-popular *Justice of the Peace and Parish Officer*, which ran through 30 editions between 1755 and 1869, and there were legal treatises devoted to settlement, which was in fact the most important branch of law, if judged by the number of lives affected and lawyers' hours expended. Parish officers faced with potentially costly additions to relief rolls consulted expert counsel and, if they thought their case a good one, went to court. To the poor and parish officers, and even to well-informed contemporaries, the Law of Settlement must often have seemed mystifying and illogical. Yet there was a broad logic to its provisions, as an outline history should make clear. Even in outline, this body of law is complex, but this is a Hill of Difficulty that must be climbed for the sake of what follows.

The care of the poor in medieval England was the responsibility of kindred, church, lord, guild, and other corporate entities, perhaps in that order of importance. No Law of Settlement established territorial bounds of responsibility, although
the poor were generally considered to be the responsibility of the
place where they had been born or where they had been long
in residence. In the Tudor period residence became of greater
importance, reflecting increased migration and increasing acceptance of physical mobility. When statutes of Elizabeth's reign
compelled English and Welsh parishes to relieve their poor, the
question of precisely who the parish poor were took on added
weight, but it was not until the second half of the seventeenth
century that parochial responsibility was specifically defined by
statute, and not until about 1800 that the Law of Settlement
achieved refinement through amendment and judicial precedent.

The well-known Settlement Act of 1662 specified 40 days as the
minimal period necessary to establish settlement by residence. It
also allowed settlement to those paying rent that over the course
of a year would total £10. However, the 1662 act did not initiate
so much as it confirmed and standardized common expectations.
That act also gave each parish the authority to remove needy
sojourners, as well as those whom parish officers considered
likely to be in need one day even if the person were at the time
self-sufficient. Yet here again the law appears to have limped
behind practice, for there was nothing new to the expulsion of
unwelcome sojourners. Still, the 1662 act was an important legal
precedent, although there is little evidence that it was carefully
enforced.

The real foundation of the Law of Settlement, one that would
stand until well into the nineteenth century, was the Act of 1691.
This statute illustrates what Charles Wilson has called in another
context "social mercantilism." This act, and a modifying statute
of 1697, was designed to encourage migration from areas of high
unemployment to areas where the poor's "labour is wanted"
and "where the Increase of Manufactures would employ more
Hands."[13] The law now allowed a poor person to earn a new
settlement through one of four forms of meritorious service: the
payment of rates or local taxes; a year's service in a regular parish

office; completion of an indentured apprenticeship; completion of a year of service to one master if one were unmarried at the time the contract was undertaken. In addition, the 40-day residence provision of the 1662 statute was kept as a ground for achieving settlement until 1795, but it was amended to require a public notice of intention to settle prior to the period of quarantine. The number of poor achieving settlement by this cumbersome process was inconsequential; indeed, I have never found a case where a settlement was so based. Also retained from the 1662 act was the provision specifying a £10 annual rental, a particularly important stipulation for those towns in which rents were high, such as London. There were thus six ways of meriting an "acquired" settlement.

To this list must be added six additional ways of achieving settlement, which may be called "derivative" settlements, based on the Common Law. (1) Children assumed their parents' settlement, and (2) a wife took her husband's settlement (lengthy cohabitation was considered sufficient). In both cases the law attempted to preserve the unity of the family. (3) Illegitimate children were usually settled in their parish of birth. (4) Ownership of an estate effectively brought a settlement, for it was an ancient principle that a man ought not to be removed from his freehold. Although a 1723 statute attempted to restrict this right by excluding purchasers of estates valued under £30, judges apparently continued to uphold Magna Carta, for freeholders with land of lesser value, although subsequently denied settlement, were considered irremovable. This seems to be a case in which the intent of a statute was circumvented by judicial interpretation. (5) It was also possible to achieve a settlement if parish authorities granted regular relief, such as a weekly allowance or maintenance in a workhouse. Such relief was considered as recognizing a right to settlement, even if later the parish officers repented of their carelessness or generosity. Finally, (6) if all else were inapplicable or undiscoverable, a pauper was considered settled wherever he or she happened to be. Such cases were uncommon and chiefly limited to abandoned children.

All twelve avenues to settlement were hedged and qualified by laws and judicial precedents as the Law of Settlement evolved, which is why Burn and other guides went through so many editions. The most important legal change in the eighteenth century was George Rose's 1795 act, which abolished settlements by public notice and by the payment of rates. More important, this humane statute prohibited removal on suspicion of future need (likely to be chargeable) and in cases where the health of the sojourner might be threatened by the move (suspended order of removal).

One final feature of the law, dating from a 1697 statute, was that a parish could give its own poor parishioners who wished to migrate a certificate acknowledging a continuing responsibility for the parishioner and his family. This provision had considerable importance in the early eighteenth century, but little in the second half, and virtually none after the 1795 statute limited removals to those who were actually chargeable, meaning those who requested and needed regular relief. Persons in need who were simply given casual relief in money or kind were not considered chargeable.

Administration of the poor law was legally in the hands of churchwardens and overseers of the poor of each parish, under the supervision of justices of the peace (magistrates). The justices played a key role in interparochial problems, such as disputes over settlement. Overseers were appointed annually; two to four were selected for each parish, generally on Easter Monday. In this matter the parish proposed while the justices disposed, although the latter generally limited themselves to the parochial nominations. In practice, each parish developed its own way of handling poor law administration, sometimes vesting extensive authority in one man, who might be reimbursed for his services, sometimes relying on annually elected officers, sometimes contracting care of the poor to a profit-seeking entrepreneur, and sometimes reserving all important decisions for the parish vestry. Technically, the vestry was composed of all parishioners paying church rates, although provision could be made for a select vestry, composed of individuals empowered to levy and administer the parish rates. Whatever the form of governance, power and responsibility in most parishes rested with a small group of men who possessed the confidence of the ratepayers and a willingness to serve. Where few were willing to serve, parishioners could be drafted and even fined if they refused their annual stint in parish office.

The most difficult and hazardous task in poor law administra-

tion for both parish officers and magistrates was interpreting the
Law of Settlement. How was a year's service to be defined? What
specific parish offices brought a settlement? What kind of evidence was required in a particular case? Of the various grounds
for achieving settlement, which applied? Most cases were simple
enough, and even the difficult ones could usually be resolved
by homework in Burn or some other manual. But the need for
precise answers in specific circumstances could bring in the lawyers, who found in the Law of Settlement a gold mine. The
complexity of the law fostered the impression that it was economically restricting (except for lawyers) and obnoxious to the
poor; it thus attracted influential critics, such as Adam Smith and
Jeremy Bentham.[14]

Yet the law was clearly meant to serve constructive ends. First,
it was intended to benefit the poor by assigning responsibility for
their welfare to a specific parish and yet provide them opportunities to change their parish of settlement if required for family integrity or deserved through meritorious action. Second, the law
was intended to encourage the ablebodied unemployed to move
to where their labor was wanted. Finally, the law was designed
to lighten the welfare burdens of the parish whose workforce
exceeded available work. Designs and realities do not always co-
incide, especially in social engineering. The law was imperfect
in operation and was often evaded or broken, yet it may have
worked better than its critics have appreciated. *How* it worked
is best approached through the case history method, to which
we return. Indeed, this dense overview of the law may be fully
understood only by examining the law's operation in individual
circumstances and at different times in its evolution.

*   *   *

9 February 1843

William Morey, laborer, now residing at No. 20, Exeter Street, in the
parish of Charles, Plymouth, saith: "I am sixty years of age, and was
born in the parish of Dittisham, Devon, as I have been informed by my
parents. My father, John Morey, laborer, deceased, was a settled inhabitant of Dittisham. When I was about seven years of age I was bound out
as a parish apprentice to Richard Pinkey of the said parish, farmer, to
serve him until I was twenty-one years of age. I resided with my master

in Dittisham several years. My master afterwards removed to the parish of Blackawton, Devon, and I resided with and served him in the said parish of Blackawton until I was between eighteen and nineteen years of age. I then left my master and went to sea in the Royal Navy, and never returned to his service.

"I married my present wife, Sarah, at Portsmouth. After my marriage, I went to Dittisham and applied for labor. I was then taken to a Bench of Magistrates at Morley, examined as to my settlement, and afterwards removed by their order to Blackawton as the place of my settlement, and was employed on the parish work.

"I afterwards went into Hampshire with my family, and became chargeable to the parish of West Meon in that county, and fourteen years ago last September, I, my wife, and four children were removed by order of the justices to Blackawton as the place of my settlement. Since which last-mentioned removal the overseers of Blackawton have bound three of my sons, namely John, William, and Richard, apprentices to farmers of the said parish.

"I have done no subsequent act to gain a settlement, and am, with my said wife and Sarah, my daughter, aged fourteen years, actually become chargeable to the said parish of Charles in Plymouth, aforesaid. My daughter has done no act to gain a settlement in her own right."

William Morey
Charles, Plymouth, Devon

Morey was from south Devon, born toward the end of the American Revolution. As son of a poor laborer, he was apprenticed by the parish officers to a farmer in his father's parish of settlement, Dittisham. When his master moved to the adjacent parish of Blackawton, Morey followed, and it was there that he earned his settlement, for Blackawton was the parish in which he completed the last 40 days of his service. It was those final days that determined settlement by apprenticeship. Then he went to sea at century's end, perhaps lured to Plymouth by some stirring recruitment poster or an enlistment bounty. His apprenticeship actually expired some time while he was at sea, but that made no difference. How long he served in the Royal Navy is left unstated, for that was not material to his settlement, but it is likely that he was discharged at Portsmouth toward the end of the Napoleonic wars and married soon after.

Those postwar years were hard times, and Morey returned with his wife to Dittisham, the parish of his birth, only to be re-

moved to Blackawton, his parish of settlement, which acknowledged its obligation to him by giving him parish work, perhaps
in the form of ditching or road repair. But he returned to Hampshire some years later and apparently found his own work for
several years. Then, in the late 1820s, he fell once again into need
and was removed yet again to Blackawton. There his sons were
bound to parish farmers, as he himself had been. He again left,
returning to Plymouth, where he was unable to manage without
relief; the result was the settlement examination provided here.

Dorothy Marshall once compared laborers under the Law of
Settlement to "the shell-fish, which cling to the rocks and let the
drifting tide bring them their daily food." [15] Morey was more like
a small fish forced back to its protective rocks in time of danger
but willing to swim forth when it saw an opportunity, which is
the truer simile for laborers such as he.

Morey's examination reflects the greater thoroughness characteristic of the Law of Settlement after the 1834 Poor Law Amendment Act. Settlement documents gain in clarity and detail, but
the colorful extraneous information often found in the earlier
records is lost as administrators of the poor law took a more
professional view of their work, although it is pleasant to read
examinations in the first person. The 1834 act did not end the
Law of Settlement, but changed it in important ways. Since
these changes were not made retroactive and did not immediately invalidate the old grounds for achieving settlement, the
1834 changes had less dramatic effects on the practice of the law
than they otherwise would have had. Subsequent mid-Victorian
legislation further obscured the 1834 act's importance in changing settlement. Yet it marked a turning point. Illegitimate children henceforth were to take their mother's parish of settlement,
which was surely a humane improvement. Settlement by yearly
service was abolished, for that was the source of more litigation
than anything else. Settlement by holding parish office was abolished. In addition, various qualifications were added to settlements based on apprenticeship, annual rental, and estate ownership. The 1834 act, in sum, pruned the mercantilistic old Law of
Settlement by reducing the merit element and by re-emphasizing
the still older principle of residence. Perhaps even more important in changing the character of the process was the greater
complexity of the removal procedures under the new law. [16]

The nineteenth-century trend toward residence as the principle for settlement, first seriously raised by a select committee of Parliament in 1817, is clearly seen in the 1834 act and subsequent legislation. In 1876 three years' residence was accepted as the basis for a settlement. Curiously, this turned the clock back to the early Tudor period, for three years' residence had appeared in a statute of Henry VII's reign,[17] although it did not matter much how settlement was determined before compulsory provision became the law under Elizabeth.

Not all aspects of settlement can be represented in this first chapter, and neither four nor forty cases could provide all possible permutations of the Law of Settlement. However, the stories of these four Devonians, placed in context, provide the main outlines of the law, and some indication of its character.

TWO

Divided Families

RECORDS OF THE SOJOURNERS are full of information on family crises. Desertion, illegitimacy, bigamy, death—whatever the cause, the poor family came to the attention of parish officers whenever dependency threatened. Even if no relief was requested and no removal was contemplated, when the divided family's fortunes plummeted, sooner or later that usually meant parochial expense.

Men and Women

19 December 1786

This deponent saith that he was born, as he has heard and believes, in or near Exeter, but in what parish he does not know, nor ever heard, but has been informed and believes that his mother was taken in labor as she was going to Exeter, but from what place he has never heard, and was delivered of him at a farm house in the road. He was baptized in the parish of Tavistock [Devon], and is now in the thirty-first year of his age. At the time he was born his mother was the wife of John Denty, who was a soldier and had been absent several years in Germany or elsewhere in foreign parts and had no intercourse with his mother for several years before his birth.

He lived in Tavistock until he was about fourteen years old with one Mark Stephens, with whom his mother placed him to be taken care of, and who was paid for the same. At the age of fourteen years he was put to live as an apprentice with Mr. John Garland, sergemaker, in Tavistock, and lived with him as such apprentice for about six years in that parish, but was not bound by indenture, as his master has told him.

He has since lived as a servant at two places in the parish of Kingsbridge [Devon], but made no agreement for a year, and did not stay three-quarters of a year in either of the places. He never rented lands of the value of £10 a year, or had any of his own, or executed any public office, or paid any parish rates or taxes. His mother's name was Elizabeth.

He was married about six years ago, and in about a year afterwards his wife eloped from him, and went to America, as he has been told and believes, and he has not seen or heard from her since. He had a child by her, named John, who is still living in Tavistock.

    Thomas Denty
    Modbury, Devon

Wars had much to do with dividing families in the eighteenth century, and illegitimate children were sometimes a consequence of long separations. There are many variations to the same theme. Denty's story is also representative of a recurring pattern of failure often reported by settlement examinees, caused by a string of misfortunes or by personal inadequacies—it is seldom clear which. He had had an apprenticeship, but without an indenture there was no settlement. He had given service in Kingsbridge, but nothing that had lasted a full year. He did not inherit a settlement and had reached his thirties without acquiring one; in consequence, he belonged where he was, in Modbury. Misfortune dogged his personal life as well, for his mother had deserted him at the outset, and his wife had run off to America.

Whatever the circumstances, whoever was to blame, desertion of one family member by another was common. Divorce was a legal impossibility for the poor, and husbands and wives who could not abide their spouse or their circumstances ran away. Britain's possession of an overseas empire beckoned the discontented of both sexes, although clearly husbands were more likely to desert and had better opportunities to seek new lives abroad.

The Law of Settlement was designed to do what could be done to keep families together. Indeed, deserters were deemed rogues and vagabonds by 17 George II, *cap.* 5 (1744) and subject to whipping or confinement—if they could be caught. Husbands, wives, and their legitimate children too young to establish settlement in their own right (under age seven) were never under any circumstances legally separated from one another, but illegitimacy could lead to long-distance separations if the mother had traveled far from her parish of settlement to have her child, although even here a child under age seven could not be separated from its mother, on the grounds that it required nurture to that age. It was not just the written law that tried to promote the integrity of the family; parish officers also did what they could, if only to keep welfare costs down. Sometimes they acted with grotesque zeal, as the following story exemplifies.

*   *   *

24 September 1793

Esther Gillingham, a parishioner of Fulham [London], whose maiden name was Herbert, being with child by Samuel Gillingham, to whom she swore it about two months after Christmas, was compelled to marry the said Samuel (who was taken up the day of her swearing) by the threat of Mr. Cheesemore, one of the overseers of Fulham, that if she did not marry Samuel she would be sent to Bridewell [Prison] for a year and a day.

By which she was frightened into a consent, and the man [Samuel Gillingham] was kept three days in the cage at Fulham, when a license was produced, and both were married at the parish church. Then the parish officers gave them a dinner at Mr. Lucas' The King's Arms, and from there they went away to the Sign of the George in Fulham, and from thence to a lodging in Hooper's Court. About eight the same evening her husband ran away from her, and never bedded with her or had carnal knowledge of her after the said marriage.

Esther Gillingham
St. Luke, Chelsea, London

It would be pleasant to think the dinner was a generous gesture, but it seems much more likely, given the preceding circumstances, that Fulham's officers were doing what they could to solidify their shotgun wedding. Plenty of food and especially plenty of free drink, and the couple would surely be ready for bed. These failed, and Esther remained Fulham's charge.

Another approach of parish officers was to subsidize a marriage as a means of reducing welfare costs. Elizabeth Lewis in 1794 wanted to marry a man from Westminster, and all she asked of her parish, St. Luke, Chelsea, was 40s., a gold ring, and a wedding dinner. Since she would then be the responsibility of another parish, St. Luke's gave the matter serious consideration. They interviewed the husband-to-be, one William Reed, and discovered that he rented a house in the parish of St. John the Evangelist at £14 a year, which gave him a settlement in that parish.

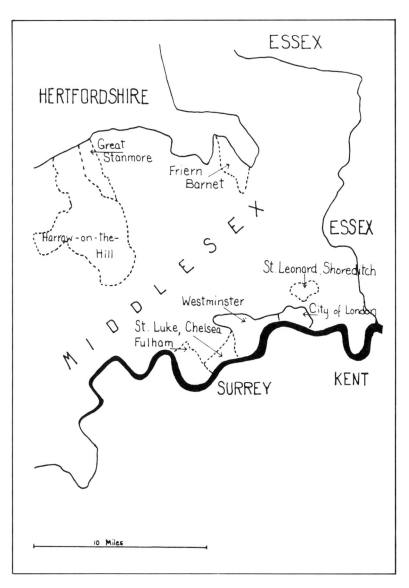

Environs of London

Hope must have soared. But then they discovered from Reed
that he was already married. Perhaps he considered himself a
free man, for his wife was then under sentence of transportation, but that did not affect the legality of the first marriage, and
the request was denied.

Although marriage negotiations and intimidations were more
common in London than in Devon, William Marshall of Beaford
in that county, thatcher by trade, was involved in such a case. He
had gone as a journeyman to Bideford in 1802, where he shortly
thereafter impregnated Frances Folland. When he refused to
marry her, the parish officers sent him to Bridewell Prison in
Exeter for three days to give him time to reconsider. While there,
he professed to have a change of heart and was brought back
to Bideford. Duly married to Frances Folland, Marshall took his
new wife to a moor four miles from the town and abandoned her.
Returning to Exeter, he joined Colonel Hall's regiment, in which
he had previously enlisted while imprisoned in Bridewell.[1] Such
cases were uncommon, however, for most parish officers realized that without the willing consent of both parties desertion
was the likely consequence of a forced marriage.

If a parish could not ensure successful marriage, it did what
it could to make the father of an illegitimate child pay maintenance for his offspring. This brought parish officers into contact
with a broad spectrum of society. Among the putative fathers in
the bastardy examinations of St. Leonard, Shoreditch, London,
between 1813 and 1832, for example, are to be found weavers,
master mariners, shoemakers, blacksmiths, gentlemen, hackney
coach drivers, yeomen, convicts, farriers, wine merchants, police
constables, gunsmiths, lace manufacturers, footmen, surgeons,
journeymen bakers, carpenters, silk merchants, and poulterers.[2]
The one thing they had in common, with few exceptions, was
a reluctance to support their offspring. Although parish officers
had legal power to secure the reputed father and extract a bond
to indemnify the parish, or failing that, a weekly allowance, it
seems to have been unusual when a parish did not end by paying most of the maintenance costs of such children, as it also had
to do for deserted spouses and their legitimate children.

*   *   *

11 August 1797

This examinant, on her oath, saith that she was lawfully married to Samuel Phillips about four years ago at Bishopsgate Church [London], and that she lived and continued with her said husband until about February 1795, when in consequence of the extreme ill usage of her said husband, he at that time having given her a venereal complaint and frequently beating her and cutting her with knives, and denying her the common necessaries of life, she was under the necessity of leaving him.

She went home to her father, who assisted her in gaining her maintenance until November last, when by reason of old age her father became incapable of continuing that assistance. She was then under the necessity of applying for relief to the overseers of the poor of the Liberty of Saffron Hill, Hatton Garden, and Ely Rents in Middlesex. They received her into their workhouse for some time, and have since her quitting the said workhouse paid her a weekly allowance of 2/6, in consequence, as she, this examinant, believes, of her said husband having undertaken to reimburse them. Her said husband for some time past has refused or neglected to reimburse the overseers, and she has never received any money or assistance whatsoever in the smallest degree from her said husband since she left him, other than through the overseers. She is now, otherwise than through the said overseers, without the means of subsistence, although her husband is very well capable, as she this examinant has good reason to believe, of maintaining her, or of affording her such assistance by which she could maintain herself.

Phoebe Phillips
Liberty of Saffron Hill, Hatton Garden, and Ely Rents, Middlesex

Brutality within the family is uncommon in the records of settlement, although that may reflect its irrelevance to settlement questions rather than its absence.

* * *

12 December 1799

Elizabeth, this examinant, was lawfully married to Isaac Tooke on or about 25 June 1791. Her husband now rents and lives in a house which he has kept upwards of a year in the Strand in the parish of St. Mary le Strand, at £100 a year, rent and taxes, as he has informed this examinant.

Near or about six years ago, at the time of him and this examinant renting and living in a ready-furnished lodging at No. 11 in George Street, Blackfriars Road, he left her, and said he was going into the smuggling trade. For about three months afterward he came at different times to the said lodging to give her money, and afterwards went away again. She went away from the said lodging, with her husband's concurrence, and worked for Mr. Blundell, a lint maker on Bethnal Green, during the space of four or five years, on and off.

About two years after leaving Blackfriars Road she went in search of her said husband, and found that he kept house in St. Martin's Lane. She went to him to ask him for maintenance. He told her it was then out of his power, and that she must give him a week's notice, in which time she met him by his desire in writing at the Green Dragon in Botolph Alley near Fenchurch Street; there he gave her half a guinea, and told her that she should have that sum every 20th of the month. She continued to receive the said half guinea monthly for about ten months, to the best of her present recollection.

About the expiration of that period she and her husband went together to his aunt's, one Mrs. King at Mr. Allen's, pattern maker in St. Martin's Lane, and while they were there a woman who now goes by the name of Mrs. Tooke, came there, and seeing this examinant's said husband with her, the said woman said she would utterly renounce him, as this examinant was his lawful wife and had the greatest right to him. He then signified that he would not live with this examinant, but would live with the other woman. Her husband then left this examinant there.

To the best of her knowledge she never afterwards saw him until today, although she repeatedly called at the house where he had moved to in the Strand, and received from the other woman silver at different times, until last Lord Mayor's Day she met her husband and the said woman with another person near one end of Holywell Street. She, the examinant, desired him to tell her why he did not allow her a maintenance, to which he signified he never would unless he was forced. She has not since had any money from her husband, and is now chargeable to the parish of St. Mary le Strand.

Elizabeth Tooke
St. Mary le Strand, Middlesex and Westminster

If Isaac Tooke rented for anything like £100 a year, he was a very successful smuggler indeed and would have been occupying one of the grandest houses in the Strand, judging by the rate books. Doubtless, he or his wife exaggerated, he to impress her or she to impress the magistrates concerning his ability to pay her a maintenance.

The two preceding examinations are fuller and more dramatic than most, yet in much of the detail one finds the ordinary and the representative in the extraordinary and the peculiar. Certainly it was common enough for a wife to be deserted by a philandering husband, with the overseers intervening to attempt to extract a maintenance allowance from the husband. Occasionally it was the husband who appealed, as in the following strange petition.

*   *   *

Gentlemen: [no date given, between 1806 and 1827]

The man, Alexander Sanders, a humble claimant on your parish of St. George, Southwark, finds himself grievously oppressed by and through a wicked wife, Elizabeth, together with her bloodthirsty accomplices, the West India planters and merchants, and their subtle agents, with many of whom she cohabits. We parted with mutual consent about six weeks ago, at which time she promised that if I would divide with her the one half of my small stock of household furniture that she was perfectly content to be held by a written agreement, signed before a witness, to never trouble or molest me again.

But a fortnight had hardly passed before she was stimulated by two Irishmen, who at that time cohabited with her, to lay an information against me to get me pressed [into the Navy], but being disappointed in this cruel and unjust project of robbing me of the other half of my furniture, she immediately resorted to a horrible invention of falsehoods, and thereby through her hellish offices made my character appear so odious before her West India friends that they, with her Irish husbands, set about every artful stratagem to deprive me of life and possess her with my house and goods. Notwithstanding that, I flung the goods into the hands of my creditors. I was obliged instantaneously to quit the house or suffer myself to be shot in the open daylight.

I implore the gentlemen who meet here this night for the inspecting of the accounts of the poor that they will be pleased, with the assistance of the magistrates, to take an immediate recognizance of a deep laid scheme to plunge me at an unguarded moment into an awful eternity. . . . While [my enemies], styling themselves gentlemen of honor and integrity, are fitting on my unfortunate brow a complicated mass of horns, my infamous wife, by their hellish plots, is made to hasten my destruction. But certainly, gentlemen, as generous Englishmen and guardians of your parish rights, you can not eye indifferently so glaring a breach or trampling on the laws of God and your country. You cannot suffer an honest man's life thus to fall, one who has worn out the best days of his youth and the best of constitutions in hard naval services to your country. I am not inclined personally to be a burden to your parish, as the business of peruke maker and hairdresser, to which I was bred in the West End of your city of London, if allowed to follow it, would afford him a comfortable subsistence, and had it not been through the drunken and whoring treachery of my extravagant wife, I should not have been compelled at so untimely a season to seek an asylum of life and death within your workhouse walls.

As for my wife, if she were sober and chaste, she could earn from 15/ to 16/ a week, for she is so good a hand at the tailoring business that she is never a day in want of work. But if in any future period she should, through her own wretched conduct, become burdensome to your parish, it will be of far less expense to the parish to be troubled with one than with two.

I do not mean, gentlemen, by this boldness of speaking, to dictate to you, but my drift is merely to convince you that it is not my wish, as a tradesman able and willing to get my bread by my business, to be numbered among your indigent poor longer than I can consider myself safe from a mischievous frame of sanguinary villainy. Therefore, if you will be graciously pleased to procure and sign for me a certificate or ticket of absence for any time that you may think proper to limit it, to enable me thereby to claim the protection of any of the four kingdoms [of the British Isles] where I may in prudence reside . . . I will ever feel myself impressed by the strongest sense of gratitude for your bountiful goodnesses, and likewise to make to you the firmest promise that I will not at any after period of time trouble your parish.

It's the common trumpet talk of those who have destroyed the union between my unfortunate wife and I that they can jointly prove my wife a whore. "But," says they, "that shall not be a hindrance of his living with her, if she chooses to live with him, to preserve him a little longer from our vengeful hands, for a West India planter or merchant, or an Irish laborer's whore, is good enough for a black fellow," and they are fully resolved, if she pleases, to force me to write and offer her any terms of reconciliation that she or they should point out.

Sanders further implores that the gentlemen of the committee will not insist on his doing any labor while he remains in the workhouse, as he is in a slow decline, and greatly afflicted with rheumatic pains, both in body and limbs.

[Alexander Sanders]
St. George the Martyr, Southwark, London

Wishing to sojourn elsewhere, Sanders had a bizarre story to tell, in form as well as in content (considerably condensed here), especially concerning his judgments of his wife's character and the intentions of her friends. Some of what appeared in Sanders's petition may be true, yet examinees and petitioners would have been less than human if they had not attempted to make the best possible case for themselves. Apparently Sanders had served some years in the British Navy, possibly recruited in the West Indies and discharged in London. Perhaps aboard ship he had been taught the rudiments of his trade, later perfected in the West End, where a black peruke maker and hairdresser might have been something of a novelty, and successful for that reason. His downfall may well have been his unhappy marriage to a white woman, which exposed him to racial prejudice, exacerbated by her apparent character. Whatever the event, Sanders's petition, with its interesting alternation of the first and third persons, illustrates that the records of the sojourners, so rich in the varieties of human experience, are a poor place to search for statistical norms.

* * *

27 November 1805

This examinant, on her oath, saith that she is the wife of James Thompson (now at sea) and was married to him in the parish church of St. George, Bloomsbury, about seven years ago. Her husband served his full apprenticeship out to one Corby of Sun Street in the parish of Waltham Abbey in the County of Essex, wheelwright, about fourteen years ago.

His master dying, she, this examinant, about seven years ago, at the time they were married, let her husband have £300 stock. With this sum he took his late master's house and business, the rent of which house was £8 a year, and this examinant's husband rented at the same time a shop opposite the house in the same parish at the rent of £10 a year, and inhabited such house and shop two years and upwards, and paid the poor's rate for such premises, and did not afterwards gain any other legal settlement.

She has by her said husband two children, namely Thomas, aged five years, and Jane, aged three years, which said children have been taken by the friends of this examinant's husband, and the officers of the parish of Waltham Abbey make an allowance toward their support. She, being pregnant, has become chargeable to the parish of St. Leonard, Shoreditch.

> Mary Thompson
> St. Leonard, Shoreditch

Thompson apparently wrecked the business his wife had financed and then ran off to sea, leaving his family to the care of his parish. Even if he had been impressed on a visit to a port town, it is difficult to see how he could have lost £300 worth of stock unless he was profligate; £20 was as much as many laborers earned in a year. Her children were maintained by their parish at the home of her husband's friends, but at whose wish or order? She was expecting a child, but whose? And why was she in St. Leonard, Shoreditch? Perhaps the answer to the last question is simply that it was only five miles down the road from Waltham Abbey, and there was likely to be more work in the environs of London than in Essex.

St. Leonard, Shoreditch, was far too pressed with paupers to fill in the details once it was clear Mary Thompson was not their responsibility. With 6,000 houses and over 50,000 inhabitants, it was the third largest parish within the Bills of Mortality,[3] and like other large parishes was constrained to get as quickly as possible to the heart of the matter. Given this situation, Mary Thompson's examination was exceptionally full, and an indication that even busy officers of a large parish could be moved by an unusual fall from economic grace.

*   *   *

17 May 1823

John Bignall, on his oath, saith that he is about twenty-five years of age, a laborer, and was born at Watford in the County of Hertford. Says he has a wife now living, named Lydia, to whom he was married this morning by license at the parish church of Great Stanmore in the county of Middlesex. Says that his said wife has one illegitimate child living, named Lucy Rogers, belonging to Great Stanmore, and about three years old.

Says that about ten and a half years ago he hired himself to Mr. Robert Dracott of Watford, butcher, to be his servant of all work for one year from Michaelmas day, at the yearly wages of £5, and his board, that he continued in his service two years and upwards, and received his full wages, and that he slept the whole of the time at his mother's house in Watford. Says that at the Michaelmas after he left Mr. Dracott he hired himself to Mr. Bailey Smith of Bushey Hall in the parish of Bushey, Hertford, as horsekeeper, for one year at £4 wages and 6/ a week for board wages and lodging, that he continued in the said service one whole year, and received his full wages accordingly. Since that time he has done no act, matter, or thing whereby to gain any subsequent settlement. Says that he has several times received relief from the parish of Bushey.

> John Bignall
> Great Stanmore, Middlesex

Settlement examinations were often conducted, as seems likely in this case, to clarify a situation, not to remove a sojourner. There is no mention here of Bignall's being chargeable, and since 1795 only those who were in need could be removed, unless there were other issues involved beyond the matter of poor relief, of which there is no evidence here. What appears to have interested Great Stanmore was that since Bignall clearly had another parish of settlement, Lydia, his new wife, would no longer be a charge on Great Stanmore. Lucy, her illegitimate child, would continue to be Great Stanmore's responsibility, for a husband was not legally responsible for his wife's illegitimate children. The most unusual feature of this examination is that Bignall was examined by the tactless authorities on his wedding day.[4]

* * *

28 September 1826

Ann Craddock says she was married to Thomas Craddock on the 24 August 1825 at the parish church of St. Olave in Tooley Street [London]. He was at that time a porter at Mr. Fry's in St. Mildred's Court, Poultry, tea dealer, and he was at that time sleeping at their house, and continued to do so until February last. She was in a situation as a servant at the time of her marriage, and continued in her situation until February last. Then she left her situation and her husband left Mr. Fry's service, and went as a weekly servant to Mr. Todd at the Red Lion Wharf, Lower Thames Street, and resided with her at No. 3 Meeting House Court, Miles' Lane, Cannon Street, for about four months, and then moved to No. 10 Pump Court, Union Street Borough, where she still lives.

Her husband entered into the East India Company's service on the 8 July last (particulars of which may be known of Captain Murray at No. 36, Soho Square), and left England in the month of August last in company with another woman whom he represented as his wife, and who formerly lived with Mr. Scott of St. Mildred's Court, and afterwards with Mr. Courleen of Sothbury. This deponent further saith that she has understood from her said husband that he lived with Mr. Fry about three and a half years, and that he had a salary of £21 a year when he first went there, and £25 a year afterwards. She expects to be confined with her first child in about three months.

> Ann Craddock
> St. Mildred, Poultry, London

To her pathetic story the parish officer added the following postscript: "This woman came under an order of removal from St. Savior, Southwark, dated 25 September, 1826. I made enquiry at Mr. Fry's and found her statement correct." A later note states: "She was delivered of a female child on the 16 December, 1826." The final postscript reads: "The child died at Peckham [Surrey], 11 March, 1831," most probably while at a baby farm. Although an examinee was the principal authority on his or her settlement, parish officers frequently sought verification, as in this case, and this was perhaps especially true of London parishes where communication among metropolitan parishes was not usually difficult and where wily examinees could and did lie themselves into a desired settlement. It is interesting that St. Mildred used the settlement examination to keep an ongoing record of the case, at least insofar as St. Mildred's obligations were concerned. Presumably they believed that Ann Craddock could fend for herself; it was the child that fell to the parish to maintain, an expense ended by its death four and a half years later.

In Ann Craddock's story the nub of the marital problem was very likely the excellent wages Thomas Craddock received at Mr. Fry's, followed by a dramatic decline in income when he left Fry's service. Probably he was forced to leave Fry's service, for it was uncommon for a master to permit a live-in servant to continue in service after marriage. Thomas Craddock, apparently finding his new job at the Red Lion Wharf and his new home at Meeting

House Court not to his liking and perhaps blaming his wife for the fall in his fortunes, escaped overseas in the employ of the East India Company and in the company of another woman. His wife was three months pregnant when he left; perhaps that too was a responsibility he was not willing to face.

*   *   *

4 January 1832

William Johnstone, on his oath, saith: "I am about forty-two years old, and was born in the island of Grenada in the West Indies. I was married at St. Margaret's Church, Westminster, to my first wife, Elizabeth, about twenty-two years ago, by whom I have five children now living, namely William, about twenty years old, Margaret, about seventeen, Elizabeth, about fourteen, Robert, about twelve, and Louisa, about nine years of age. My said wife died nearly ten years ago, and was buried at Great Stanmore. The eldest boy has been apprenticed. Margaret is in business. Elizabeth is hiring with a milliner, and the youngest boy is in the Caledonia School, and the youngest girl at Bluecoat School.[5]

"About five years ago my children left me at Aix-la-Chapelle [Aachen]. I was married at Cologne in Germany, according to the Catholic forms, to my present wife, Catherine, about seven years ago, by whom I have one child, named Alexander, about thirteen months old; my wife is a Catholic and I am a Protestant. About fourteen years ago I took to rent a house and premises at Great Stanmore of Mr. Learmouth at the yearly rent of 200gn. I occupied the same about four years, and paid three years' rent for the same, since which time I have done no act to gain a settlement."

William Johnstone
Great Stanmore, Middlesex

200 guineas a year! Johnstone had clearly been a wealthy man at one time, perhaps heir to a West India planter's fortune. He had rented the Great House in Stanmore, which was available at the time given in the examination and was the only house in the parish that would have rented for such a sum.[6] One must assume that he had then employed servants and enjoyed all the trappings of life in a great house. Perhaps since those halcyon days he had experienced some business disaster, but his second marriage in Germany, followed by his children "leaving" him at Aachen, is suggestive. At that time his oldest child could

only have been about fifteen years old, and Louisa, the youngest, would have been about four. It is much more likely that the father deserted his own children. Someone then stepped in to befriend the children, as they all seem to have been well placed back in London. Once again, the story is tantalizingly incomplete. Whatever the precise circumstances, it seems certain William Johnstone had a vein of irresponsibility, and that could lead even the wealthy to chargeability.

It is interesting that the parish officers recorded the religious confessions of Johnstone and his second wife. Given that the marriage was according to the Catholic rite, they may have been uncertain as to the status of the child, Alexander. They need not have been (if the marriage act took place), for English law recognized marriage in a foreign country so long as the law of the country in which the marriage took place was observed (although there were some legal problems with clandestine marriages in Scotland). Alternatively, the clerk taking down the examination may have been intrigued by the story itself, a not uncommon thing, as examinations are often fuller than any legal consideration can explain, even when one considers that clerks were not always certain what was or was not germane to the settlement. It is enough to assume that clerks were human, although one often wishes, as with Johnstone's story, that the examination had been even more complete.

* * *

7 February 1832

This examinant, on her oath, saith that she is the wife of William Taylor, and was married to him in the parish church of Ancaster in Upper Canada [Ontario], 6 April 1824, and by him has two children, lawful issue, namely William, seven years, and John, five years and upwards. Since her marriage to him he has not done any act to gain a settlement by renting a house or otherwise (produces an indenture), that her said husband has informed her, and she believes, that he was bound as an apprentice by indenture about 22 February 1814 for seven years to John Giscard of Swaffham [Norfolk], a clock and watchmaker, and that he lived with and served his said master the whole of the said term, and that during the last six or eight months of such service he was residing with his master in the parish of St. Stephen in the City of Norwich in the County of Norfolk.

Her said husband is under sentence of transportation for seven years, and herself and children have become chargeable to the parish of St. Leonard, Shoreditch.

Sarah Ann Taylor
St. Leonard, Shoreditch, London

Her story was confirmed by a visitor to her husband, then aboard the convict ship *Ganymede* at Woolwich. A letter from Giscard also confirmed the details of the apprenticeship, the indenture for which was clearly a carefully treasured document of the Taylors, their passport to settlement. But not all the stories examinees and petitioners told were or could be confirmed. Did they usually tell the truth?

Settlement examinees were under greater pressure to be truthful than petitioners, for an examination was a formal process, conducted in the presence of the magistrates, an intentionally intimidating situation, at least for most of those subjected to this experience. There was the fear of commiting perjury, or of doing so and being caught. In addition, the examination often occurred during some personal crisis—unemployment, the desertion of a spouse, illness—when the examinees were most vulnerable. Quite apart from these considerations, examinees could not always know what evidence they might give or withhold would help or hinder their good future. It seems likely that the most frequent lapse from truth was omission of evidence the examinees thought might be to their disadvantage. Elizabeth Terry, for example, had never heard her husband say where he was born, or where he belonged, or where he came from. She had not heard from him for almost three years, and she had last seen him on board a frigate at Portsmouth about five years before. Recently she had been told he had been lost at sea on His Majesty's ship *Crescent*.[7] Perhaps her husband had indeed been the silent type. On the other hand, what if he had mentioned to her a parish far from her home? Why should she say? What justice was there in forcing her to move? Who could prove perjury?

Petitioners, on the other hand, and here may be included the poor who were subjected to informal examinations, as in the case of Harriet Williams, were in a better position to go beyond omitting facts to gilding the truth. They were not giving testimony under oath, and there were usually not so many intimidating auditors. An elaborate story might move parish officers to generosity, as Alexander Sanders undoubtedly hoped. Of course, there were cases that went well beyond omission and exaggeration to the assertion of blatant settlement-determining falsehoods, a subject to which I shall later return.

The Children

An important patrimony of any poor child, for good or ill, was a parish settlement, to be guarded if judged a favorable one, to be discarded if judged unfavorable and there was opportunity of acquiring a better settlement elsewhere. There were a few, however, like Thomas Denty, who could name no parish as theirs; here is one more such case.

*   *   *

Michaelmas, 1784

Ann Godfrey, single woman, aged twelve years, and a vagrant, on her oath saith she has neither father nor mother, nor knows where she was born or where her father was settled, and that she never was bound an apprentice nor done any act to gain a settlement.

Ann Godfrey
Exeter, Devon

Examined before the Devon Quarter Sessions, she was simply discharged. She was probably judged harmless and reasonably healthy and likely to move on. Moreover, unless the authorities could discover something of her background, she belonged to no place. Where no specific settlement condition could be met, an examinee was settled in the place where he or she then was. In short, Ann Godfrey would have been Exeter's responsibility —good reason to let her move on. Yet a twelve-year-old child should have been someone's responsibility; this was surely a case where the Law of Settlement was inadequate to the circumstances, and it boded ill for Ann Godfrey's future.

*   *   *

19 January 1773

Judith Rideout, on her oath, saith that her maiden name was Baker, and that she was born in Totnes in Devonshire. About thirteen or fourteen years ago she was delivered of a male bastard child in Portsmouth in the County of Southampton, who was afterwards baptized there by the name of William, and hath since, as she has heard, gone by the name of William Baker. Upon her marriage with Thomas Rideout, her sister, Mary Baker, now the wife of John Dikes, offered to take care of the child, who was then about four years old—and accordingly took William and carried him to Sturminster Newton in the County of Dorset, where this examinant saw him about six years ago.

She is informed her said child is now in the parish of Modbury, Devon, but how he came there she knows not, but is rather surprised to hear he is there, her sister having promised in case she found herself unable to take care for him, to send or carry him to Portsmouth where he was born. And lastly this examinant saith that when her child was of very tender years he lost the use of one of his legs, and she believes he is in that state at present, as it was at first thought he would never recover the use of his limb.

Judith Rideout
Southampton

William Baker was thrice-cursed: illegitimate, abandoned by his mother, physically handicapped. Her account, cold and factual, suggests the physical mobility of even the least fortunate, for Sturminster Newton was approximately ninety miles from Modbury and sixty from Portsmouth. This does, of course, represent unusual mobility, even for an ablebodied boy.

*   *   *

15 March 1773

About fourteen years since she was married to John Webber in the parish of St. Sidwell, Exeter, by whom she hath had five children, four of whom are now living—and one of them, now aged eleven years and upwards, whose name is John, was born in the parish of St. James in the City of Bristol.

About six weeks ago, being at Brompton Ralph, Somerset, to which place John Webber belonged, she was taken before a justice of the peace, together with a former wife of the said John Webber. On their examination it appeared, due proof having been made, that John Webber had been married to his former wife about a year and three-quarters before he was married to this examinant.

She was accordingly sent to the parish of Alphington [Devon] as the place of her legal settlement before her marriage, and her son was removed to St. James, Bristol, where he was born a bastard, his last legal place of settlement, and that the said John has never done any act to acquire a settlement.

Rebecca Edmunds
Kenton, Devon

Although bigamy was a felony until 1795 (when the crime was reduced to "grand or petit larceny"), concurrent marriages were extremely common. This is not to be wondered at, given the lack of a legal way for the poor to obtain a divorce; moreover, a sojourner in a place where no one knew his background might marry a second time with an excellent chance of avoiding discovery.[8] What was Rebecca Edmunds doing in her husband's parish of settlement, which was a small village on the edge of the Brendon Hills, some twenty-five miles northeast of Exeter? Had she gone to check on her husband, or had he audaciously taken her? It seems unlikely she would have visited Brompton Ralph, or been discovered, if one or the other explanation did not apply. The number of detected cases could represent only a small fraction of those that went undetected, for only curiosity, temerity, or ill-fortune was likely to expose the sojourner who put prudent miles between his marriages.

Bigamy, like all felonies, assumed "evil intention," and yet many concurrent marriages clearly lacked that element. A husband might go to war or a spouse might desert to the colonies, and be presumed dead, only to reappear years later to invalidate a subsequent marriage of the spouse who had stayed home. In such cases prosecution would be most unlikely, but the second marriage would nevertheless be invalidated, and any children thereof would be considered bastards, a charge on the parish of their birth. There is no question that the frequent victims of bigamy found in the examinations were treated by the Law of Settlement in barbarous fashion.

*   *   *

21 June 1775

Please yoe Reverence this beabe is Chrissened in the name of Sofia Brooks I [undecipherable] will lift up my eyes to god to Enable Me to Pelease my Drest Beabe & now as god sees my grate grivence which compelles me to lave her to the compasione of the charitey which has been desined I am in Dutey boud to pray for the Bishop of Linkione

Anonymous
St. Martin, Ludgate, London

Legal phraseology in settlement papers often masks the anguish so evident in this unedited petition on behalf of Sofia Brooks. To be sure, it takes little imagination to sense the human suffering in many of the stories, however laconically they were recorded. Ann Richardson, for example, reported to the officers of St. Leonard, Shoreditch, in 1784 that her mother had died the year before and her father had now deserted his three daughters. Ann, the oldest, was nineteen years of age and could fend for herself, but not so her younger sisters, Eleanor and Comfort.[9] George Bonfauche of St. James, Westminster, boarded four of his children with Lucy Laws, a nurse in Harrow-on-the-Hill, and then moved away in 1789, leaving no forwarding address and owing the nurse about £15 in fees and expenses.[10] Yet there is a human element in the few extant petitions and letters written by the poor themselves that make them especially valuable to the social historian, as illustrated by the words of Sofia Brooks's mother above and by William Smith's petition below.

*   *   *

29 December 1822

Kind Sir,

I have taken the opportunity of writing to you concerning the ill-treatment I have received since you sent me here. As soon as he [the master] saw me the first night I came, he took hold of me by the collar and kicked me in such manner that I had a swelling in my groin, so that I could not walk well until the doctor gave me something to bathe it with. When he [the master] found it was swollen in such manner he began to be very kind to me, but as soon as I got a little better he began to ill-use me every hour in the day. He has kicked me seven or eight times in one day. If I am playing with any of the boys, I am doing wrong, and if I stand still I am doing wrong, so I am first beat for one thing, then for another, and thirdly for he don't know what.

Really, Sir, the ill-treatment I receive makes me always very ill. If, Sir, you would be so kind as to consider into it I should be extremely obliged to you.

When I came in I had the Itch [an infectious skin disease, often caused by mites burrowing under the skin], which I told him, and he gave me something to rub in with. If, Sir, you would be so kind as to give me a blue jacket and trousers, which would be as reasonable as any other suit, and give me leave to go out, I can soon get a ship and I will promise you I never will trouble the parish any more, for live in this manner I cannot.

Therefore I hope, Sir, you will take it into consideration, and please excuse my taking the liberty to write to you, but really it is a case of necessity, for if you saw how I am treated I know you would feel for me.

William Smith
Southwark, London

This letter to one of the parish officers of St. Mary, Aldermary, is part of a collection of correspondence dealing with this parish apprentice. His master, Thomas Willis, a manufacturer of worsted collar cloth, tilting, and yarn, had twice previously written the parish on occasions when the boy had run away. Master and apprentice did agree on two things: the latter's need for new clothes and for treatment of the Itch. Presumably the parish provided these services, and the boy ran off to sea, as he suggested he would, for the following February a letter arrived from the deputy governor of the Chelmsford House of Correction: "A lad calling himself William Smith has been brought into my custody as a vagrant—says that he was formerly in your service, but has latterly been at sea. Will you have the goodness to inform me what you know of him so that I may see what can be done for him when the term of his imprisonment expires?"

It is not always clear from correspondence where the fault lay in master-servant conflicts, but here it seems likely that Smith had reason to run away. In contrast, E. Champion of Gravesend had written a few months earlier to Mr. Prosser, a tea dealer in Cheapside and a parish officer, expressing disappointment with a parish apprentice that Prosser had sent. A saucy and intimidating boy, Champion found him to be: "I am sorry that I ever had anything to do with him, and would not keep him upon any account, for by what I hear him say I should be turned out of doors in a little time. He intends calling upon you to tell you how cruel I have used him."[11]

Various other forms of importunity occasionally surface in settlement records. Benjamin Forbes, born a bastard in St. Mildred, Poultry, in 1823, applied to his parish 23 years later to be fitted out to go to Australia; not surprisingly he was refused.[12] Ann Coxhill of Bicester Market End, Oxford, insisted in 1829 that the overseers of the poor of Harrow-on-the-Hill, Middlesex, pay an allowance for her illegitimate child, son of a deceased resident settled at Harrow. Otherwise, "if you don't think well to send me the money according to this letter I certainly will let the child fall on Biscester parish, and have him brought home with an order [of removal]." To which the overseers responded: "You are requested when you again trouble the officers of this parish to use a little more civility [for your letter] is not to your credit."[13] But parish officers had great discretionary power, and for every occasion a pauper spoke or acted boldly, there were a hundred in which he spoke and acted humbly and hoped for a generous heart.

*   *   *

12 September 1834

Frederick James saith that he has heard and believes he was born in the parish of St. James in the borough of Taunton. Sometime after he was removed from Taunton to Kenton; when he does not recollect. When he was about five or six years of age he was sent from Kenton to London to his mother, who was then married and living in London. He lived in Sloane Street, Vauxhall, and in another street, which he does not recollect, with his mother and father-in-law [stepfather], Mr. Bannister, a schoolmaster. About the beginning of the year 1827 his father-in-law, mother, and himself removed to Bristol where his father-in-law kept a school for day scholars. About four years after they had been living in Bristol his mother died, and he was then sent to his uncle, Benjamin Teague, schoolmaster, Bradfield, Berkshire, to assist him in his school, and remained with him about three and a half years, when my uncle told him he must go with him.

About 4 August he left Bradfield on horseback, my uncle riding in a cart with me, and in four days we reached Taunton, and stopped at the Wagon and Horses Public House. Soon after we arrived my uncle went out, leaving me behind in the public house, and soon after returned with his nephew, Robert Garland. My uncle then told me to lead the horse I had rode from Bradfield through the street outside the town, my uncle and my cousin, Robert Garland, riding in the cart. When we got through the town my uncle told me to go with my cousin and let the horse I had rode run by the side of the cart. My cousin took me to the workhouse in Taunton, where they refused to receive me. My cousin afterwards saw the overseer of St. James, who refused to receive me. I was then taken before the magistrates by my cousin, Robert Garland. The magistrates said the overseer must give me money to take me to my friends at Kenton. My aunt, Mrs. Garland, went to the overseer and applied for relief for me, when he gave 7/ to take me to Kenton.

>   Frederick James
>   Kenton, Devon

Kenton had been willing to give a few shillings to Harriet Williams to see her on her way to Exmouth five years before, but to be saddled with an illegitimate teenager who was clearly the responsibility of Taunton was quite another matter, and he was returned to Taunton by a removal order. Still, it was doubtless worth the try; Frederick James's grandmother Rebecca Teague lived in Kenton, and she might have been willing to help the boy, but as it turned out she either could not or would not. Why was this fourteen-year-old not apprenticed by his relatives? Why the anxiety of Taunton to be rid of him, when they might have made him a parish apprentice? It seems likely that something more than money was involved here. One strong possibility, supported by the tenor of the examination, is that the boy was subnormal in some way and would have been difficult to place.

*   *   *

21 January 1856

"I," the said examinant, says, "I am the son of the late Mr. Josiah Davey, of Stogumber, Somerset, cordwainer, deceased, by Mary, his late wife, also now deceased, and I am the grandfather of the orphan children, Leah Mary Davey and Charles Thomas Davey, now in the Southampton workhouse.

"My father . . . was apprenticed to a Mr. Hobbs (whose Christian name I cannot recollect, but who used to be called Sergeant Hobbs) of the parish of South Molton, Devon [about twenty-five miles west of

Stogumber, across Exmoor], cordwainer, and during his apprenticeship resided in that parish. I have often heard my father speak of it. My father never to my knowledge acquired any settlement in any other parish. My father died in 1828 or 1829. I have always heard that my mother was relieved by the parish of South Molton after my father's death. I have often heard her speak of it. Also, that my late sister, Ann Davey, was taken into the South Molton workhouse, and died there about twenty years ago. About March of 1849 my late mother, having become chargeable to the parish of Stogumber was, on complaint of the churchwardens and overseers of that parish, removed by an order to South Molton, which order was not appealed against. And my mother afterwards, and while residing with me, received parish pay for a certain time from South Molton. My mother died about December 1850.

"The late William Davey, who belonged to the band of the 59th Regiment of Foot, the father of Leah and Thomas Davey, was my son by Ann, my wife, to whom I was married at Marston, Somerset in 1820.

"My son, during my absence from England in the year 1831 or 1832, was apprenticed by the parish of South Molton to Mr. Cochran, a farmer of Tanhouse in South Molton. On my return to England in July 1835, I found my son living with Mr. Cochran in South Molton, as such apprentice, and he continued to reside in that parish during the whole of the time he served under his apprenticeship. Mr. Cochran now resides at No. 7, Somerset Place, Taunton. I saw him a few days ago. He informed me that he had some time since destroyed my son's indentures, with other papers.

"The children, Leah and Charles, are, as I have always understood, the children of my son by Leah Alice, his late wife, deceased—formerly Leah Alice Luscombe, spinster, to whom he was married at the parish church of Portsea [adjoining Portsmouth] on 5 February 1844, but I have never seen them till now. My son informed me of his marriage by letter. My son died at Hong Kong in China on 13 August 1853. I never did any act to gain a settlement in any other parish, nor did my son do any such act after his apprenticeship."

Josiah Davey
Stogumber, Somerset

Davey, a mason by trade, had come all the way from Stogumber to Southampton to give his evidence concerning the settlement of his grandchildren, Leah, aged eleven, and Charles, aged four, both of whom were titled "infant orphans." Betty Luscombe, the maternal grandmother, was also called to testify. She confirmed Josiah Davey's account and added a few additional details. Leah had been born at Portsmouth, and Charles in Hong Kong. After their father's death the family had embarked for England, but the mother died on the passage home. The orphans had on arrival been placed in the care of grandmother Luscombe. After three or four months of looking after them, however, she was no longer able to do so and had put them in the Southampton workhouse. She was able to produce certificates of her daughter's marriage and her grandchildren's baptisms. The evidence in the case also included affidavits from the master of the Southampton workhouse and from an overseer of the Southampton parish that had been maintaining the children there. The papers for this case are among the records of South Molton, to which the children clearly belonged.

Leah and Charles derived their settlement from their father's apprenticeship in South Molton; so there could be no doubt of the settlement, the story was taken back to the children's great-grandfather, also of South Molton. This was somewhat unusual, but it illustrates that not every generation achieved a new settlement. Indeed, it became increasingly difficult for sojourners to acquire one, as the Law of Settlement evolved in the late eighteenth and early nineteenth centuries, partly because statutes closed some loopholes and partly because parish administrators became more efficient in seeing that sojourners did not fulfill requirements for a new settlement. Before and after 1834, sojourners thus increasingly looked to fathers and grandfathers, even great-grandfathers, to provide settlements.[14] Yet there is another reason for this trend. Sojourners did not always have an incentive to lose ancestral settlements, and this may well have been true of the Davey family. South Molton appears to have been generous to the Daveys. The grandfather giving testimony in this case was clearly an intelligent artisan, very conscious of family ties to South Molton. It would have been foolish to risk the connection.

The extensive documentation in this case reflects the added complexity of pauper removal under the post-1834 poor law, partly because of changes in the law and partly because administration was in the hands of professional bureaucrats rather than amateurs filling out their year in parish office.

The Law of Settlement recognized the integrity of the legally constituted family and the right of all English and Welsh residents to receive relief in time of need, whatever their family status, and whether they were a settled parishioner or sojourner.[15] But the law also recognized the right of each parish to remove unwelcome sojourners, although that right was variously restricted and after 1795 was limited in most cases to those actually in need of relief. The law also exacerbated the unfortunate, even tragic, circumstances so often associated with divided families, and it was particularly harsh in its treatment of bastards and the victims of bigamy.

In its treatment of the family the law promoted a moral code. In this respect the legal provisions were attuned to the predilections of the men charged with enforcement. Was there not biblical authority for visiting punishment on the offspring of wrongdoers? Perhaps few officials consciously thought about it, yet perceptions of good and bad conduct undoubtedly shaped attitudes not only toward settlement—who was a welcome sojourner and who was not—but toward every other aspect of the pre-1834 poor law. The Old Poor Law, as it has been called, may be epitomized as the "relief of the poor within a framework of paternalism."[16]

THREE

Employment

THE LAW OF SETTLEMENT, as it evolved from the late seventeenth century, awarded industry and perseverance in various ways; settlements could be earned by completing an apprenticeship, by serving the same master for at least a year, by renting or buying property, or by paying rates. A quintessential expression of social mercantilism, the law worked as it was designed, some of the time. Like most laws designed to mold human behavior, the clay could prove stubbornly resistant. Sojourners found ways to avoid unwanted settlements, and employers and parish officers found ways to deny settlements to sojourners they did not want: informal apprenticeships, eleven-month contracts, rents that fell just short of the minimum £10 in annual rents, remission of rates, refusal of parish office, lapses of memory. No simple pattern emerges. Just as Machiavelli's prince needed *virtù* and fortune to succeed, so too did the sojourner need ability and luck to retain or find a desired settlement. The result of innumerable calculations was an extraordinarily complicated yet dynamic system.

Apprentices, Artisans, and Laborers

23 November 1775

Joseph Polyblank, now about the age of sixty-five, saith that he was born in the parish of Churchstow [Devon], where his father had gained a settlement, as he has heard, by renting. His father died when he was about nineteen—that about the age of fourteen his father had placed him with his brother-in-law, Peter Drew, a carpenter in Churchstow, with whom he lived two years in the nature of a servant, and received wages. About the age of sixteen he quitted Peter Drew, and lived at different places by the week until he was about nineteen or twenty years of age. Then he married at Tiverton [Devon], and lived there with his wife several years, working at his business as a carpenter by the week, but being warned out of Tiverton [threatened with removal], he came to Exeter, and lived there two years, working still by the week.

From thence he removed to Combe Royal in West Alvington, where he worked as a carpenter by the week for several years. While there his wife died. He then removed to Plymouth, where he worked several years by the week, in which town he married a second wife. Being much respected, he was appointed Cryer, but had no salary. He continued in that office some years, but never executed the same whenever he could get a deputy, and the office was mostly executed by a deputy.

Having lent some money to Peter Drew, his uncle, to carry on work at Centry Quarry [West Alvington], and in order to serve himself, was influenced to become a partner in the work. Accordingly, by articles of agreement, dated 23 January 1755, between Elizabeth Fortescue of the one part, the said Peter Drew, Henry Drew, himself, and Sampson Weeks of the other part, whereby they took lands at the Quarry for a term of years at £24 rent—Peter and Henry each having a sixth part, while Sampson and he each had a third. Later the sum was increased to £27, and the partnership paid that sum for several years before he left. During the partnership he lived at Centry House with his wife, and had several children born there. While there, he looked after the work on account of the partnership. [Details are given on West Alvington properties rented, the examinee's share totaling £15.13.4 per annum.]

He never gained any settlement in any other capacity. Thereafter, his family remained at Centry, but he went to Plymouth for work, and would return to Centry as his home.

    Joseph Polyblank
    West Alvington, Devon

The officers of West Alvington took down Polyblank's story (abbreviated here) for their records; he was clearly theirs by virtue of his rented properties, and there was no need for a formal examination before magistrates. This was an unusually efficient and enlightened parish—efficient because it found profitable employment for its paupers; enlightened in the scope of relief granted the poor in their own homes, both in money and in kind, and also in the provisioning of the suggestively named "carehouse" where Joseph and Elizabeth Polyblank spent their last days.[1]

It is likely that Polyblank, clearly a shrewd man, arranged to retire in this pleasant parish on the Kingsbridge Estuary. He dis-

paraged his services as cryer of Plymouth, for example, although
that office might have been sufficient to qualify for a Plymouth
settlement, if it were judged a public and annual office and he
had served the same, for the law recognized all manner of offices
as meriting a settlement—parish clerk, landtax collector, constable, ale-conner, sexton, hog-ringer—but Polyblank's deputizing undercut that settlement basis. He also took pains in his later
years to keep West Alvington as his home even while working
in distant Plymouth, for sixteen miles separated the two places,
and in the days before mechanical transport such a separation of
home from work must have represented a major inconvenience.
That suggests calculation, although it is not possible to prove
intent. A poor person, be it remembered, was generally the
principal witness to his own settlement, and his testimony took
precedence over that of a former master or of any other parishioner (excepting magistrates) who paid poor rates and could therefore be judged to have a vested interest in denying a sojourner a
settlement. That doubtless emboldened some examinees to em-
broider or omit to their advantage, as previously suggested, but
the simplest route of all was the one Polyblank apparently took
—avoid earning a settlement where none was wanted, which in
this case was Plymouth, where he had spent so many years as
carpenter and cryer.

*   *   *

11 September 1784

Upwards of five years ago he was hired as a yearly servant to one
William Wiltshire of the parish of Walford, Hertfordshire, farmer, in the
capacity of plowman, at the yearly wages of £8, and lived with his said
master there under that hiring for twelve months, and received twelve
months' wages, and did not afterward gain any other legal settlement.
And hath a wife named Sophia, to whom he was married at Walford
Church, and three children, namely Sarah, aged four years, Austin,
aged two, and Ann, aged one year and upwards.

Jonathan Tooley
St. Leonard, Shoreditch, London

Tooley's examination was far more typical than Polyblank's in
its brevity and simplicity; indeed, it is one of the most typical

to be found. Only the key facts were included; the children's ages were important in order to establish that they were still too young to earn a settlement in their own right. Tooley's circumstances were unexceptional; no employment engaged more hands than agricultural labor, and an annual hiring was the second most common ground for achieving a settlement, exceeded only by marriage (the wife taking her husband's settlement). In addition, the most common sort of examinee was the father of young children because of the prospect that the father might earn a new settlement and thus make the parish where he sojourned liable for the entire family.[2]

Polyblank had achieved settlement in a rural Devon parish by paying rent, which was somewhat unusual for that location, although quite common in the environs of London, even though Tooley had managed to avoid rents of £10 a year. Rents were, of course, much higher in the cities. All that was needed before 1819 was 40 days' occupancy at a rent that would, if continued over the course of a year, total £10. Minimally, only a little over £1 was actually needed, or 3/10½ per week for six weeks.[3] Since scrutiny in a large metropolitan parish would be imperfect, it was usually not difficult to become settled through rental payment before parish officers were aware of what was happening. The question is why anyone would wish to do so. Sojourners ordinarily preferred to retain an earlier settlement in another locality than to become a permanent charge on a large metropolitan parish, seldom a happy fate. There were, however, metropolitan parishes where the level of care might have made them attractive, St. Luke, Chelsea, and some of the City of London parishes, for example. Early nineteenth-century reforms of settlement law that made settlement by rental payment more difficult are indicative that at least some authorities thought urban parishes were abused by the relative ease with which a sojourner could achieve settlement by this means. To return to Tooley, it is quite likely he chose not to fulfill, or at least not to report, a settlement in St. Leonard, Shoreditch, in order to guard his connection with Walford.

* * *

2 September 1793

He was born in the parish of Tiverton, Devon, as he has been informed and believes, and lived with his parents, who are legally settled in Tiverton, till he was about twenty-eight years of age. From thence, he removed to Honiton, and kept a school, where he rented a room for £3 a year, but as a boarder. From thence, he removed to Harpford [Devon], where he kept a school for about eight years, but under no certain agreement for any rent except a few shillings for the school room, not amounting to above 1/ a week. From thence, he removed to Newton Poppleford in the parish of Aylesbear [Devon], where he lived about a year and a half in a house for a rent not exceeding 2gn. a year. From thence, he removed to Otterton [Devon], where he lived about one year for the rent of 2gn. or thereabouts. From thence, he came into East Budleigh, where he keeps a school, and gives £2.10 a year for rent. The examinant is now married, and has a wife called Maria, and one child called Maria, aged about three-quarters of a year. . . .

Thomas Thomas
East Budleigh, Devon

It is unlikely that this peripatetic schoolmaster concerned the parishes in which he had taught while still a bachelor, but a wife and young daughter aroused East Budleigh's interest, as in the case of Tooley. Most teachers, like most plowmen, fell within the economic range where adversity could quickly lead to dependency, and it was accordingly not an uncommon employment to turn up in records of settlement.

*　*　*

22 June 1798

She was born in the parish of Dawlish, Devon, but her parents' settlement was then in Kenton. About the age of ten years she was bound apprentice by a parish indenture to Benjamin Tanner in Kenton, and lived with him there about one year. Her master then ordered her to go and live with his father in the parish of the Holy Trinity in the City of Exeter. She lived with her master's father in that parish about three months. She then ran away and came again to Kenton. Her master was then living at Dartmouth in the said country. Her master then sent for her to live with him at Dartmouth, and she lived with him there about one week. She then ran away from him, and came again to Kenton. She was then committed to Bridewell [Prison in Exeter] for running away from her master. Then she was sent back to her master again, at Dartmouth, and continued running away from him at different times afterwards. She was then discharged from her master by the mayor of Dartmouth, and was then ordered by him to come home to Kenton, where she has resided ever since. This examinant has not done any other act whereby a settlement might be gained, according to her knowledge or belief.

Jane Torr
Kenton, Devon

If Torr had not rebelled, her settlement would have changed from Kenton to either Holy Trinity in Exeter or to a Dartmouth parish. Her determination to stay in Kenton led to her discharge from her apprenticeship, allowing her to retain her parents' parish of settlement. This may have been simply a case of a homesick girl, extraordinarily stubborn or courageous, and very possibly both, but the fear of permanent alienation from Kenton if she lost her settlement there may have been a factor in her thinking.

*   *   *

[no date given, ca. 1816]

Gentlemen to whom this writing may concern:

I, Samuel Rowe, was bound apprentice to John Shepherd to be taught to be a hellier [a worker with slate and tile], and if he should happen to die before my time was expired, Philip Shepherd, his son, was to teach me the business (that is, if his father should die, not else). Then John Shepherd, son of the aforesaid John Shepherd, being out of his apprenticeship, came home to his father to learn to be a hellier. But the old John Shepherd, knowing he had not employment for both of us, would rather that I should go off, and accordingly asked of me whether I should be willing to go along to his son Philip at Plymouth to work. I replied "yes" in hopes I might learn more at Plymouth than I could at home. And having been in Plymouth some time, Philip and I fell out. And our master, Mr. Eastridge, seeing and hearing us fall out and differ so much (at the pay-table at the Pack-Horse) took my part, and told Philip that he had no right to my wages (which were 10/ per week), nor would he pay them to him, but accordingly, Mr. Eastridge paid to me my week's wages.

Then Philip sent home to his father, and by the next Saturday night my old master, John Shepherd, came to where we were paid up, at the

Four Castles in Old Town, in order to take my wages. Where Mr. East-ridge held a dispute with him, saying he could not have any right to send me there, for if he had no employment for me, as he was alive, I was no longer his apprentice.

But then I, thinking they might lay a snare for me, left Plymouth, and came home to my father's house, and resided there (and thereabouts) for six weeks and upwards. But still fearing they would trouble me, I went to Plymouth to pick up a few books I had there where I lodged in order to elope off from this country. Then the people where I lodged asked how I went on, for I had not been there for some time. So I told them about my affair with my master, and that I was of a mind to elope off. Then they persuaded me to agree with my master for my remaining time [of apprenticeship], saying that my master might throw up the in-denture for two or three guineas, which if he would, they would spare me the money.

Then I came back that same night, and acquainted my father of it —and within a few days I, with my father, went to John Shepherd, and asked him whether he was agreeable to resigning my indenture, on condition, and he was very agreeable for the sum of 3gn. A few days later, after the money was paid, my indenture was resigned up at the Half Moon in Modbury [Devon]. This, Gentlemen, is the truth and nothing but the truth, which I am ready to make oath to.

Samuel Rowe
Modbury, Devon

Rowe, an unusually literate man for his position in life, had in effect volunteered his own settlement examination in order to show that Modbury, not Plymouth, was his parish of settlement. Like Jane Torr, he knew where he wished to be. The key here was that Rowe claimed that his old master had violated the terms of the apprenticeship and then had surrendered the indenture for a price. If Rowe had simply eloped, as he considered doing, the case would have been more complicated; it might have led to a Plymouth settlement, depending on the precise wording of the indenture and if he had had 40 days of service in one particular Plymouth parish.

Rowe may have felt that his master had misused him, but in fairness to John Shepherd senior, and other such masters, it should be pointed out that long hours and much cost might go into the training of an apprentice, only a portion of which was covered by whatever fee had been paid the master (a master might later hope to benefit from the apprentice's labor as the latter became more experienced). There was a natural conflict of interest. Apprentices, as they gained in years and employability, often considered themselves held down by their apprenticeship and rebelled. Masters thus had some incentive to treat mature apprentices reasonably well or agree to the sort of arrangement Rowe reached with old John Shepherd. Yet it did not always work, and runaway apprentices helped staff the Navy and colonize the Empire. Rowe himself would have left if he had not had unusually generous friends in Plymouth.

*   *   *

[no date given, ca. 1821]

He was born at Bulkington [north Warwickshire or north Wiltshire; which Bulkington is unspecified] 1 February 1786, and was the illegitimate son of Ann Randle by John Southern.

At about the age of five years pauper was brought up to London by his mother, who took lodgings in Webb Square, Shoreditch. Afterward, they moved to Bethnel Green, and then removed to Castle Street, Shoreditch. About the age of eight years (1794) he was bound an apprentice to Mrs. Jane Richardson, then living at King's Head Court, Fish Street Hill, chimney sweeper, for seven years.

Pauper was sent previously for a month to see how he liked the business,[4] and upon the expiration of the month some writing was entered into by which he was to serve Mrs. Richardson for seven years, but whether it was an indenture pauper cannot say—only that he, together with his mother, mistress, and her daughter, Jane Worden, went to the Guildhall, and were taken into some office; but what was said or done pauper cannot say or whether he signed a paper or not, don't know.

Pauper continued with Mrs. Richardson for about four years at King's Head Court, and then moved with her to George Lane, Pudding Lane, and remained there about twelve months—then removed with her to No. 1, Pea Hen Court, Bishopsgate, and remained there about three years, remaining with her about three months after the expiration of the seven years.

At the end of the seven years his mistress produced some paper, but whether an indenture or not, don't know, and told pauper that his time was up (Jane Worden being present), and told pauper that she would take care of the paper for pauper.

Soon after, pauper was pressed into His Majesty's Navy, and served first in the *St. Albans*, 64 guns; afterwards, the *York*, 64, then the *Dicta-*

tor, 64, then deserted and went to his mother at Bulkington. Soon after pauper's return to his mother she proposed that pauper should learn her business, and that she would find a loom and house, room, board, lodging, clothes, and every necessary, and that she was to receive the earnings of pauper. Under such arrangement pauper continued with his mother about eighteen months, when he married his first wife, then Elizabeth Lovett, at Bulkington Church, now about twenty years ago, but has no children by that marriage, and did not occupy apartments at a greater rent than 1/ a week. His first wife lived about two years after their marriage.

About a fortnight before Christmas sixteen years ago he married his present wife, Sarah Orton, at Bulkington Church, by whom he now has five children.

Upon his marriage with his second wife pauper rented a house of Richard Hewit at Ryton in Bulkington at £4.10 rent, and paid all taxes, continuing to hold that house about twelve years. For the last two years pauper paid a rent of £9.9.

About seven weeks ago he became chargeable to Bulkington, and was removed to St. Ethelburga.

John Randle
St. Ethelburga, London

Randle's story suggests that it was sometimes easier to gain than lose a London settlement; he was returned to the parish in which he had completed an apprenticeship almost thirty years before, his birth and long residence in Bulkington being inconsequential to the settlement. Note the care taken to determine that it was a true apprenticeship, which entailed a notarized document or indenture, although for the purpose of determining settlement oral testimony attesting to the existence of such a document was considered sufficient. If he had rented and paid taxes in Bulkington *before* 1795, he would have obtained a settlement there, but legislation of that year abolished settlement by ratepaying.

This was obviously an inequitable way of treating Randle and his family, but it was a common occurrence: it was not always easy for a person, Londoner or otherwise, to acquire a new settlement after military service and marriage, no matter how many years he or she had lived and worked in a parish, especially after legislation in 1819 made settlement by rent payment more difficult to achieve. Randle was fortunate in one respect—the apparent conscientiousness of his former mistress, Jane Richardson. Chimney sweeping in London was the most notoriously exploitive form apprenticeship could take, with excellent prospects for early death or permanent deformity.[5] That he survived until the age of sixteen and was then considered worth pressing into the Navy suggests good treatment by his former mistress, and good luck.

It is, of course, possible that Randle *wanted* to be in London, for it was only his testimony on the details of his apprenticeship that brought him back to a small parish in the City of London, where care of the poor may have been tolerably good. Motivation is the most difficult thing to determine, whether of actions of today or of a century or more away. All one can say is that a middle-aged man of broad experience in London streets and ships' decks, where a certain wit was a precondition to survival, was the sole witness to his own settlement, contingent on a single and relatively simple point—was he formally apprenticed or not.

* * *

23 December 1823

He is about twenty-four years of age, and was born at Great Stanmore, was married about two and three quarters years ago at Paddington Church by banns to his present wife, Elizabeth, by whom he has no child living. Says his father, William Clark, at the time of his death about twelve years ago, was settled at Great Stanmore. To the best of his belief, soon after his birth, his father ran away, and left his mother, and they were put into Stanmore Workhouse, where his mother died. He was there maintained till he believes the year 1813, when Mr. Nightingale, the overseer of Stanmore, sent him by Hawks, the farrier, to a public house at Greek Street, Leicester Fields, where he was employed as a potboy for nine months, his master finding him clothes, board, and lodging, he finding himself washing and mending.

After he had been there nine months the waiter went away, and his master asked him if he would like to take the waiter's place, as he might have it, which he accepted. He served in that place, his master still finding him clothes, board, and lodging, and he himself washing and mending. No wages were ever mentioned or ever paid. His master and he disagreed, and he left the place without giving or receiving notice. He then came back to Stanmore Workhouse, where he was maintained some time, and then went to live with Mr. Beaumont of Stanmore, carrier, at 1/ a week, board and lodging. He served him about six months, when he asked his master to raise his wages, which he did to 2/ a week for about four months, and then left him.

Thomas Clarke
Great Stanmore, Middlesex

Great Stanmore removed him to St. Martin-in-the-Fields, the parish in which he had served first as a potboy and then as a waiter, but St. Martin appealed to Quarter Sessions and the order of removal was quashed. Back to Great Stanmore went Thomas and Elizabeth Clarke.

In a case rather similar to this in 1774, it was held that "if a boy be hired as a boot-catcher and post-boy, but no term for which he was to serve is mentioned; and he is found in board and lodging, but receives no wages: this is a *general hiring*,"[6] which meant that it could be the basis of a settlement. What was lacking in Clarke's case was a complete year of service in the same position, something on which the law was very particular. Still another ground for quashing the order was that Clarke had been maintained in the Stanmore Workhouse *after* he had ceased working at the public house. If any case could have been made for his settlement in St. Martin-in-the-Fields, it ought to have been made when he returned to Great Stanmore. Setting up a pauper child as an alehouse potboy was a questionable proceeding in itself, and St. Luke, Chelsea, in another instance, considered it most improper.[7]

*   *   *

4 February 1826

James Radford, shopkeeper, saith he hath heard and believes he was born in the parish of St. Sidwell's, within the city of Exeter, and was regularly baptized in the parish church, as will appear by the parish register of baptisms. He derived this information as to the place of his birth from his mother, who has told him of a particular house in Longbrook Street in which he was born. As long since as he can recollect he was living with his parents in the parish of St. Thomas, in a small tenement of two rooms, his father working as a journeyman grounder of leather.

When deponent was about six or seven years old his father left his mother, and deponent continued to live with his mother in St. Thomas. When he was about ten years old he was placed at a blue coat school in Northernhay Street in Exeter, where he remained until he was near twelve years old, when a Mr. Scoble of Totnes came to the school, saying he was in want of a boy, and deponent being pointed out by his master, was asked if he was willing to go with Mr. Scoble as an apprentice. Mr. Scoble the same day sent for deponent's mother, and it was agreed between them that deponent should go a month upon trial, Mr. Scoble promising to keep him at school and bring him on in his learning, and it was understood that if the parties liked each other at the end of the month that he should be bound to him until he was twenty-one years old. With this arrangement, deponent went to Totnes and remained with Mr. Scoble during the month, when Mr. Scoble told him that if he behaved well during the time of his apprenticeship he would at the end of it give him £5 and two new suits of clothes. Deponent remained with him under this arrangement until he was twenty-one, and he verily believes he bound himself by an indenture an apprentice to Mr. Scoble, but from this distance (deponent being now a man sixty-seven years of age) he does not immediately recollect the execution of the indentures. He, however, recollects that when he was about twenty years of age, under the impression that he was one year older and that his apprenticeship was then nearly expired, his master procured from the parish of St. Sidwell's the register of his baptism, and he continued to live as before until he was twenty-one years old, when his master gave him £8 and a suit of clothes for good behavior during his apprenticeship.

Deponent, on expiration of his apprenticeship, left Mr. Scoble and hired himself with one Mr. Luscombe, an attorney of Totnes, having previously married at the close of his apprenticeship, and lived with Mr. Luscombe about six months, after which he returned and lived with Mr. Scoble about a year and a half, his wife renting two rooms during the time. He then removed to the parish of St. Andrew, Plymouth, and lived as a servant, and worked with one Mr. Hodge for about six years, renting rooms during that time, from £4 to £5 a year. Deponent then went to Tavistock, and kept a tollgate there for several years. He afterwards hired himself as a servant or bookkeeper to Mr. Lang of New Quay in Tavistock for three years at the wages of £20 a year, with a house to live in, for which house deponent procured a license as a victualler, and the business was conducted by his wife. The taxes, if any, were paid by Mr. Lang. He lived with Mr. Lang under this agreement, with a progressive advance of wages, for eight years, when he again took a tollgate, which he kept for some time.

He then took a house and shop in which he now resides. In 1819 he was appointed overseer of the poor of Tavistock, which office he performed for three years, and has since purchased some property for £200 and upwards in Tavistock. While living in Plymouth and working for Mr. Hodge, his son, James Radford the younger, was born, and removed with this deponent to Tavistock when he was about four or five years old. At the time deponent was living and keeping a tollgate he placed his son, who was then about eleven years old, with Mr. Martin, cordwainer, of Tavistock, as an apprentice for seven years to learn the art and trade of a cordwainer, deponent finding him everything (except shoes and aprons) and Mr. Martin paying deponent a certain sum weekly during the term. This agreement for the apprenticeship, though perfectly understood by the parties, was parol only, no indenture being prepared between them. Deponent's son served the seven years with Mr. Martin, living and boarding with deponent until about the last year and a half of his time, when deponent, having removed from the tollgate to New Quay, as before mentioned, his son slept and boarded with his sister in Tavistock. After his son left Mr. Martin's service he worked some time in Tavistock, and then enlisted in the North Devon Regiment of Militia, in which he served three or four years, during which time he married, and he afterwards turned out from the militia into a regular regiment, in which he remained several years, returning to Tavistock with his wife and child about 1814. At the time deponent kept his tollgate subsequent to his leaving Mr. Lang. His son has ever since resided in Tavistock, working as a journeyman cordwainer.

James Radford
Tavistock, Devon

Clearly, the elder James Radford was settled in Tavistock several times over (though not when he operated a tollgate, the law making an exception to any occupancy involving that occupation). The son's settlement was in question because the father had set his son up in a spurious apprenticeship, there being no indentures, and the younger James Radford had then gone on to serve some twelve years as a soldier, with no opportunity to establish a new settlement of his own. Veterans of Britain's many wars of the eighteenth and early nineteenth centuries were cruelly victimized by the Law of Settlement, for during their term of service they could not acquire settlement in their own right, the prime years for doing so. Those who survived the fighting and the diseases often returned to social insecurity.

This particular case went to the midsummer Quarter Sessions in Exeter, where justice and law parted company, the son's settlement being adjudged to be in Totnes, where his father had long before served his apprenticeship. Although the father had later obtained a new settlement in Tavistock, that was well after the son was legally emancipated through marriage and military service. So now a man, his wife, and four children were the legal charge of a strange parish that could have felt little real sense of responsibility toward them.

The story is also interesting in showing how far a man could rise. The senior James Radford appears to have had a caring mother and a good first master. He himself was clearly energetic and ambitious. From a broken home in an Exeter tenement, he had become a prosperous shopkeeper in Tavistock. Bad feeling between the senior Radford and his son seems likely, for the father was certainly in a financial position to help his son. Perhaps, like many self-made men, the father thought the son should make it on his own, not appreciating the differences in circumstances. The father had been fortunate in missing the wars; at a different time his residence in Plymouth might well have been cut short by impressment. Moreover, the mother of the senior Radford had done much more for him than he had done for his own son, for she had placed him in school and saw to it that he was properly apprenticed. Another deposition in the case stated that the irregular apprenticeship of the younger Radford to Martin, the cordwainer, was specifically designed to prevent the boy from achieving a settlement by apprenticeship, because Tavistock penalized masters who took apprentices from outside the parish by saddling them forthwith with a parish apprentice as well. This was a common procedure for restricting the number of new settlements. Nevertheless, a man as enterprising and prosperous as the senior James Radford could have made better provision for his son.

Few of those whose stories appear in settlement records did as well for themselves as the senior James Radford. Failure and tragedy are immeasurably better represented than success. There was John Tribe, who crisscrossed southern England in search of work as a sawyer. The father of fifteen children by the same wife, only three of whom were still alive, he was a widower in

1826 when he told his tale "on a bed of sickness" in the Totnes poorhouse.[8] And Sarah Paxton, apprenticed to a mantua maker in central London, was deserted by her mistress only a year after Paxton was indentured, for a fee, of course—it was not only apprentices who ran away.[9] And Ann Packer, apprenticed to Farmer Blake of Kenton, had to leave in 1825 at the age of fifteen because Blake's son impregnated her. Eight years later she was examined yet again, after being discharged from service a second time for being in the "family way."[10]

The whole system of deciding settlement on the basis of an apprenticeship or a premarital annual hiring was more suitable to a preindustrial economy. Apprentices appeared in the factories of early industrial Britain, but the logic of the factory system favored weekly wages to workers who were dischargeable at the discretion of the employer, not seven-year indentures and annual contracts. A worker could spend years in a factory, only to find in sickness or age that his settlement lay in a rural parish where he had been born or raised or done some act earlier in life to earn a settlement. That was not necessarily to the pauper's disadvantage, but it deprived him of choice, sometimes resulted in great personal hardship, and was unquestionably unfair to the rural parish that had not benefited from the factoryhand's labor, except under a transient contract years earlier. The women who worked in John Berry's factory in Chagford, Devon, lived in a rural village on the edge of Dartmoor, but they were employed at weekly wages. No matter how long they wove for Mr. Berry, when they were no longer needed or able to work, Chagford could give them settlement examinations and send them home.[11] There was an important alternative to removal (see Chapter Seven), but for now it is sufficient to note that wherever industry employed labor, whether country village or industrial town, there might be jobs for sojourners in good times, but there might not be settlements. In this way, agrarian England contributed to the takeoff phase of the Industrial Revolution.

Domestic Servants

A quartet of domestic servants' stories illustrate the peculiar problems created by the Law of Settlement for members of one of the largest of all occupations at the time of the Industrial Revolution.

*   *   *

10 November 1791

Ann Clossen, otherwise Barker, aged twenty-four years or thereabouts, and baptized at the parish church of St. George in the East in August of 1782, by name of Ann Barker, upon her oath saith that she was never married, that she was brought over from Africa to England by Captain Moore, with whom she lived in Kent Street in the borough [of Westminster] about six years, having diet, lodging and clothes, but no wages—and quitted his service when baptized. She then hired herself as a yearly servant on Midsummer Day, 25 June 1790, and continued in her said service with Mr. H.S.L. Neale, a surgeon in John Street, Adelphi, in the parish of St. Martin-in-the-Fields, for the space of three months at the yearly wages of 7½gn., diet, and lodging, and then discharged herself from her said master's service in order to live with John Clossen, a black man, at Mr. Molton, Red Deer, Bethnal Green, with whom she continued about a month.

In consequence of some words, she left him and applied to Mr. Neale to know if he wanted a servant, and he again hired her, on 20 October 1790 at the yearly wages of 8gn., diet and lodging, and continued with her said master under that hiring until 20 September last, and then was discharged [for on that day she was] delivered at the house of Mr. Brown in Off Alley in the same parish of a male bastard child, since baptized Robert, yet living, and chargeable to the same parish, and that Robert Allen, who lived servant with Mr. Neale, did beget of her body the said male bastard child, and is the true and only father thereof and no man else.

Ann Barker
St. Martin-in-the-Fields, Westminster

Chief Justice Mansfield declared in 1772 that slavery within England was "so odious that nothing can be suffered to support it but positive law." [12] There was no such law, but Mansfield's ruling was narrowly couched in the landmark case of James Somersett, and slaves continued to live in England for years after. It may have been in that capacity that Ann Barker first served Captain Moore, considering the circumstances outlined in her examination. Black servants were in demand in eighteenth-century London, and certainly her material fortunes improved dramatically after baptism and a new master.

Barker's story, quite apart from that, illustrates a central dilemma in the settlement stories of domestic servants—how to reconcile a master's expectation that the servant would remain unattached with the servant's desire to marry or at least to have a relationship with a person of the opposite sex. If such a relationship led to an illegitimate child, or if the master became aware of a marriage before a child was born, the consequence was usually loss of employment.

*   *   *

18 October 1800

She is the widow of Richard Toms, deceased, who has been dead six years, and was married to him in the parish church of St. George, Bloomsbury, about fifteen years ago. Her husband was a yearly servant to Godfrey, Esq., of Charlotte Street, in the same parish, in the capacity of footman, at the yearly wages of £24, and served his master, under a hiring, for some years. This examinant was also a servant to the said Godfrey in the same house in the capacity of cook and housekeeper at the yearly wages of 12gn., in which service she had been for eight years.

This examinant and her said late husband quitted such service, and were married. They had three children, living, namely George, aged fourteen years, now at school at Mitchum; Peter, aged eleven, now on board the *Tiger*, commanded by Sir Sydney Smith; and Amy, aged about seven, now at a friend's house at Woolwich. This examinant further saith that she nor her late husband did any act whereby to gain them any subsequent legal settlement. Having been lately discharged from prison, and wandering abroad, and being found in the street, she was by the officer put in the workhouse of St. Leonard, Shoreditch.

Margaret Toms
St. Leonard, Shoreditch, London

In this case, the end of domestic service seems connected to the beginning of marriage. Although how the Toms fared after leaving Godfrey is unclear, it is likely that things had not prospered for them, for they achieved no settlement elsewhere and the widow had sunk low. Since domestic servants who married usually faced loss of employment and a precipitous decline in living conditions, it is little wonder they were given to liaisons, as in the preceding case of Ann Barker. Even if a domestic servant were permitted to marry, the family had to be divided in a manner convenient to the employer and destructive to family life.

There was still another hardship visited on domestic servants. Because they often moved with their employers and might in the course of their service earn several successive settlements based on annual hirings, they could find themselves at the end of their working lives in strange surroundings, without friends, relatives, or the benevolence that long-established paupers might receive from more generous neighbors. To be sure, a fortunate servant might be helped in time of need by a former master, but the settlement examinations suggest that all too frequently the former domestic servant, whatever the reason for leaving service, suffered a dramatic decline in status, income, and security.[13]

*   *   *

19 May 1827

He was born, as he hath heard and believes to be true, in Kenton, Devon, where his parents then resided. He never was bound apprentice, but worked with his father in Kenton as a shoemaker till he was about fourteen years of age, when he agreed to live with Mr. William Jeffrey at Huntspill in Somerset at £10 a year, and served him about seven months. He then agreed with Mr. Dougan at East Teignmouth for 16gn. a year, and lived with him under that agreement about eight months. He then went to London for about two months, and returned again to Kenton, and agreed to work with Mr. Landers in Kenton for six months at 6/ a week. He worked about four months and left. After that he agreed to live with Mr. Boulton in Kenton for 18gn. a year, and lived with him one month.

He then went to work for Captain Ash in Kenton as a laborer on board lighters, and worked for him about two years. He then worked in Starcross for different masters as a laborer for about five months. He then went to London to get service, and hired himself to a Mr. Barnet, No. 16, Lower Berkeley Street, for 30gn. a year, and lived with him about nine months, and then left.

Since that time he has never lived as a servant, nor never did any act whereby to gain a settlement but as above stated. He married Jane, his present wife, in the parish of St. Paul, Exeter, by whom he has three

children. When he married he was about nineteen years of age, and that
when he married it was after he parted from the employ of Mr. Landers
and before he went to live with Mr. Boulton.

   William Warren
   Kenton, Devon

How does one account for the succession of good positions,
briefly held? It seems likely he was a prepossessing young man,
but whether he was restless, shiftless, unable to adjust to domestic service, or shrewdly avoiding the loss of his Kenton settlement is unknowable. Very likely, it was some combination of
these.

Although he married while still attempting domestic service,
it is probable that his wife saw little of him while he served Mr.
Barnet in Lower Berkeley Street. Marriage *after* the annual hiring
had begun would not in itself invalidate a claim to settlement,
so long as the annual hiring was completed under the master's
roof. That was not done in this case.

Warren's examination suggests how mobile a young man could
be if he seemed promising material for domestic service.[14] Like
the Empire, like the sea, domestic service offered the qualified
young man and woman an opportunity to escape a humdrum
and parochial life, as well as good wages, travel, and a way of
life likely to appear romantic to the child of laborer or artisan.
The price in potential marital grief and personal insecurity later
in life would not have deterred a young teenager like Warren,
bored with his shoemaker's last. At any event, in Warren's case,
through luck or calculation, he did not lose his native settlement
for some strange new parish far from home, as so many domestic
servants did.

*   *   *

22 February 1829

This examinant says he has heard and believes he was born in the
parish of Hill Ridware in the County of Stafford. When he was about
sixteen, he hired himself as a postilion to Thomas Thornhill, Esquire, of
the parish of St. George in the City of London. He served him, partly in
London and partly at Finby Hall in the parish of Huddersfield in Yorkshire, for about five years, by the year. The latter part of his time he

was at Finby Hall. Mr. Thornhill afterwards took Riddlesworth Hall in
the parish of Riddlesworth in Norfolk. He continued as a yearly servant
with him for a year and three-quarters afterward. For nearly the last six
months of that time he was at Riddlesworth Hall.

He afterwards was hired as undercoachman to the Right Honorable
Earl Fortescue in Grosvenor Square for a year at the wages of 25gn.
[Hugh, First Earl Fortescue, 1753–1841]. He continued with his lordship
about fourteen months. He was sometimes in London and sometimes
at Castle Hill in the parish of Filleigh, Devon. Then he served Lord
Yarborough for a year. Then he served Lord Granville Leveson-Gower
two years, by the year. Then he served Lord Fortescue six years, by
the year. He was usually in London with his lordship some months in
every year, and he served the latter part of the six years in Grosvenor
Square. He was then married, and had since done no act whereby to
gain a settlement.

    William Shaw
    South Molton, Devon

Shaw had traversed England many times as a young man in
service to the aristocracy. Later in life he found himself in a pleasant north Devon parish, but he, like Harriet Williams, appears
to have had his legal settlement in St. George, Hanover Square.
Since this particular examination is preserved in the Fortescue
Papers, not in a parish records collection, it is likely that Lord
Fortescue gave material assistance to his former servant. Such
support was not always forthcoming, as we shall see in the case
of Lady Audley's sick cook, but it is unwise to be too skeptical of
the fruits of private benevolence. This was an age of paternalism,
and that influenced both peers and parish officers.

FOUR

Travelers

LONDON WAS EXCEPTIONAL in its ability to attract sojourners from all over the British Isles, but only a small number ever
ventured more than a day's journey or two from their parish
of settlement. Indeed, generally the number of sojourners in a
particular parish from another parish was inversely proportional
to the distance between the parishes. Yet some sojourners did
travel far; most commonly they were associated with three occupations: soldiering, seafaring, peddling. This chapter studies
such sojourners and the special problems they and their families
sometimes faced when it came time to determine the parish of
settlement.

Soldiers

11 August 1762

He was born in the parish of Sampford Peverell [Devon], and lived
there with his parents until he was thirteen years of age. Then he was
bound an apprentice by the churchwardens and overseers of the poor
of Sampford Peverell to Francis Surrage of the said parish, and served
him as an apprentice about nine years, and then went away by his master's consent. He went into the parish of St. Thomas the Apostle, near
Exeter, and worked to day labor about six weeks. Then he came and
served his said master, Francis Surrage, as a covenant servant for half
a year. Then his master yielded up to him his indenture. He then went
into the parish of Mamhead, Devon, and lived with John Soaper for a
month. At the expiration of that month he agreed with the said John
Soaper for a year to serve him in husbandry affairs, and lived with him
three-quarters of a year.

He then entered himself a soldier in Colonel Watson's 60th Regiment
of Foot, and served a year and a quarter under him as a soldier, in

which time he had his right arm shot off by a cannon ball in taking of Guadeloupe. He then was admitted back to Chelsea Hospital, and got his discharge. He was asked what parish he would go to, and said Sampford Peverell. He came back into the said parish, and soon after was married. He has done no other act to gain a settlement than as aforesaid.

Joseph Wadland
Sampford Peverell, Devon

This veteran of the Seven Years War, styled husbandman by the parish officers, was probably examined soon after his marriage, but it is clear that he belonged to Sampford Peverell, if he told his story truly. He had as a young man stretched his wings in the Vale of Exeter, but it was his military service that had led to distant travels.

* * *

23 June 1783

About seven years ago she intermarried with Joseph Welch, her present husband, who was then a private soldier serving in America in His Majesty's 44th Regiment of Foot, and was married at New York in America. Says about three months ago she came with her husband from America to England and came to reside in the parish of Harrow-on-the-Hill, but has no children now living by her said husband. And further says she has heard her husband say, and she believes it to be true, that the place of his last legal settlement is the parish of Harrow-on-the-Hill, and that he gained such settlement by being an apprentice to James Smith of the parish, tailor. About seven days ago her husband went away and left her, and she believes he is gone to America, as she has neither seen nor ever heard from him since.

Sarah Welch
Harrow-on-the-Hill, Middlesex

Doubtless there is a dramatic tale behind this flimsy outline, and certainly it is ironical that this American woman should end as a charge on her husband's English parish, while her English husband apparently sought a new life in the former colonies, among people with whom he had once been at war. We do not know if this was a case of desertion. Perhaps he asked her to come with him and she refused; that she should think he had gone to America suggests some discussion before he left Harrow-on-the-Hill.

* * *

To John B. Cholwich[1]

8 December 1789

Dear Sir:

The woman who now waits on you says she is wife of Joseph [John] Oldfield, a private in the 1st Regiment of Dragoon Guards, quartered here, who also waits on you. This woman applied on Sunday last to our overseers for relief, who refused her any assistance. The sergeant who accompanies these people will give you a particular account of their characters, by no means in their favor. Be so good as to order what must be done, as the woman is big with child, and probably not married. The man was removed from Sidbury here as a disorderly person, and as such he is not fit to be continued here, as we have no officer to keep proper order. Our overseer attends.

I am, dear sir, your obedient servant

W. Jenkins

The Vicarage, Sidmouth, Devon

Cholwich, a magistrate, took John and Mary Oldfield's settlement examinations. The private claimed to have married Mary two or three years before at Linlithgow in Scotland, but "about six months after he was married, when he was in liquor, he destroyed his certificate." He also claimed to have been married a few years earlier in Lincoln to a woman whose name he could not quite remember. Ann or Elizabeth, he thought it was. But in a day or two her real husband claimed her as his wife, "and, on a complaint to John Oldfield's captain, he was obliged to give her up." Oldfield was a Yorkshireman, and his presumed wife, Mary, was from Northumberland. Cholwich's response was practical and forthright.

To W. Jenkins

10 December 1789

My Dear Sir:

Excuse want of paper; I am at the White Cross; there is none in the house. I see nothing better that can be done than to give the woman such necessary relief as she wants. She and her child will remove with the regiment. It would cost you much more to send her either to Northumberland or Yorkshire. You will keep the examinations in case of an accident. I am in great haste, being engaged to go to Tidwell [an estate in East Budleigh].

Ever yours sincerely,
John B. Cholwich
[Farringdon, Devon]

The White Cross was a public house located in Colaton Raleigh on the Exeter–Sidmouth road, and it was destroyed by fire in 1818. One can picture this busy, conscientious magistrate scribbling his note in a small, cold parlor on the only scrap of paper that came to hand, treating the matter in the same fashion as the clerk at Kenton had dealt with Harriet Williams. Here, too, there would be no lasting charge on the parish, for the regiment and its camp followers would move on. The solution was to give them something for their immediate needs rather than to undertake an expensive and problematical removal (although it might have been a kindness to Mary if the parish had intervened to separate her from her husband).

*   *   *

14 January 1806
Ann Jones, aged forty-five years, maketh oath and saith that she was born at Morden in Surrey, and came to live with Mrs. Scott of Colney Hatch in the parish of Friern Barnet in the year 1783, with whom she lived sixteen months at the wages of 9gn. a year. In June of 1785 she was married to Walter Tudor Jones, who was then a soldier, and had been nine years in the Royal Artillery at Woolwich. The general of that company, seeing the said W. T. Jones was so very assiduous, engaged him as his livery servant at 12gn. a year, with whom he lived in that capacity for twenty-three years, but did not obtain his discharge. He therefore received his pay as a soldier, being 4/6 per week, and from his later indisposition, was placed with the invalids at Woolwich about two months before he died.

The said Ann Jones went to service several times during her marriage, first to live with Mrs. Vachell of Holly Street, Cavendish Square, for two and a half years at 20gn. for the first year and 10gn. for the second, and at the same rate for the half year. From thence, she went to live with Mrs. Wheatly of Lesney [Park], near Lessness Heath [Kent] for three years, for the first of which she received 20gn., and 10gn. for each of the others. From thence, she went to live with Mrs. Moonyer of Baker Street, Portman Square, three years for 13gn. a year. She continued in her little house, for which she paid 3gn. a year till about 20 December 1805, being two months after her husband's death, up to which time she paid rent, property tax, and poor rate. Ann Jones has now living three children, namely Walter Tudor, aged nineteen, Lucy, aged sixteen, and Charles, aged three. She never heard her husband say what parish he belonged to, only that he came from Hereford.

 Ann Jones
 Friern Barnet, Middlesex

After her examination, Ann Jones and her youngest child were removed from Kent to Friern Barnet, where she had earned a settlement by service before her marriage. Presumably, her older children were already apprenticed or in service. Her husband's long service to the general was inconsequential to settlement, as was her own employment after her marriage. The family probably had ample income while both parents worked, although it would have been a fitful sort of family life they occasionally shared in the "little house." (If that house was in Friern Barnet and she had paid rates there before 1795, she had a still later claim on the parish.) The Law of Settlement did provide two concessions to soldiers, although neither was of any use to Ann Jones. First, the time spent in military service might, with a master's consent, count toward the fulfillment of a year's contractual service. Second, soldiers, sailors, and their families were entitled to relief in transit to the parish of settlement on presentation of a certificate or pass, and they were not liable to fines or penalties under the vagrancy acts. Since this last right was generally accorded to all reasonably well behaved sojourners, all this did was affirm that soldiers and mariners should be treated in like manner.[2] A few veterans qualified for hospital and pension benefits, but most could expect relief only under the poor law. Since the law was administered paternalistically, there were, no doubt, many instances in which a parish officer was generous to a former soldier or sailor. Veterans were legally entitled to few benefits, however, and suffered the great disability of being unable to qualify for a new settlement while drawing pay, a disability dramatically affecting Ann Jones and her three-year-old son, Charles. Her examination illustrates yet again the perils of domestic service, as well as the curious limbo reserved for those in military service and their dependents.

Mariners

28 November 1740

Honorable Sir:

With humble submission I beg leave to acquaint your honor that my husband, William Morton, did formerly belong to His Majesty's Ship, the *Prince of Orange*, then under the command of Captain Davies, and was sent up to London in one of the tenders in the room of a pressed man the latter end of November last—but being taken ill of a fever and ague, which continued upon him almost three months, he could not repair on board to his duty.

Soon after his recovery, his ship having sailed for the Mediterranean, he entered voluntarily on board His Majesty's Ship, the *Cambridge*, where he now remains, under the command of Captain Whorwood, who has been so good as to give me the certificate you will herewith receive. As I have already two children to maintain, and probably may have more, I hope your honor will consider me, and get his name off the *Prince of Orange*'s books, for the better support of myself and poor family, for which favor I shall ever be bound in duty to pray.

Mary Morton
St. Helen, Bishopsgate, London

This petition, almost certainly written for Mary Morton, is part of a collection of documents concerning William Morton among the pass warrants and pauper examination papers of St. Helen, Bishopsgate. Also included are Morton's power of attorney and will, dated the previous July, giving his wife full authority and benefit. The presence of the Morton papers in a parish collection illustrates how the sojourner, and those he left behind in the parish of settlement, turned to the parish in times of distress.

Four years after Mary Morton wrote for help, her husband, describing himself as shipwright and mariner, wrote a remarkable journal of an adventure, and sent it to his wife, with this note: "My Dear, you may show this on occasion if anything be said against me, as to how I have served my King and country, and the merchants in England. And I think it very hard to receive such hard usage as I do, when I have done all that lay in my power to save the ship and cargo, and have saved her by my own hands." Written in his own hand, the prose is rough and occasionally obscure, but it displays a clarity of mind and a vigorous independence of spirit that may explain the British Navy's victories in the eighteenth century.

7 November 1744

This day, being the 7th November, I, William Morton, being then on board the good brig *Speedwell* in Antigua, commanded by Captain Bagwell, Irish-bound, from thence to London in the kingdom of England, laden with sugars and consigned on several merchants, Mr. Thomas Perkins, merchant, being authorized as part owner, we sailed in company with the *Ellen*, man-of-war, Captain Durell commanding, with several other merchant ships under his convoy for the Island of St. Kitts to take water, and on the 10th day of that month set sail again to proceed on our voyage.

On the 17th November he put Commodore Knowles' packet on board us, and so hailed away north, and we to the east, taking leave of each other, with two merchant ships and a snow [a small sailing vessel, resembling a brig] in company of us, one bound for Bristol, and the snow for Dublin. Meeting with hard weather, we parted and lost sight of each other.

On the 15th December in the morning we spied a vessel which proved to be a French privateer, called the *Enterprize*, belonging to Bayonne, 12 carriage guns, 24 swivels and 150 men, and gave us chase until seven the night of the 17th. Coming up with us, she fired nine guns on us, and obliged us to strike. They boarded us, and took the captain and mate [line obscured], and put on board eleven men, captain and mate, to navigate the vessel to France, being then their prize.

We then kept in company with the privateer until the 19th. After the plundering and shipping of us, the weather proving bad by a great storm, we parted from them, and on the 23rd, about ten in the morning, beating the seas, our foremast, fore-topmast and main-topmast were carried away, and three of the French carried overboard, two we saved and one drowned, with my [countrymen?] cutting the lanyards, hoping we should meet with a man-of-war during all that day.

On the 24th we got up a jury mast and made what sail we could but driving hard the same night we fell in with the Haskets [Blasket Island?] about ten, where we spied land, and seeing the breakers flying, we stood off till the next morning. Then we spied Loop Head [northern mouth of the River Shannon], where the French gave up the ship and all to our care. Upon which I told the captain and the rest of the French that they were my prisoners. Then they begged of me to let them have the boat to make off, which I refused. Then I stood in for land.

On the 25th [Christmas], we came to anchor under Loop Head, being the entrance to the River of Limerick [Shannon] and hoisted a signal of distress halfmast high, and lay at anchor, with two anchors down, both cables at an end, where we lay all night. Next morning we took down the signal of distress, and hoisted a signal for a pilot. About ten in the morning of the 26th a boat came on board with a pilot and six hands more, who refused doing service until I produced a note for 20gn. in order to bring me into a harbor where I could get a mast and rigging for the ship.

Then I told the French captain they were my prisoners, and demanded his papers, whereupon he took them out of his pocket, and desired me to grant him the favor that he should keep them until he came to a magistrate, which I granted, and then proceeded. Weighed our anchor, the pilot at the same time said he would lay her ashore in the mud and make sail for Limerick, to save the trouble of weighing anchor, which I refused, and he brought her to anchor at Carrigaholt, where I took the ship's boat, one man, and the French captain and mate in her with me ashore in order to find a magistrate to make my condition known to him.

I met with a man who talked broken English and French, who told me that he would carry me to one Mr. McMahon. The gentleman immediately came to me, and finding the condition we were in, provided refreshment for us. We refreshed ourselves, and invited him on board, and two other gentlemen, to take a glass of wine with me. On coming on board with me, they told the French that they were their prisoners, which I refused, and desired to affront no man on board. One of them, in French, demanded the French captain's writings, who gave them to him. Nevertheless, I made a demand of them, as my property, being the bills of lading, on which they quarreled with me, and forced me out of my cabin. A little time after [an officer from] the King's yacht [words unclear] boarded us, and finding that he was surveyor and captain, having His Majesty's [orders?] on board him, I gave up the vessel into his charge, and told him that I had twelve French prisoners on board, and carried him into the cabin where I had them confined, and delivered them to him as prisoners of war.

I desired him to carry them to some castle or place where they could be secured, and at the same time made another demand of the papers from Mr. McMahon. Whereupon Mr. Thomas [the King's officer] and he had hot words, Mr. Thomas telling him he had no right to them, and assuring me that the place where the ship lay was not safe, if it should chance to blow a hard gale, and told me that he had His Majesty's pilot on board, whereupon I gave the vessel in charge to the pilot, telling him his life was at stake if anything should happen to the vessel. Upon which, he weighed anchor the same night and brought her in tow with Mr. Thomas's vessel to Admore [?], where we cast anchor next morning, being the 27th. Mr. Thomas took her in tow again, and brought her up to the River Limerick Quay, where she now lies, and gave up the prisoners in custody, who were put into the King's castle, and supplied me with everything I wanted in favor of my merchants and owners, and still continues them credit.

But in his zeal for praise and profit Morton had offended men of a higher social order, and he himself landed in prison. Six months later he wrote from Dublin to his brother in London.

Dear Brother: 22 June 1745

I hope these few lines will find you in health, and my wife and children together, as I am at present, thank God. I am released out of my confinement by the government, and I do expect in less than ten days to have a trial for the ship and cargo together, and in our side a legal prize.

Dear brother, I think it very strange that my wife never these twelve weeks did send me word how she or my children were, or how affairs went with them, for to hear from them would be a great satisfaction to my mind. And to the contrary, in rejecting me, they may be highly mistaken, for I hope I shall be the making of them, even though they paid no mind to me in my confinement. I believe I shall be at home in less than two months, and, by God's assistance, unbeholding [sic] my blessing to my children. I hope I shall see them soon, and I with my wife may do well.

My dear brother, if there be any secret, I hope you'll let me know it in your answer to me, to the Sign of the Ram in Aungier Street, Dublin, by next post, fail not. My love to Johnny and Betty, not forgetting my sister, and all well-wishers.

    William Morton
    Dublin

And in the margin he wrote: "I am uneasy. Do not neglect. As soon as you can." Among stories of desertion, bigamy, and neglect, it is refreshing to find one that shows familial devotion, although we are left to wonder with William Morton if his wife's silence held meaning.

It is unlikely that much came of Morton's project. His case would lie with the High Court of Admiralty in Dublin, but it was not a good one in law, for although a ship that was taken as a prize could be claimed as salvage by the recaptors, there was an exception. As William Pritchard writes, "Seamen of the saved ship in the ordinary course of things, in the performance of their duties, are not allowed to become salvors, whatever may have been the perils, hardships or gallantry of their services."[3] What does seem probable is that Morton received some reward from the merchants who benefited from the recapture, for the parish records contain no further mention of the Mortons until twelve years afterward when the vestry book of St. Helen, Bishopsgate, records the appointment of Mary Morton as "searcher of the parish."[4] A settled parishioner and most probably a widow, her job was to examine dead bodies within the parish and report the cause of death. The plague had long since departed London, and the position, however unenviable, was probably not onerous, but it does suggest that William Morton's reach had exceeded his grasp.

* * *

Michaelmas, 1777

Michael Frederick Murray, a Hanoverian, on his oath saith that in the year 1739 he entered the service of the King of Great Britain whom he continued to serve on board His Majesty's ships during the two last wars, and in the year 1761 was discharged from the service on account of his having had his left arm wrist cut through, the first joint of his right thumb jammed off in pursuit of a French ship, a gun shot wound in his right leg, and other wounds.

He lived at Boston in America from the year 1762 till the present year as a sugar baker, when being pressed to take up arms against the Government he had his sugar house and other buildings leveled with the ground, and he with his wife, Esther, and a daughter called Catherine, about a twelve-month old, quitted America and came to England in the Lisbon Transport.

Michael Frederick Murray
Exeter, Devon

Examined as a vagrant at Quarter Sessions, Murray was simply discharged. The law gave magistrates power to whip and imprison vagrants, but in such circumstances anything other than a discharge, unless the authorities thought he lied, would have been unthinkable. Murray had a story to move the paternalist to benevolence, but of that there is no record.

*   *   *

25 April 1795

Ten years ago, three weeks before last Christmas, she was married to Luke Calvin, at Haverfordwest in the Principality of Wales. She hath heard her husband say he was born in New York in North America, and was brought up at George's Quay in the City of Dublin within the Kingdom of Ireland, and served his apprenticeship with a captain of a ship belonging to Liverpool in Lancashire. And this examinant further saith that she was delivered of Catherine Calvin, her daughter by her husband Luke, at Hatherleigh, Devon, four years ago the day after Christmas last.

Ann Calvin
Warkleigh, Devon

Mariners were sometimes part of a transatlantic community, as was revealed to the officers of this rural, interior, north Devon parish through Ann Calvin's examination. Her husband was even then in His Majesty's service, and there is no indication she was in need or that she was removed. The sea was moat and wall, but it was also an avenue, bringing world travelers to England's parishes, not all of them mariners or merchants. One strange case was that of Isaac Furness, a "China man" who had earned his settlement in St. Michael, Crooked Lane, London, by renting a house at £42 per annum in the early nineteenth century, for which he paid rates for thirteen years. He later earned another settlement in Islington by the same means. A hairdresser by trade, perhaps, as in the case of Alexander Sanders, he found his ethnic difference a positive advantage. He must have been a humane man, for he had brought a boy from Copenhagen, the illegitimate offspring of a Danish shipowner and servant girl, and had himself raised the boy and given him an apprenticeship.[5] Even the foreign-born could earn an English settlement by renting, one of the easiest ways in large cities to acquire settlement. It is intriguing to read settlement cases with an international dimension, and perhaps nowhere were they more frequent than in the gentle county of Devon where so many men went to sea, or across it. Here are three.

*   *   *

6 July 1825

He was born, as he hath heard and believes to be true, in Kenton, where his parents resided and were legally settled. When he was about fourteen or fifteen years of age he went to sea with Captain Sheppard of Starcross, and sailed with him about four months. Then he left him at Sunderland [Durham], and went to sea with another Captain Sheppard, of Sunderland, for 15/ a month, and served him about six months, when the vessel was lost. He then agreed with Captain Clark of the ship *Boddington* to go with him to the West Indies for 25/ a month. He remained in this service during one voyage, which was about nine months, and left the vessel on her return to London. He then agreed to go in the *Europa*, a voyage to the East Indies and back, for 26/ per month. He performed this voyage in about twenty months, but before he returned to England he was impressed into His Majesty's service.

After that he agreed to go a voyage to the East Indies in the *Exeter*, Wilson commander. He performed that voyage, and was again impressed on his return to the Downs [a roadstead off the Kentish coast that affords a good anchorage behind the natural breakwater of Goodwin Sands], and remained in His Majesty's service ten years. Since that time he has sailed in different vessels as a master, his place of residence being at Starcross. He never rented £10 a year nor did any act whereby to obtain a settlement but as above stated.

Charles Tucker
Kenton, Devon

*   *   *

7 February 1828

He was born at a place called Marlborough Head [Marblehead, Massachusetts?] in North America. When he was about the age of eleven years he entered the American merchant service as a common seaman, and continued in that service until he was about twenty-one years of age, when he was taken from the American ship and pressed on board the *Crescent*,[6] frigate, where he remained seven years, when he was drafted on board another frigate, where he remained four and a half years, when he was discharged.

He then came to Totnes, where he remained two months, when he entered into the Newfoundland service in the employ of Messrs. Blacker and Cranford. He was in their employ nine months, when he returned to England and got into the employ of Mr. Henry Holdsworth of Dartmouth as a seaman. He continued in that employ four years, when he went into Mr. Henry Pinsent's employ, and went to Labrador. He was in that employ four years, when he went into the employ of Mr. Thomas Pinsent, and remained five months. He then returned to Totnes where he has resided ever since. About the year 1816 he married Sarah, his present wife, in the parish church of Totnes, by whom he has no children.

Richard Renur
Totnes, Devon

* * *

10 December 1832

I am about forty-three years of age, and I was born, as I have been informed and verily believed, in the parish of North Huish, Devon. When about twelve months old I was taken by my uncle to live with him in Ugborough, where I resided till I was about eleven years old, when my uncle died, and I was sent to Plymouth to live with my parents.

After the expiration of about three months, I was bound apprentice by a voluntary binding by my father to Mr. William Norris, a tailor of Ugborough, to serve him as an apprentice till I was twenty-one. The indenture was duly stamped and prepared by Mr. Andrews, solicitor, Modbury, and signed by myself, my father, and my master at his office. I served my master in Ugborough under this indenture till I was about nineteen, when I ran away, and agreed to bind myself to Captain Fry, captain of a merchantman. My master found out where I was, and came to Plymouth and claimed me. My aunt paid £10 to my master to get him to give up the indentures, and they were burnt. I then bound myself to Captain Fry for three years as a sea apprentice. I served him one year, always sleeping on board the vessel. Captain Fry then handed over my indentures to Captain Sergeant, but they were not transferred. I served Captain Sergeant one year, always sleeping on board. The vessels in which I served were employed in coasting.

At the end of the year I entered the merchant service, and then was impressed into a man-of-war, and I served in a man-of-war or in the merchant service from that time till the present, with the exception of some short periods. I married my present wife at Ashburton about fifteen years ago, and have one child by her. I have often been relieved by the parish of Ugborough, both in and out of the workhouse. I have done no other act to gain a settlement. During my absence on the last occasion, and whilst I was in the Brazils, and after I had been absent more than a year, my wife had a child named Joseph, which is now living.

> Denny Ryde
> Ashburton, Devon

As these three examinations suggest, all long-service mariners could expect impressment, at least if their time at sea coincided with Britain's wars for trade and empire. Such forced recruiting took place on both land and sea, and even landsmen and sailors on foreign ships were not safe if the need for hands was great. The right to impress rested on no statute, but, in the words of Lord Mansfield, on "immemorial usage, allowed for ages"; it was justified only by the "safety of the state" under "that trite maxim of the constitutional law of England, 'that private mischief had better be submitted to than public detriment and inconvenience should ensue.'"[7]

Service at sea could be extremely diverse, with a man alternating between the Navy and merchant service, and the voyages varying from coastal shipping to trade or conflict in the most distant seas. One very common pattern was for a boy to learn the ropes in coastal shipping, and then graduate to ocean voyages in his late teens or early twenties, concluding his life at sea some ten to thirty years later by returning to coastal service, perhaps as master of his own small ship—that is, of course, provided he survived the hardships of his earlier voyages. Sea apprenticeships encouraged this pattern.

A mariner's settlement was often difficult to determine, especially if he had begun with a sea apprenticeship, as so many did. The great advantage to boys, captains, and shipowners of entering into a formal apprenticeship is that such apprentices could not legally be impressed into the Navy until they were eighteen years old. In 1834 Captain Chappel of Appledore, Devon, offered Robert Parkhouse the sum of £30 to serve as his apprentice for four years. Although at the last moment Parkhouse decided to stay on land and become a tailor, such enticements, this one admittedly larger than most, could well lure a young man to sea, if he had any taste for adventure.[8]

Years later the details of an apprenticeship were likely to be of great concern to parish officers faced with the problem of determining which parish a boy had been in that last crucial night of his apprenticeship, provided it was also a place that the boy had dwelled in for at least 40 days during the time of his service. (The 40 days did not have to be consecutive.) This sounds complicated, and was. William Anning's 1834 settlement case, for example, required the most detailed investigations of coastal shipping to establish that he had spent 40 days altogether in the Bight of Exmouth, located in the parish of Kenton, including the last night of service. To reach that conclusion, the examination included information on ports of call, cargoes carried, the time needed to load and unload various cargoes, and the use of false apprenticeship indentures, after Anning's legal apprenticeship was completed, in an effort to fool impressment officers. All this, in order to determine where a 44-year-old seaman belonged.[9] Even his old master was called on to recall utterly unmemorable events that had happened thirty years earlier. The Poor Law Amendment Act of 1834 did not abolish settlement by apprenticeship, but it did away with this particular kind, for perhaps in no way did the Law of Settlement work so illogically as in the case of former sea apprentices.

*   *   *

5 August 1833

Mr. Merrill, Merchant
Pudding Lane, Lower Thames Street, London
Sir:

Your humane and gentlemanly manners seem to require an immediate explanation of my peculiar case. Not having had occasion to apply for any such assistance, I felt much depression of spirits at the thought of requesting parochial relief. I was regularly educated in the medical profession, and after my apprenticeship with one of the principal surgeons in Hull, I became a pupil to Mr. Abernethy at Bartholomew Hospital for two years. I then settled at Brigg in Lincolnshire, but, there being an old established practitioner in the place, I did not succeed to my wishes.

My father, having been an oil and coal merchant, was acquainted with and had some dealings with Mr. Jones of Fish Street Hill, and, after I had been in business a considerable time, with an accumulation of bad debts, he wrote to Mr. Jones, and I was appointed his assistant in business, where I remained about three years. Then a gentleman procured for me the appointment of surgeon to a free-trading Indiaman, where I was very comfortable, and have continued in that employ the chief part of my time since.

But most unfortunately on our return in December last, intending to [words unclear], we were overtaken by a very heavy gale, and in spite of every exertion our ship, *The Perseverance*, was cast away before daylight on the Isle of Ascension, and before we had time to save a single article, she became a complete wreck, and I with the other officers and men lost everything we had. I had saved in my different voyages a few hundred pounds, with a most excellent chest of clothing for different climates, two small boxes of dollars, my instruments, books, etc.—all were lost.

We were taken up by an American ship, and put ashore near Plymouth. Thus, from a respectable employ and rank in society, in one moment I was reduced to the greatest distress, and, having no relations in London, being a native of Lincolnshire, I am perhaps the greatest sufferer in body and mind of all that met with this misfortune. At present, I have no resource until my health and strength may be restored, if Providence permits, but the temporary help, Sir, which you and the gentlemen of the vestry may generously be inclined to favor me with, as my case is not a common one. It is the first time I have been so distressed. I most respectfully trust your generous feelings will sympathize with my situation and assist me as your superior judgment may direct.

Though my family is very respectable, most of my nearest relations are dead. Yet I will no longer be a burden upon the parish than absolute necessity requires. Not having been settled anywhere since I left Fish Street Hill, I can claim no other place [of settlement]. With sincere respects and the most humble feelings, I am, Sir, Your unfortunate humble servant.

Robert Kidson
[Plymouth?]

To this supplication Kidson added a postscript: "Having unexpectedly met with a gentleman from the country who gave me a small assistance, I have deferred troubling you, Sir, as long as I could." His story gives point and poignancy to the old saw of shipwrecked fortunes and indicates that at a time when few persons had insurance, shipwreck, fire, theft, or other disaster could easily reduce even a person of some means to dependence on the only comprehensive social security then available.

Peddlers

Whether one was judged a vagrant or a sojourner depended on length of residence, previous employment history, and the parish officers' estimation of the person in question, according to a process that was easier to apply in practice than to define in law. Begging was the best passport to a vagrancy classification, but there is an enormous range of activity between insistently requesting charity and subtly presenting oneself in such a way as to intimidate or arouse compassion. Peddlers were particularly likely to inhabit this borderland.

*   *   *

17 January 1818

He was born in the parish of Farringdon [Devon], where his parents were legally settled. When he was about nine years old, he was bound apprentice to Mr. Lake, who occupied Sparns estate in Farringdon, with whom he lived till the said Lake left Farringdon, and went to [East Budleigh]. He, this examinant, went with him. Mr. Lake occupied a small estate there, but he is not certain how long he lived with Mr. Lake in [East] Budleigh. When he left Lake he was not twenty years of age. He then went to work with a miller about ten miles from Exeter, but does not know the name of the miller, nor of the parish where he lived. He continued there about a quarter of a year, when he fell out of a hayloft and broke his shoulder. He was brought to his father in Farringdon and, after some time, sent to the Exeter Hospital, from whence he was discharged as incurable. He believes this was about twenty-seven years since, and that he is now, as he believes, about forty years of age.

He then returned to Farringdon, and worked as a day laborer. He never saw his master Lake from the time he first left him. He then went to London, where he was employed to assist the watchman, but when he was to be sworn in they objected to him as a cripple. He then bought a basket to sell cotton thread and rabbit skins, and traveled the country, which he has done ever since, never having had constant residence.

He married Sarah Richards at St. Martin's Church in The Strand, who lived about seven years after she was married, and died at Ramshill in Kent, where she was buried. He continued a widower about four or five years, and then married Elizabeth Hancock, 25 May 1807, his present wife, at Barrack Street, Dublin, in a Roman Catholic chapel, called Barrack Street Chapel. By his first wife he had one still-born child only, and by his present wife three children, two boys and one girl. The eldest, called John, is now living in Romney, in Kent with his wife's uncle, John Dulay; the second, called James Dawe, who is now living and with him, who was christened at Eltham in Kent, and was three years old in August last; the third, called Elizabeth, is dead. He has done no other act whereby to gain a settlement, other than above stated.

James Dawe
East Budleigh, Devon

Dawe's old master, Nicholas Lake, was still alive, and was asked for his version of the relationship. He claimed that Dawe had run away. Shortly afterward, Dawe's father and uncle promised Lake an indemnifying bond so that Dawe would not be chargeable to the parish of East Budleigh during the remainder of his apprenticeship if Lake would give up Dawe's time. Lake arranged a meeting at his house to draw up the bond, even recruiting the schoolmaster's services, but the Dawes did not appear. About a year later the young Dawe came to his master's house to say that if Lake would let him go to get his living elsewhere he "would never be troublesome" to Lake again; Lake told him "he might go where he pleased." That was the last Lake had heard of Dawe until asked to make his deposition over twenty years later.

Memories falter, and the two men may honestly have remembered different things, although Lake's remembrance of the indemnifying bond sounds suspiciously like what the officers of East Budleigh would have wanted to have happened. But Lake's story, even if true, was probably insufficient to place Dawe's settlement anywhere other than East Budleigh, where the last 40 days of Dawe's service to Lake had taken place. That Dawe had not completed his apprenticeship was irrelevant. All that was necessary was that the apprenticeship had lasted 40 days in one parish, as it clearly had in this case, that it had never been canceled, and that the master had given Dawe permission to go where he pleased. A peddler, his wife, and three-year-old son were thus the responsibility of East Budleigh.

* * *

9 January 1830

I was born in the parish of St. Nicholas in the City of Cork in the Kingdom of Ireland. I am now about thirty-five years of age. I have heard and verily believe that my mother's maiden name was Mary Barry, but I do not know whether she was ever married. I have heard and believe that a person called John Busby was my father, who I have heard and believe entered into the marines before I was born, from Cork. I never saw him until about nine years since, when I came from Ireland to England, and went to Totnes. John Busby acknowledged me to be his son.

I have heard and believe that I was put out to nurse and taken into the Foundling Hospital at Cork. When I was about a year and a half old my mother embarked on board a ship then lying in the Cove of Cork, bound for England, for the purpose of joining John Busby. While on board ship in the Cove my mother met with an accident, and was re-landed, dying shortly thereafter. I did not go on board ship with my mother, but remained in the Foundling Hospital at Cork until I was almost seventeen years of age, when I was bound an apprentice by the governors of that institution to a person named Benjamin Phillips of Rathcooney in County Cork, corduroy weaver.

I served him as an apprentice under an indenture for a year and a half, when I ran away and went to Clonmel, where I worked for about four years on board the barges at half a guinea per quarter, and my meat, but I did not continue with any one master a year at Clonmel. When I was about twenty-two and a half, Patrick Hogan, a person I had worked with in the barges, took a public house at Clonmel, and hired me as a clerk and waiter. I lived with him off and on three or four years, part of the time at £4 a year, and part of the time at £5. I served him the whole of the last year, and received from Hogan £4 for the year's wages.

In 1820 I left Hogan's service and came to England. During the time I have been in England I have maintained myself by selling of things about the streets of London and in the country. While I have been in England I have never hired myself to any person as a yearly servant, nor have I rented £10 a year in any parish at any time. On 12 November 1823, I married my present wife, Eliza, in the parish church of St. George, Queen Square, London, by whom I have three children now living with me, John, aged about five years, James, aged about three, and Mary, aged about eleven months.

During the greater part of the time I was in London I resided in a house near Gray's Inn Lane in the parish of St. Andrew, Holborn, Above the Bars, in the County of Middlesex. While I resided there I became chargeable, and received from the parish officers parish relief, sometimes 1/ a day, and sometimes 18d. I was never taken before any magistrates by the parish officers of St. Andrews to be examined as to my settlement, but I was examined by a Mr. Wilkes, who was clerk of the workhouse of St. Andrews.

I applied to the parish officers of St. Andrews for a pass to take me to Totnes, but that was not granted. The beadle of the parish paid the fare for me and my family by wagon, from London to Totnes. He gave me 15/ to pay my expenses on the road. He paid the money by the order of the parish officers of St. Andrews. Mr. Payne of Holborn is the acting bursar of St. Andrews, and the person who advised my being sent to Totnes with my family in the way we were. I have done no other act whereby to gain a settlement.

    Simon Busby
    Totnes, Devon

The Busbys' experience parallels that of Harriet Williams. St. Andrews chose the easiest, cheapest, and most humane method of dealing with this Irish family—casual relief, followed by assistance to go somewhere else—without invoking the law.

Devon, as well as London, had a particularly severe problem with sojourners and vagrants, the latter being persons Paul Slack has identified as "far from any past reality or present hope of respectability," who were often distinguished by broken families and long-distance mobility over a period of years.[10] Devon's many ports funneled into the county unemployed persons from North America and Ireland. Plymouth, in particular, was plagued with destitute immigrants. Vagrancy cases, tried before Exeter Quarter Sessions, are a barometer more of the magistrates' zeal than of anything else, although it is not difficult to relate the ebb and flow to international events and economic distress. The peak of 65 identifiable cases in one year occurred in the wake of the American Revolution, in part because of an influx of Loyalists, like Michael Frederick Murray. There was also an increase at the time of the great turn-of-the-century corn dearth. The years following Waterloo and the late 1820s saw increases;[11] both were periods of rising unemployment.

What is particularly interesting about Dawe and Busby is that they were treated as sojourners, not vagrants, and examined for their parishes of settlement. Dawe may not have been in need at the time, and his crippled condition may have aided his cause, whereas Busby, although subject to removal to Ireland, together with his family, was treated to a cheaper and more humane alternative by the officers of St. Andrew, Holborn,[12] although the overseers of Totnes could not have been happy with this metropolitan parish's dumping its Irish poor on them.

Dawe and Busby pursued a most suspect occupation, one that almost any wanderer might claim, including beggarman and thief. However, they were judged to be merely poor men and treated accordingly.

FIVE

Responsibilities

WHO WAS responsible for whom? Answering that fundamental question was the whole raison d'être of the Law of Settlement. On one level parishes and townships negotiated or litigated with one another self-servingly, whereas on another level local officers and self-supporting families cooperated or conflicted in caring for a dependent. Illness or disability was especially likely to be the occasion for the initiatives of parish officers, employers, family members, and the poor to intersect. In answering this fundamental question of responsibility, the petitioners and parish officers produced some of the most human documents of the Industrial Revolution, disclosing the gamut of responses—benevolence, integrity, evasion, cruelty, fraud.

Relatives

The responsibility for dependents begins with the family, and British poor law authorities in the eighteenth and early nineteenth centuries were in no mind to change this immemorial obligation. Indeed, the laws of settlement and maintenance promoted family responsibility by linking members of the nuclear family to a common settlement and by compelling family members to care for their own. Problems arose when family members defied law or morality by refusing to provide assistance. Of course, in many instances they were themselves paupers or on the edge of pauperism. Problems also arose when the family tie went beyond the parent-child relationship, as in the following case.

* * *

Marystow is a west Devon parish located near the Cornish border. On 18 August 1786, Elizabeth Rowe was given a settlement examination there; she was then twenty years of age. She claimed to be legitimate, and although born not in Marystow but in the parish of Tavistock, her father was legally settled in Marystow. It is not clear if her father had died or run away when she was quite young, but when she was seven she was in the care of her mother, who apparently was living in Marystow. Mr. Tremayne, an officer of the parish, ordered her apprenticed. That implies that her mother was then on parish relief. It was quite common for a parish to apprentice such children to ratepayers, a kind of compulsory billeting whose cost did not appear in parish account books. In this case, however, a great-aunt, Christian Collings, befriended Elizabeth by placing the child with Gilbert Rowe, the child's uncle and a yeoman living in the neighboring parish of Milton Abbot. There she lived until she was eighteen, but not entirely at her uncle's expense, for the parish of Marystow provided her clothes and paid Rowe 18*d*. a week to support his niece until she turned sixteen.

Marystow ceased support at that age, but the uncle no doubt found the teenager a useful worker and so provided Elizabeth a maintenance for the next two years. She left her uncle after a disagreement. Another aunt then came to the rescue by telling her that William Atwell, a yeoman living in Meavy, about four miles to the south, was in want of a servant. Elizabeth went there, and after a week's trial, she was hired. She asked for 30*s*. a year, but Mr. Atwell did not hire servants by the year in order to prevent their acquiring a settlement. He offered instead to pay her 7*d*. a week, and under that arrangement she lived with him for two years, receiving her wages as she wanted them. She left Atwell's service at Lady Day (25 March), a common time to begin and end service, and soon after hired herself to John Williams, a yeoman living in Lew Trenchard, a parish adjoining Marystow. On this occasion she got her asking price of 30*s*., but for only fifty weeks of service, not the full year needed for a settlement, and for the obvious reason. She served Williams a little over eight weeks when she hurt her leg and had to leave. She returned to her uncle Gilbert, who had since moved to Brentor, a parish east of Marystow. He allowed his niece to stay under his roof for only a little over a week. He then had a servant take her to the churchwarden of Marystow, where she remained another week before her examination was taken.[1]

Because Elizabeth was a pauper child, it was considered improper to allow her to stay with her mother. However, her uncle was quite satisfactory from the standpoint of the parish, especially since he lived outside Marystow. This created the possibility that Elizabeth might acquire a new settlement and cease to be a charge on Marystow. Perhaps that explains Mr. Tremayne's fairly generous support of Elizabeth until she was sixteen. The uncle then entered into an agreement with his niece that was almost certainly exploitive, for she was to continue to work for him for nothing more than a bare maintenance. No wonder they disagreed. She did better for herself at William Atwell's, but it was still a poor service, all the more so because Atwell adopted the common ploy of evading the law's intent by hiring only on a weekly basis. Over two years later when she returned to her uncle, in need of rest and care, his avuncular concern lasted little more than a week before he sent her to a Marystow parish officer; the law did not require an uncle to maintain a niece.

Six noncontiguous parishes were involved in the girl's story— Meavy was over ten miles from Lew Trenchard—yet they were all in the Tavistock area, and within a day's journey of one another. Although Elizabeth was a parish ward, not all members of her extended family were so circumstanced, and they were willing enough to help find her a place and use her services. Her week's residence at the Marystow churchwarden's home suggests, however, that her relatives were reluctant to step in when the parish could be held accountable for her maintenance.

*   *   *

2 March 1790

John Kingston of Diptford, yeoman, saith that about eighteen years since Francis Kingston, his brother, came to this deponent and desired to take a part of this deponent's estate, which he refused, but offered to take his said brother into the house and that he might stay there till he had got another place. Francis accepted, but absolutely refused to agree for any time. Without anything further passing, Francis lived with this deponent sometimes there, sometimes absent, for about five years . . . and at the expiration of this time Francis asked this deponent for some wages. Deponent asks what he demanded. Francis answers, what deponent pleases. Deponent then throws said Francis down 40gn. and tells him to pay himself. Francis takes up the whole money, and further saith not.

John Kingston
Diptford, Devon

It seems likely that Francis Kingston had a grievance over an inheritance and that the two brothers did not get along, but another deposition suggests that there was more to it.

2 March 1790

Mr. John Cholwich of Blackawton, a relation of Francis Kingston, lived with deponent about nine years since. About that time Francis Kingston came to this deponent's house in Blackawton, and appeared to be a great object of charity. This deponent asked him whether he would live with him or not, which Kingston accepted, but said he would not live with him constantly nor make a bargain for any certain time at all with this deponent or any other person. He accordingly lived with this deponent about a twelve-month. This deponent never paid him any certain wages, as he was frequently wandering about the country during the time he lived with him, for some days at a time, and he never followed his work regularly. This deponent sometimes gave this Kingston a little spending money and sometimes some clothing, but cannot recollect anything particular about the matter.

John Cholwich
Blackawton, Devon

Unless there was collusion between the two relatives, it seems certain that Francis was a shiftless sort, and he was forthwith removed to the parish of Slapton, where presumably his parents had been settled. According to the two accounts, Francis had been treated generously by his brother and then given a second chance by another relation, John Cholwich, nine years later. (This was the uncle of John B. Cholwich, who figured in the Oldfield case in the preceding chapter.) But on this third occasion, in 1790, Francis received no help from his relatives. As is so often the case, the story has intriguing omissions, and one must beware of concluding too much from too little.

*   *   *

7 September 1800

Four years ago she was sent from Milton Damerel, Devon, to Shebbear, Devon, by a [removal] order [the two northwest Devon parishes bordered one another]. Soon after, she went back to Milton to the house of her grandmother, who kept a cow and a pig or two, and occupied two or three fields to grow potatoes and a little barley. Her grandmother said to her that she was a friendless creature, and if she would do the work of the house for her, if there were anything left at her own and husband's death she would treat her as her own child, and give it to her. She agreed to it.

She did the work of the house, milked the cow, etc., and had her meat, drink, and washing. She went to summer work, and applied the money she got in buying her clothes. But the spinning work she did in the winter her grandmother had the money for. She made no other bargains, and has continued with her grandmother . . . for four years, until a week ago, when, being with child, she came into the parish of Shebbear.

Mary Fishly
Shebbear, Devon

Four years before she had been removed from Milton Damerel to Shebbear and then she had returned again to Milton; she was liable to imprisonment for so doing, but this law, like so many others, was only sporadically enforced.[2] Of more interest is her second exile from the neighboring parish of Milton. Did her grandmother turn her out, or did Milton Damerel's officers warn her off? Perhaps she left of her own accord, to return to her most certain refuge, her parish.

*   *   *

11 December 1810

About the month of May 1809, she received into her care three children belonging to her brother, William Hill, late of Chancery Lane in the Liberty of the Rolls, Middlesex, and received for each of them 5/ a week to May 1810, but has not received anymore since. Her brother lived in the parish of St. Dunstan [in the West?] upwards of twelve months, and rented apartments at £10 per annum, from which he was removed into the hospital, where he died, and left the three children in the care of the deponent—the name of the eldest being Mary, aged eleven, the middle one named Caroline, aged seven, and the youngest named Sarah, aged five, all of whom are now dependent upon this deponent, Mary Higgins, who prays they may be passed home to their parish forthwith, for the three children have become chargeable to the parish of Friern Barnet.

> Mary Higgins
> Friern Barnet, Middlesex

Taken by itself, this deposition suggests Higgins was a callous aunt, but it may provide a good example of the danger of concluding too much. Sixteen years after making this deposition, Mary Higgins was herself examined for her own settlement. She reported that she was then aged 68, and the mother of eleven children, six of whom were still living. She was a widow, and had been one at the time of the earlier deposition, when she had been caring for her brother's children. She had also at that time had five or six of her own children living at home. Somehow she had made do, for her own examination in 1826 revealed that her parish of settlement was Grimsthorpe, Lincolnshire, where her husband had been born and served his apprenticeship. That she had managed to stay in Friern Barnet all those years suggests that she had practiced rigorous economy in avoiding removal, perhaps earning her living by boarding other people's children.

Given these circumstances, she did what may have been the most human and humane thing, not only for herself but for the majority of her charges, by placing the burden of supporting her nieces on their father's parish of settlement, presumably St. Dunstan in the West. Indeed, she most probably had no choice, given her own precarious situation. When she was finally examined, all her children were grown, and she was too ill to be removed from Friern Barnet.[3] It was a victory of sorts.

* * *

To the Gentlemen Parishioners of Kenton
Gentlemen of the Committee:

I taking the liberty of writing to let you know our distress, which I hope you will not be offended at it. Gentlemen, the whole cause that I do not keep up my poor rates, it is for want of labor and credit. But ever since my father's death, and long before, I have had no credit, which is four years ago. I have taken it upon me to maintain my mother for living in this house, a woman in her eighty-fifth year of age. You must think, Gentlemen, that there must be proper care took of such old, infirm woman. Through that my wife is not able to serve a penny because she must always be home attending. Myself without credit and without a friend: this is my condition, Gentlemen.

But, Gentlemen, Mr. Curier hath told me several times that if I could get a gentleman or a man of fortune to pass his word for me, he would let me have a lot of goods for six months' credit. If I could gain that I should have nothing to complain of concerning the poor rate, nor yet be obligated to go potato digging.

Gentlemen, I humbly ask a little favor of you, when you will be so kind as to pass your word for a little lot of leather for that time, that I might be able to maintain my mother and keep up the poor rate, which I have done for twenty-seven years past, and brought up my family in honesty. And as for myself, I can defy any person to speak a dishonest thing against me. But I have met with so many bad debts that I could not keep up my credit. Thanks be to my God that I have got my health and strength. And if, Gentlemen, you will be so good as to grant me this favor, I would sign anything that you would desire. I do not want to wrong the parish of a penny.

Gentlemen, if you will grant me this kind favor, I should return you my sincere thanks, and remain your most obedient and humble servant. [Postscript] If this favor is granted I would do anything for the parish that is wanted, either new work or old, in shoe trade.

Samuel East
Kenton, Devon

Kenton appears to have denied the petition; at least there is no record of assistance in the overseers' accounts. Although the parish had often employed East in the past, they were at that time remarkably cautious in granting casual relief, and then only for illness and distress that went beyond the avoidance of potato digging.[4]

Children were legally obligated to maintain needy parents, just as parents were obligated to care for their children. Even grandparents were liable for grandchildren.[5] Yet few areas of the poor law were more spottily enforced, perhaps for the same reasons that it is difficult to enforce comparable laws today—those legally responsible were themselves too poor to maintain fellow family members, or the responsible party had irresponsibly deserted, or the authorities decided that providing relief was less costly or troublesome than compelling relatives to pay.

East's petition illustrates the reluctance of the independent artisan to apply for poor relief, particularly when he had been a long-settled ratepayer, as in East's case. It is true that sojourners may have been somewhat less restrained by pride, but for them there was, of course, another constraint: fear of removal.

*   *   *

2 May 1822

To: Mr. [Wilshire]
Greenwich Road Academy
Madam:

I have seen Mrs. Sheppard, and my sister [Sarah] is to go to her house when she leaves you because we don't mean to trouble the gentlemen of the parish any more with her; so as soon as you can spare my sister she may come, either the latter end of this week or the beginning of next, but if you please, don't send her to the parish.

Eleanor Neek
16 King Street [London]

There followed a postscript to Sarah: "When you come you're to enquire for the flower pot, and then when you get there you will know your way, and be sure you mind where you cross the road, and you come straight on to Mrs. Sheppard, and be sure you thank the lady for her kindness to you."

This letter has obscurities, such as the disparity between the address and salutation, but the letter unquestionably breathes sisterly concern. Whether Eleanor Neek's concern was benevolent or tyrannical in spirit, or some combination thereof, is not possible to determine, but she obviously wished to provide for her own sister. Sibling relationships, then as now, could be ambiguous in just this way. Another instance follows.

* * *

29 November 1827

About nine years ago she was hired as a yearly servant to live with Mr. Thomas White of Wormwood Street in the parish of St. Ethelburga at £6 per year wages. She lived with her master four years and ten months, and she left Mr. White's to lodge at apartments taken by her brother in Dukes Street, Union Street, Spitalfields. Afterwards she removed to Mr. Greenwood's, No. 3, Worship Street, at 4/ per week, which was paid by her brother, who dined in the house and paid the expense of housekeeping, but her brother slept at the banking house of Sir John Lubbock and Co. That pauper lived at Worship Street for about five years when she met with an accident which compelled her to go to the London Hospital. Upon leaving the hospital her brother boarded and lodged her at a house in Long Alley, Bishopsgate Street, and paid 7/6 per week for her board and lodging. Her brother afterwards allowed pauper 9/ a week for her board and maintenance, and pauper took lodging in Chapel Street, Holliwellmount, where she was living at the death of her brother's wife, and paid a rent of 3/6 per week.

Upon the death of her brother's wife, her brother called upon pauper and informed her that his wife was dead, and said: "You will dress yourself and come straight home." Accordingly, she went to her brother's apartments in Worship Street, and after living there about [space left blank] months, pauper removed with her brother to No. 18, Paul Street, where the latter paid a rent of £22.1 a year. Pauper had to take care of the apartments and nurse her brother's child. After she had [moved] to her brother's lodgings in Worship Street she asked her brother what he would give her a year. He answered: "You may think yourself well off to have board and lodging found for you." Pauper remonstrated with her brother, telling him it was keeping her quite under, so she would never have a farthing in her pocket. This conversation occurred soon after she went to live with her brother. Pauper's brother lived at Paul Street about six months, when he died. Pauper then went to live at her present residence, and pays a rent of 3/ per week.

Ruth Bridcutt
14 Fuller Street, Bethnal Green Road, London

Perhaps it was benevolence that led her brother to take her out of her service to Mr. White, although he may have wanted an inexpensive housekeeper. Whatever the initial motive, it was a relationship that soured after her sister-in-law died. Ruth Bridcutt's transient lodgings in various east London streets (many of which are no more) served to cut her off from neighborhood and make her more dependent on her brother, a dependency he apparently exploited.

There is no way to prove that family ties were more or less strong then than now. Certainly many relatives looked to the poor law to relieve them of a burdensome relation, whereas others did what they could to help. Much the same is true today, although the forms of public welfare and attitudes toward it have changed markedly, making it easier for families today to draw on assistance for dependent members without the onus associated with poor relief. Family ties in that earlier time were often strong, thus lowering the poor rates by an amount that will forever be undeterminable. There were also, of course, relatives who evaded the responsibilities they might well have undertaken. Yet Mary Higgins may have represented the norm. Her ability to stay off the rates was her only assurance of not being removed to a Lincolnshire parish she had probably never seen. For when there was so little to share, the poor law, whatever the onus, provided the final resort.

Illness and Disability

17 July 1790

My wife's name is Sarah. I have two children, twins, females, of six months old. My wife is in Bartholomew's Hospital. I pay 8/ a week for nursing my children, and being out of place, apply for relief, having parted with all my goods before this application.

Henry Hathaway
Harrow-on-the-Hill, Middlesex

Hathaway, a coachman by trade, starkly and tersely summarizes the consequences of sickness and unemployment—abject dependency. Even that was not necessarily enough, however, if the pauper happened to be a sojourner, as the following case illustrates.

*   *   *

5 February 1817

Upwards of twenty years ago he lived two years as a yearly servant with William Jackson of the parish of East Budleigh in the county of Devon, gentleman, and that he hath not since done any act whatever to gain a settlement in any other parish or place, and this deponent verily believes that his place of legal settlement is in the said parish of East Budleigh.

John Truck
Bodmin, Cornwall

This brief examination was accompanied by a note from a doctor: "The above deponent is in great distress, having a wife and five children to maintain. From an accident in cutting his foot, he is not able to work." Apparently the authorities in Bodmin had genuine concern for the Truck family, for the doctor's testimony was supplemented by a letter from Joseph Fayner, the parish clerk and master of the grammar school in Bodmin.

John Truck is a very industrious sawyer, but in spite of his industry he is unfortunate. His wife is very sickly. Had it not been for the charitable of this town all his family must have starved, or you must have had them sent to your parish. He expects to get work again as soon as he recovers, and it would be most judicious in you to afford them relief through our overseers, who now afford him some temporary relief in the hope that you will refund it. My wife has done much for the poor man's wife in her sickness.

This compassionate letter was still further complemented by an official note from Bodmin's overseers, demanding "an answer as soon as possible to say what allowance Truck is to have." Otherwise, the family would be returned to East Budleigh by a removal order.

None of this was deemed sufficiently satisfactory for the officers of East Budleigh to embark on an outparish allowance for the Truck family. They frigidly replied: "The parishioners do not acknowledge John Truck to be settled in this parish, as after he left Budleigh they are informed by his father he lived in Exeter and many other places; and until he is brought to us in a regular way, we know nothing of him."

And so the Trucks were removed to East Budleigh, there to render another settlement examination, which unequivocally showed that East Budleigh was their parish of settlement. The hardship this imposed on the Truck family must have been great, and one wonders why Bodmin did not resort to a "suspended order" (see below). Presumably the family, although too ill to work, was able to move the eighty miles separating the two parishes. Quite apart from that, the expense to all concerned, especially to East Budleigh, was the greater for want of the out-parish relief Bodmin had requested. Now East Budleigh was indefinitely responsible for relieving this poor family, unless work could be found for them when they regained their health.

Most parish officers had sense enough to realize that outparish relief was the cheaper way of supporting the parish's poor who were sojourning elsewhere, an important subject explored more fully in the following chapters. Yet there was always the fear of providing unnecessary relief by trusting the honesty and competence of the officers from another parish. In this particular case, East Budleigh may have been seriously misled by Truck's father. Moreover, Bodmin's unusual concern for the Truck family may have aroused East Budleigh's suspicions.

The suspended order, a procedure introduced in 1795, prevented the removal of paupers until they were well enough to travel. Even parish officers immune to humane considerations might be constrained to help sojourners in need in order to avoid suspended orders. "Believe me, it is bad policy to suffer the family to want," an Exeter lawyer told the assistant overseer of Cheriton Bishop in 1833, "as the health then becomes impaired and they are obliged to apply for medical assistance, and then comes a suspended order."[6] Although the law prescribed reimbursement by the parish of settlement when an order of removal was suspended on medical grounds, getting the money could be tedious and troublesome. Sometimes it was too little, and most times it was too late. Parish officers dreaded suspended orders, which provided some incentive to resident doctors and magistrates not to invoke the new law except in the most extreme cases. This may have influenced Bodmin's treatment of the Truck family, although the packet of materials Bodmin sent

East Budleigh suggests a parish that would not have permitted the Trucks to travel if there had been serious risk to their health.

It is as difficult to generalize about the motivation of parish officers as it is about paupers, and on such really important questions numbers have no relevance. One is left with the fallible impressions of scholars, preferably those with close familiarity with the original documents. My impression—it will never be anything other than a scholar's impression—is that paupers and parish officers behaved in a reasonably intelligent and responsible way. Paupers usually tried to stay off the rates, and parish officers usually relieved the distress of the settled and sojourning poor by a compromise between charity and economy that varied with the officer, the parish, and the specific situation. Apart from the humane feelings many parish officers quite certainly possessed, the law, as it in fact worked, meant a measure of charity was economical; this became increasingly so with the growing sophistication of settlement law in the late eighteenth century. Gross abuse of authority could involve trouble and expense, which most human beings naturally seek to avoid. The cruelty and stupidity of the few, so often visible because of those qualities, should not obscure the plodding competence of the many.

*　*　*

19 November 1826

Churchwardens of St. Mary, Aldermary
Watling Street, Bow Lane, Cheapside, London
Sir:

As you have solicited Mr. Douglas to enquire into the justness of my claim upon you, the following is a statement of facts which I gave him when he called upon me, with which he appeared satisfied.

Namely, that after my father died in Bow Lane in November 1793, I carried on the business about four months. When I gave it up I took to tramping about the country near fourteen years, during which time I never paid higher than 2/ per week for my lodging, nor rented a house of any kind whatever. In 1806 I married in London and took a room at No. 87, Wardour Street, Soho, at the yearly rent of £8, where we lived above two years, and then came to Reading where we remained ever since in the house we now live in, above eighteen years, at the weekly rent of 3/ per week. This makes up the lapse from my father's death to the present time and is a true and correct statement which I can safely confirm upon oath if required.

Thomas Bell
Reading, Berkshire

This letter was followed by a long postscript.

I must beg you will take to the boys till you can get them places, as we can get them nothing to do at Reading. Likewise, must solicit you to continue your allowance in pay to me for another month as I cannot possibly get to work sooner, having got such a weakness settled in my limbs. I should never have thought of troubling you had not this sickness happened to me, and as it is the first time, I hope you will not be against granting my request. I would have come myself, but could not possibly bear the fatigue of the journey.

The following June a letter from one Sarah Terry of Datchet, Buckinghamshire, informed an overseer of St. Mary, Aldermary, that the allowance she received for maintaining Bell's daughter was due.[7] In September, Bell wrote again concerning his two sons.

Mr. Beton, Sir,
This is to request you will inform me if my sons John and William Bell are in places. I wrote to a relation of mine, who is a wine merchant in the city, to look out for them. He promised he would, and if they behave well and are steady I have no doubt but he will be their friend. I have some hopes of the younger, who is a sharp, active boy. The elder need not have troubled you at all if he had been steady. The gentleman above [J. B. Monck] got him a place, but he ran away from it. I am sorry he has given you so much trouble. He called on me six weeks ago on his road to Oxford, where he said he had got work. My work has been all the summer very dead, and is *still* not getting half enough to employ me. I cannot get the money for what little I do. I feel myself much obliged to you and the gentlemen acting in office with you for what you did for me in my sickness and what you have since done for my family. But for that sickness, the debts from which I have not recovered, you would never have heard of me. Twelve months ago I little thought I should ever be compelled to apply for parochial assistance.

Thomas Bell
Reading, Berkshire

A postscript adds: "My wife, who is still in place, informed me you came down to Datchet and paid my daughter's board. I return you my sincere thanks for your kindness."

Bell appears to have been an educated man whose London business had failed, leading him to "tramp" the country for some years before settling in Reading. He very probably was a shoemaker, as his home parish, St. Mary, Aldermary, was especially noted for the trade, and his life since leaving there suggests the tramping artisan. The outparish relief granted Bell was unexceptional, but the parish showed prudence and apparent humanity in deputizing someone to see Bell and to visit the Buckinghamshire parish where Bell's daughter was, both to pay her expenses and to check on Sarah Terry's arrangements for the girl.

*   *   *

Mr. [Pearsons]   13 April 1828
Overseer of Harrow-on-the-Hill
Mr. Pearsons:

I am very sorry to trouble you again, but I am sorry too that my husband has gone on worse than ever, as he has been in constant work for this past twelve months, and [yet] is head over ears in debt as he spends all his money on drink. I don't know one moment from another that I may not be turned out in the streets, as we owe so much money for rent, having a young child. I have not a person [from whom] I can get night refuge. I am sorry to trouble [you], but I have neither money nor clothes, or else I should have come down myself, [but] I own no linen or the necessaries. I hope I shall soon hear from you, as else I must apply to Manchester parish. I never shall be more trouble and expense.

Margaret Pissey
23 East Street, Manchester

There is a breathless urgency to this petition, as is so often and understandably the case, and the rules of composition mattered not at all so long as the writer's meaning was conveyed. The Pisseys had traveled far from Harrow-on-the-Hill, although migration to and from the environs of London was frequently long-distance, and Harrow was well along the high road leading northwest from London to the industries of the Midlands and more distant Lancashire. What is much less frequent is to find alcoholism mentioned in a pauper petition or examination, partly because it was usually irrelevant and damaging to a claim for relief (the sins of the father, or whomever, being visited on the entire family), but partly also because sojourners lived life on probation. Self-engendered problems, such as alcoholism, most likely led to unemployment, followed by removal, at best, and possibly an application of the vagrancy acts. Sojourners, of necessity, had to achieve a somewhat higher level of sobriety and industriousness than the average magistrate or overseer, because for the sojourner there was always the threat of removal. This was true even after 1795. A statute of that year, Rose's Act, did limit removal to those who were actually chargeable, but there was a significant exception. A person adjudged undesirable (which by definition included pregnant unmarried women) could be removed, even if not actually in need of relief.[8] Not necessarily in skill but in application, the sojourners very probably represented the cream of the work force.

* * *

21 April 1830

Overseers of the Poor
Cheriton Bishop, Devon
Gentlemen:

I am sorry my wife has been under the painful necessity of applying to you for parochial assistance during my absence. It's with the greatest reluctance I lay my unfortunate case before you, but as I am compelled so to do I humbly trust you will be so good as to meet the merits of the case accordingly.

I have been laid up ever since last July, and, having a family to bring up by my labor only, it could not be expected I could save much money, and not having the benefit of any Sick Society, my father and friends have occasionally assisted me.

As I understand some doubts have arisen as to my parish, I beg to observe I have not, to my knowledge, gained any settlement by renting or otherwise since I left; if I had, I would readily state it.

Should you be so good as to assist me now in my unfortunate situation, I wish it to be understood as a *loan only*, and at some future time I may be enabled to repay the same with thanks, as I am in hopes of receiving here a perfect cure. My coming here was by the advice of my surgeon, to receive the benefit of my native air, but it appears I had not taken medicine sufficient, which caused a relapse of the disorder.

I now most respectfully leave my case in your hands, trusting you will not fail to take the same into consideration. I beg to observe I have three children, the oldest a cripple. I beg most respectfully to subscribe myself, Gentlemen, your obedient, humble servant.

James Fewins
Plymouth Ward, Devon and Exeter Hospital
Exeter, Devon

This letter is in a beautiful hand; that and the obsequious and florid style strongly suggest Fewins hired an amanuensis to communicate with the overseers. This pauper may have been the son of the James Fewings chronicled in Chapter One, who had peddled in Devon during the Napoleonic Wars. Perhaps the son had earned a settlement in Cheriton Bishop through an apprenticeship, as this parish seems to have been lax in preventing such occurrences before 1830.[9] Geography and chronology are favorable to the surmise, but it remains only that.

Were James Fewins's hopes of a "perfect cure" at the Devon and Exeter Hospital misplaced? Eighteenth-century English hospitals doubtless often fell short of any number of standards, but the Devon and Exeter was exceptionally good. Founded in 1741, the hospital had a remarkable record of helping the poor from all over Devon. Parishes subscribed to ensure admission of paupers in need of the hospital's services, an insurance that could cost a parish as little as 5 guineas a year in 1830.[10] Careful screening of patients before admission and an ample diet and good care during hospitalization were no doubt important to the hospital's success.[11]

* * *

25 August 1834

She was born, as she hath heard and believes to be true, in the parish of Wolborough, Devon, where her parents then resided, and were legally settled. She never served any apprenticeship. In 1805 she was married at Brixham Church to Thomas Williams, who was then in the Montgomery Militia. Her husband died soon after the Battle of Waterloo. She had three children by him living at his death. One of them died soon after. The other two have been off from her care for many years.

Sometime about the month of January 1825 she went to Sidmouth.

Her children were off her hands. She agreed with Lady Audley to serve as cook at £20.4 per year wages, and to receive it half-yearly. She served under this agreement about six years and eight months, going with Lady Audley from Sidmouth to Brighton on one occasion, where she stayed two months, and then went to Weymouth and stayed another two months. She was afterwards with Lady Audley in Exeter, and stayed one month. Lady Audley did not travel again for four years.

On 10 May 1832 she went with Lady Audley to Cheltenham, and was in lodging in Oxford Street for one week. She then went to lodge with Lady Audley at No. 1 in Exmouth Place in Cheltenham, and served Lady Audley there from 17 May until the beginning of October following. She was ill there, and Lady Audley told her she must leave her service. Lady Audley gave her notice to leave, and told her she should stay until she could suit herself to go. When Lady Audley left Cheltenham she took examinant with her as far as Bath, and there left examinant. Lady Audley went from Bath to Sidmouth in her own carriage, and in two or three days examinant, at Lady Audley's expense, went to Sidmouth in the stage coach. Lady Audley took down a cook from Bath with her. When examinant got to Sidmouth, being ill, she went to Lady Audley's house there, and remained about four or five days. She did no work during the time.

Lady Audley then caused her wages due up the day of leaving her house at Sidmouth to be paid her, and she left. She has done no act since to gain a settlement.

Mary Williams
[Sidmouth, Devon]

The detail of this examination was due to the uncertainty over where Mary Williams actually ended her service, Sidmouth or Cheltenham, but the historical interest of the story is primarily in Lady Audley's treatment of her sick cook. Williams could stay until she "could suit herself to go," and her wages were reckoned from her last day under Lady Audley's roof, not from the last day of actual service. This was generous, but go the cook must. Perhaps if Williams had been a servant of longer standing she would have been pensioned or reassigned, although her almost seven years with Lady Audley may have been recognized by the severance arrangement. Nonetheless, Williams joined the ranks of former domestic servants who had once been in fine homes, earning wages far beyond what they could hope to receive else-

where. There remained the recourse to poor relief. Just as some
relatives looked to the parish to assume responsibility for a kins-
man in need, so too did some members of the aristocracy on the
discharge of servants.

As for her parish of settlement, the legal and moral obligation
fell to Sidmouth where she had served most of her time, not
Cheltenham, where she became ill and was told she would have
to leave Lady Audley's service. The courts took a generous con-
struction of the law in the case of illness, counting it as service
even if the servant were incapable of any actual work. That her
last night under Lady Audley's roof was in Sidmouth and her
wages were reckoned up to that time established that parish as
her place of settlement.

*   *   *

21 November 1857

I am the widow of James Wallbank, who died 10 October last at
4, Wrestlers Court. I was married about thirty-eight years ago at Bishopsgate. About thirty-one years ago I was passed [by removal order]
with my husband and three children from Bethnal Green to St. Michael,
Crooked Lane, and was delivered to Mr. Marrial in Crooked Lane. He
carried on the business of a wire worker. Thereupon 5/ was paid to my
deceased husband, and afterwards, for about the space of two months,
either myself or my husband went to the church of St. Michael and received there 10/ per week, and on my confinement the parish officers
allowed 5/ per week for a fortnight for a nurse, and sent 5/ to me to
obtain nourishment during the period of my confinement. After the
two months I went to the parish officers and informed them that my
husband was then in employ and could do without further pay, but
upon my saying that myself and children were badly off for shoes, St.
Michael, Crooked Lane gave me £1 for to obtain them. Since I was
passed I have never rented any house by the year, nor has my husband
gained a settlement since.

Martha Wallbank
St. Ethelburga, Bishopsgate, London

This was a case of settlement being determined by presump-
tion. St. Ethelburga, Bishopsgate, learned nothing from Martha
Wallbank about the Wallbanks' settlement in a direct sense, only

that the family had received relief from St. Michael, Crooked Lane, over three decades before, and that nothing had happened since to affect the Wallbanks' settlement. What was important was not that they had received relief, for sojourners often were given casual relief by parish officers, but that the relief they had received was sustained and included a regular weekly allowance. The decisive evidence is that the Wallbanks had been removed to St. Michaels and had then received extensive relief. Whatever other grounds there may have been, and surely there were others, the facts stated here were sufficient to prove settlement.

It is interesting that the Wallbanks received such generous treatment and had responded by removing themselves from the relief rolls after the husband had found work. It is not difficult to find among settlement records such instances of humane and honest dealings among parish officers and paupers, but it is no less easy to find quite the opposite, as in the cases that follow.

Frauds

10 March 1819

He has heard and believes he was born in the parish of South Molton, Devon. He served James Joce of Swimbridge, Devon, for eight years under hirings by the year. Then he served William Lock of Bishop's Tawton one year under a hiring for a year. Then he agreed to serve William Dale of Georgenympton for a year, from Lady Day. At the Christmas following he was married. About six weeks before his year was up his master told him the parish [officers] wanted him to turn him off because he should not gain a settlement there. This happened on a Saturday.

The next day he and an apprentice boy of Dale's went to South Molton Church. They returned about half past six o'clock in the evening. His master blamed him for staying out so long and making the apprentice drunk. His master and he had some words, and his master told him he should go about his business. The next morning he left the said William Dale's service, and he has done no [other] act whereby to gain a settlement.

James Dodds
Georgenympton, Devon

This examination greatly interested the conducting officers at Bishop's Tawton, because Dodd's evidence suggested that Georgenympton had deliberately attempted to deny Dodd a settlement based upon hiring and service, the officers of that parish having entered into some collusive arrangement with Dodd's master. Accordingly, they had Dodds swear again to the truth of his account and submitted the case to legal counsel.

Counsel advised them not to proceed with the matter, even though the circumstances were suspicious and carried "some appearance of fraud," for "where there are other sufficient reasons to justify the discharge [making the apprentice drunk], fraud cannot be presumed." The evidence here was too slender, and they were told that "there is no decided case in which fraud has been found without some stronger proof of it than this case affords at present."

It was, in fact, very difficult to prove that a master or parish had deliberately defrauded a sojourner of a settlement, although it certainly happened.[12] The commoner approach was "settlement-avoidance"; all over England annual hirings gave way in the late eighteenth century to hirings for shorter periods of time, not infrequently only a few days shorter than the full year. Under such arrangements contracts might be renewed for several years, and service duly rendered, without ever conferring a settlement on the servant. Even so, settlements by hiring and service were exceedingly common, for the gates were only fitfully guarded. Of course, there were doubtless those masters, and even parish officers, who thought good yearly servants deserved settlements.

*   *   *

30 May 1825

Sarah Jones, single woman, aged about sixty-six years, being sworn and examined as to her settlement in the parish of St. Mildred in the City of London, saith that she lived and resided as a yearly hired servant with Mr. Cowling in the Poultry in the parish of St. Mildred for about four years. She had 12gn. a year wages as cook, and always slept in his house at the Poultry, aforesaid, during such service. She left his service about twenty-six years ago, and has lived principally in Half Moon Alley, Bishopsgate ever since at a rent never exceeding 2/ a week, and has been getting a living by making caps. She believes she has not gained any settlement since she lived with Mr. Cowling in the parish of St. Mildred.

Sarah Jones
St. Mildred, Poultry, London

The parish of St. Mildred investigated this story up to a point, but there was little it could do. Jones had been legally removed from Bishopsgate to St. Mildred two months earlier, and the Quarter Sessions had confirmed the removal, thus preventing St. Mildred from appealing. In addition, an inquiry conducted by a Mr. Burton, presumably acting on behalf of St. Mildred, confirmed Bishopsgate's case. Yet only a year later St. Mildred's officers discovered "this woman to be an imposter," who "had been removed to several parishes, and received relief from them under false statements."

Fraudulent claims to settlement were naturally more frequent in London and other large cities than in rural parishes where there was less possibility of anonymity. They were also more likely to involve an older pauper, such as Sarah Jones, who could invent a tale from long ago concerning masters long dead. Yet it is still rare to find outright fraud such as this in settlement records. Just as masters and parish officers practiced settlement-avoidance, sojourners presumably did so as well, either by avoiding the conditions of a settlement they deemed unfavorable or by having a convenient lapse of memory. Of course, it is also well to remember that the number of frauds exposed may have been a small percentage of the number actually committed.

* * *

John Northway was born in the parish of Kingsteignton and claimed that as a boy he was bound an apprentice to his uncle of the same name, living in the parish of Ilsington, a few miles to the west. He testified to serving his apprenticeship until he was around fifteen years of age, when he was told he might go where he liked. So off he went to serve other masters, including Mr. Richard Wills of the parish of Highweek, under a year's hiring and service, at 5 guineas. After completing that contract, he claimed to have gone to sea, continuing in the sea service for about fifteen years. He further claimed to have married his present wife soon after and never to have rented at £10 or more a year.

These facts came out in his examination, taken at Ilsington in 1831. The important question here was whether he had in truth been formally apprenticed. If he had been bound to his uncle and then been given permission to go where he liked, the apprenticeship would have remained in force, expiring sometime during his years at sea, but the last crucial days of actual service would have been in Ilsington, since his uncle had not specifically assigned him to another master or employed him in another parish. If, however, there had been no actual binding, then Highweek was his parish by virtue of his year's service there (such service did not count if at the time he was still legally the apprentice of another man).

The uncle then gave his testimony in the case. He claimed to have taken his nephew on as an act of charity when the boy was about three years old, maintaining him until he was fourteen or fifteen, at which time he ran away.

Ordinarily, the testimony of the person being examined for settlement weighed more heavily than any single witness to the contrary, at least if the witness were a ratepayer and therefore presumed to have an interest in denying a settlement. Clearly the uncle in this case was just such an interested party. On the other hand, a young child could hardly be expected to remember things as clearly as his uncle, and it is likely that the magistrates would have assigned the nephew to Highweek if there had not been a third witness.

Her name was Mary Beer. Her relationship to the Northways is not clear, but it is likely that she was a former servant of the uncle. Living in Ilsington, she apparently heard of the differing testimony, and three weeks later decided, or was persuaded, to step forward. She claimed to have found a paper on a shelf where she kept her books about three weeks earlier, whether before or after the uncle's deposition is not clear. Opening it, she remembered seeing the words "this indenture" and the name of John Northway in different places in the document. She also noticed four seals, with names near the seals, although she did not remember what names they were. She stated that she had given the paper to Mr. Barnes, the overseer of Ilsington.

Someone was lying. What seems most likely is that the uncle was in collusion with the overseer. Whatever the truth of the matter, Ilsington could not hope to win the case unless further witnesses could be produced to negate Mary Beer's testimony. Since no further documents are attached to the case, it is likely that the uncle and Ilsington conceded defeat.[13]

No one could deny that the Law of Settlement was often inequitable in assigning responsibility for a person or for a family's welfare and that this resulted in hardships, evasions, and frauds, as well as the contempt of those who saw the system, at least by the early nineteenth century, as a rickety remnant of mercantilism. But the law *did* identify responsibility. The very existence of a workable system of poor relief depended on just such a law to define and assign responsibility and that process had to begin on the local level. The wonder is not that the system led to hardships, frauds, and extensive criticism, the wonder is that it worked so well.

SIX

A London Parish:
St. Martin, Vintry

ST. MARTIN, VINTRY, is a City of London parish bordering the Thames. With some sixty houses and a population of 205 in 1821, the parish was small, even for the City, where small parochial units still partly reflected the densely packed medieval London. In the early nineteenth century, the parish had a number of problems characteristic of all metropolitan parishes, large and small—prostitution, unemployment, urban improvements that displaced low-income inhabitants (the City approach to the Southwark Bridge was built through the parish in 1817),[1] and a collection of settled and sojourning poor to relieve or remove. Although two of its parish officers, Messrs. Spendlove and Scattergood, had evocative names, the parish was not exceptionally generous toward its poor.

But St. Martin, Vintry, differed markedly from larger metropolitan parishes, such as St. Leonard, Shoreditch, in being sufficiently small for its overseers to know and follow the individual fortunes of their paupers. What is truly exceptional is the survival of a parish document containing 103 reports of pauper cases between 1815 and the 1830s, with character sketches and judgments seldom found in parish records. These reports relate both to the settled and sojourning poor. Nineteen are included here, for they provide an unusually vivid perspective on the poor of London between Waterloo and the 1832 Reform Bill (there are some later entries as well). The most valuable feature of the reports is that they are not one-time entries but running accounts of pauper lives and of how the poor law was applied in each case. Many require no commentary.

17 August 1820

John Carr, Dinah, his wife, and John aged 15, Dinah aged 11, Elizabeth 9, and Sarah 6 years old, passed from Queenhithe—lodger in

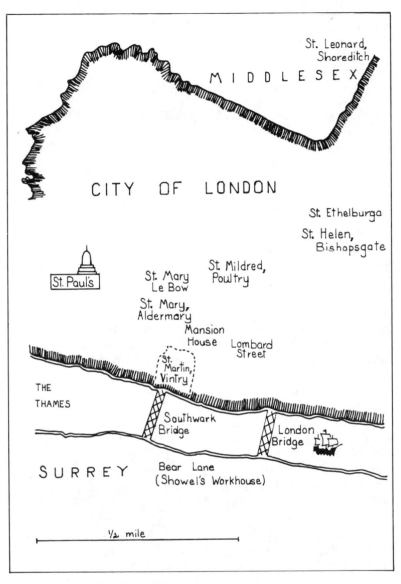

St. Martin, Vintry, and Beyond

London's Tenements, 46 Queens Street, at 4/ per week about a year [it required 3/10½ per week to attain settlement by £10 annual rental]—a blacksmith, earns 30/ per week, sometimes more.

The boy, John, having been in Vintry Ward School, but an idiot, wants the parish to put him in the workhouse—gave him an order for Bear Lane [location of Showel's Workhouse in Southwark, which was employed by this parish], 21 August 1820.[2]

Relieve them occasionally.

March 1823: John Carr, Jr. bound apprentice to Claud Neilson, one of the firm of Fraser & Co., to go to sea—paid £5 to fit him out—returned again after going one voyage to Demerara [river in what was then British Guiana], not having been in any harbor in England six weeks, gained no settlement by his apprenticeship—sent again to Showel's, where he is likely to remain for life.

* * *

[no date] 1815

John Cleghorn and Eleanor, his wife, both near fifty years of age, reside Brick Lane, Spitalfields [outside the parish, and a center of silk weaving in London]—have three children, all girls, learning the business of silk engine windster—does not send them to school—has had twelve children. He is troubled very much with rheumatism—an idle man. She is very troublesome. Nearly twenty-four years a pensioner.

4/ [relief] per week.

1816: 6/ per week—no work and ill.

2 August 1817: Removed to Mr. Clark, No. 24, Hope Street, Spitalfields, at 2/6 per week.

1822: Removed to Mr. Warner, Tabernacle Row, Finsbury.

1823: Removed to Willow Walk, where they remained a few weeks, then removed to No. 4, York Street, Bethnal Green.

1824: Removed again.

1827: Mrs. Cleghorn died—sent J. Cleghorn to workhouse, Bear Lane.

These "removals" were clearly voluntary and suggest how little parish boundaries mattered to the poor of metropolitan London. Outparish relief was regularly given and was indeed indispensable for a parish like St. Martin, Vintry.

* * *

Elizabeth Davies, a widow, aged sixty-eight years.
Resides No. 13, Worcester Place.
Rented house, No. 13, College Hill, about sixteen years since.
Pensioner, 3/6 per week.
1821: Sent to Showel's Workhouse, Bear Lane, where she died.

*　　*　　*

6 May 1815

Reuben Hartley, aged twenty-eight years. Occupies apartments in Heywood's Tenements, corner of Little Elbow Lane. Has resided there two or three years. Pays 6/ per week; a wife, but no family. Committed a violent outrage a few nights since in breaking open Mr. Coleman's door, Little Elbow Lane, about twelve o'clock.

The Lord Mayor considers him insane, and directs the churchwardens (verbally) to provide for him in a mad house. Having a certificate to that effect, Mr. Jon Miles's lunatic asylum has agreed to receive him at 10/6 per week. He was taken from Giltspur Street Compter [City prison used primarily for debtors] this day in a hackney coach, and put under Mr. Miles's care, with a note from the churchwarden requesting him to provide for him on account of the parish of St. Martin, Vintry, at the weekly sum agreed on by John Fisher, overseer, with Mr. Watts, the keeper.

Mr. John Haslam, the physician to Bethleham Hospital, was ordered by J. F. [John Fisher, here and hereafter] to visit and report when he would be in a state to be safely discharged, and upon his certificate, dated 1 June to that effect, the churchwarden sent J. F. with an order for his discharge [also called Bedlam, the Hospital of St. Mary of Bethlehem in Southwark was London's well-known facility for such cases]. 2 June, when J. F. paid Mr. Watts for Sir Jon Miles £2.7 for [Hartley's] board and care. He was discharged accordingly, and restored to his wife, and went to work next day at his usual occupation, Messrs. Wrights, the packers in Little Elbow Lane.

Since the foregoing account, he left Mr. Wright's service in 1816, and took large premises in Manchester (but left his wife in London); consequently, has gained a subsequent settlement.

June 1817: Was taken by the City officers (insane), and confined in the Giltspur Street Compter. The Lord Mayor, finding that he had a lodging at the Sugar Loaf, Little Elbow Lane, and that was the last place he slept in, sent to J. F. to attend him, when he gave us a letter for Bethlehem, where we took him Thursday, 5 June, the bond to cost us £5.4.6. We wrote to Manchester, but could get nothing there without passing him, so considered we had better put up with the least expense and trouble. He was discharged from Bethlehem 24 September following, when we paid about 6/6 more for shoes, etc. He says he paid rent at Manchester, £20 for about sixteen months, No. 14 Cannon Street, and at the bottom of Back Sugar Lane, Manchester.

* * *

30 July 1817

Elizabeth Hutchins, alias Marsh, in a forward state of pregnancy, came passed by order of removal with her son, William, from Heston Parish, near Hounslow. Gained a settlement here by living servant about a year with Mr. P. Shrub, No. 42, Queen Street. She has since that time lived a few months at Chertsey [Surrey], where she was married to Charles Hutchins, discharged from the 15th Huzzars, and was deserted by him on the road near Chertsey. It proved that he was taken into custody by the parish officers of Cadley, near Chute, near Salisbury [Wiltshire], he having deserted a former wife residing in Cadley, and was taken to Fishington Gaol. Consequently, we were obliged to take care of her, this being her maiden parish.

Her son, William, about eleven months old, was born at Chertsey, and consequently belongs to that parish, but being so young and in a very weakly state [our parish] was obliged to take care of him with the mother, the law not allowing them to be separated—sent them both to Showell's Poor House, Bear Lane. J. F. wrote to the overseers of Chertsey. They came to London, and offered to pay 2/ per week, but he died 7 September following, when he was buried at Christchurch, Surrey; the whole expense for him amounted to £2.17.8, which account was sent to the overseers at Chertsey.

Elizabeth Hutchins, alias Marsh, was delivered of a girl, 30 September 1817; was baptized at Christchurch, Surrey, Sarah Ann. On 10 November, Elizabeth was discharged the house, and after clothing her, she went to live cook at Dr. Smith's at Chertsey, taking her daughter with her, which we agreed to pay 3/ per week to Miss Marriott, 74 Old Broad Street, to put the girl to nurse at Bagshot.

November 1818: About two months since, [she] left Dr. Smith's place and lives now with Miss Haines, Chertsey Bridges.

1819: Left Miss Haines, and went to live housemaid with Captain Bradburns, Westcroft, at Chobham, near Cobham, Surrey.

1820: Where she was got with child by William Learwood, the footman, and after much trouble and expense, got an agreement to pay 2/6 per week to this parish for the child.

1821: She laid in at Showels of a boy, who, with the child Elizabeth, is placed out to nurse at J. Buckland, Brox, near Chertsey, and [we] pay 7/ per week with them. She took a cook's place at Mr. Burrows, Lower Thames Street—left there after living about six months; afterwards, took a place at Weybridge about November 1821, and at James Esq., Chertsey, 1 March 1822.

October 1822: Came again pregnant, by Josh. Keaste; when she had lain in February 1823 of a girl named Caroline, at Showell's. After much trouble and expense, he [Keaste] came to London. It was agreed by the churchwarden, Israel Phipps, to take an acceptance of William King [presumably a parish officer], Chertsey, at six months for £15, paid February 1824.

February 1824: Letter from Dr. Smith informing us of the death of the child, Caroline, at John Bucklands, Brox, near the Otter, near Chertsey, Surrey, who receives 7/ per week of this parish for Sarah Ann and William.

Married to William Bunce of Chertsey at Byfleet last day of November or 1 December 1830 or 1831.

11 May 1833: The boy, William, came up by Chertsey Coach, and went to Mr. George Mason, baker, No. 5, College Hill, upon liking [the common trial period].

Elizabeth Hutchins was clearly a problem pauper through misfortune and through her own actions. She had had two children by a bigamist, adjudged bastards on that account: William, who died, and Sarah Ann, who lived. She then had two additional bastards by separate fathers: Caroline, who died, and her second William, who lived to be apprenticed by the parish. The parish must have heard with relief of her marriage to Bunce of Chertsey, presumably ending at last their responsibility for her.

*   *   *

18 November 1815

Elizabeth Lancaster, age twenty-seven years, was passed from St. Mary, Whitechapel. Gained a settlement by being born (and residing with her mother, L. Lancaster, upwards of twenty years) in Delight's

Tenements, No. 64, Queen Street, and removed (when they were pulled down to build the present warehouse belonging to Messrs. Muggeridge and Tucker) to Goodacres, Sugar Loaf Court, in the Parish of Holy Trinity, Queenhithe, and paid 4/ per week for three weeks only, and afterwards 3/9 per week; lived there three months, then in [blank space] Court, Little Trinity Lane; paid 2/6 per week for a few weeks, when her mother left her to take care of herself. After three weeks [she] went to service for about eight or nine months, and had two places in that time. Since then [she has] lived by prostitution, for four and a half years. Sent [her] immediately to the workhouse, and from thence to Guy's Hospital on 24 November.

Removed to Braintree [Essex] in 1817, where she lived with Leonard Allingford of the parish of Leigh; she came sundry times and had relief, saying she was going to be married to Allingford, and wanted a Parish Portion [a pauper dowry; see Chapter Two], but the churchwarden declined giving or promising any.

On the 22 October 1817 they both came, saying they were married, and produced a copy of an extract worded as follows [relevant extract from the marriage register of Raying, Essex, showing their marriage took place on 4 October 1817], on which we gave the man 25/ toward buying furniture.

From domestic service to prostitution to matrimony: this surely was a common progression and brought no condemnation here. The 25/ she and her husband received after proving their marriage was hardly unalloyed philanthropy; it was in the parish's interest to maintain a reputation for rewarding marriages that transferred settlements to other parishes. Elizabeth Lancaster was now the responsibility of Leigh, her husband's parish, and that was well worth 25 shillings from the poor rate.

* * *

17 October 1818

Elizabeth Lively, eighteen years of age, gained her settlement by her father, Philip Lively, who about three years ago rented the bottom part of 45 Queen Street of John London at £36 per annum, lived there about three-quarters of a year. She says she has gained no subsequent settlement, but has lived in sundry places at weekly wages ever since. This last two months [she] has been unfortunate, and taken from a house of ill-fame in St. Mary Newington, and passed to us.

NB: Gave her an order for admittance to Showell's, Bear Lane, until she is cured, and can get a place of service.

24 March 1819: Discharged and clothed, her father promising to take care of her.

28 February 1820: Came again in great distress, having lived five months in a *Respectable* place, Miss Green's Boarding School, Kensington Square, and left there to go and live with a young man in Westminster; gave her an order to Showell's, Bear Lane, when she was found upon examination to be *injured*; sent her to Guy's Hospital to be cured.

September 1821: She went into the Magdalen [Hospital for Penitent Prostitutes, then located in Southwark]. The father received an order to go into one of the houses in Sion College.[3] Bond signed by the church-wardens, Messrs. Sills and Magnay, 14 March 1822.

The parishioners of St. Martin, Vintry, were concerned with prostitution, as the judgmental underlinings in the document suggest, although misfortune rather than misconduct is stressed. That Elizabeth Lively was admitted to Magdalen Hospital indicates that she sought to change her life and was adjudged worth saving, for entry into that famous charity was voluntary and competitive. Although there was indeed a punitive element in ordering paupers to enter the workhouse in Bear Lane, in this and the preceding case proper care of the women appears to have been the primary consideration, and it is noteworthy that both were soon transferred to Guy's Hospital for medical attention.

That the moral dimension figured less strongly for parish authorities than the cost and trouble to St. Martin, Vintry, is indicated by a memorial of 26 July 1816, signed by 26 parishioners, in which two houses in Great Elbow Lane were singled out for having "extended their notoriety to all parts of the City of London as receptacles for prostitution." The business was conducted around the clock, and respectable females in the vicinity were being insulted. Between midnight and one A.M. on the day the memorial was written, "so great was the scene of riot" at those houses "that most of us left our beds in the expectation that nothing but a conflagration could have occasioned the piercing shrieks that were then heard." But the memorialists made it clear that their intent was not to disturb vice in "its hidden retreats," but to curb the open abuse of daylight prostitution and the sort of troublesome incident prompting their memorial.[4]

*   *   *

4 June 1816

Daniel McCarthy (an Irishman) has a wife and four children, viz: one girl (the oldest), and three boys, the youngest two years old, the girl eleven. Lodges in one of Mr. Jn. London's tenements, No. 44, Queen Street, front room, up one pair of stairs—pays 2/6 only per week rent. Has lodged there between three and four months; previous to which [they resided at] Mrs. Butler's, Allhallows Lane, about one month, and paid 3/ per week—before that, in a court between Holywell Lane and Shoreditch Turnpike three or four months [for which they] paid 3/ per week, to which he removed from No. 2, bottom of Plough Street, Whitechapel, where he lived about a year and a half, paying 2/4 per week, etc.

He came to England very young, about the time of the American War. His father was a soldier. Never was a yearly servant, only a jobbing man. Worked at Harford, Payne & Co. about twelve months at 20/ per week; previously with Froggatt and Shillitoe in Steel Yard, about two years at 18/ per week; previously a bricklayer's laborer. Does not know where he belongs in Ireland, having come away so young. Is not certain whether [he was] born in England or Ireland. Has neither brother or sister, father or mother. Never had occasion for parochial relief before. His wife was born in Limerick, but does not know where.

NB: He served the churchwarden with a warrant to appear before the Lord Mayor to show cause why [the churchwarden] would not relieve them.

Allowed them temporary relief for the present, they being Irish, and gaining no settlement in England. Where they reside, the parish becomes liable to relieve [them], during their residence.

Removed (on account of the premises being taken down by the Southwark Bridge Company)—out of the parish, so ceased relief, but not without the earnest endeavors of C. Martin, Esq. to fix them in this parish.

Those last lines reflect the common rivalries among local authorities; the economic interest of each parish was to reduce the number on its welfare rolls by "fixing" paupers in other parishes. Still another Irish tenant of 44 Queen Street in 1816 was Mary Carty, whose husband had gone off five weeks before to seek work, leaving her and their two children in want. She applied to the parish officers for relief, but was refused. As bold as her compatriot Daniel McCarthy, she served the parish with a warrant from the sitting alderman at the Guildhall, who ordered that she receive relief.

The parish probably knew she was entitled to relief, but there was often a good chance a pauper such as she would not appeal. Denials and delays were common ploys of economical parish officers, to the hardship of those in need and in despite of the law.[5] Paupers had a right to appeal and may on occasion have abused that right. Indeed, one authority, W. H. Bodkin, wrote: "The power which paupers at present possess of dragging before magistrates the parish officer who conscientiously withholds relief is one of the most pernicious parts of the system."[6] But although there may have been abuses from every quarter, the right to appeal was surely one of the better features of the English poor law. It would be interesting to know, but impossible to discover, how often appeals, whether between pauper and parish or between parish and parish, arose over genuine points of law as opposed to the intricate games of bluff and counterbluff undertaken to save a parish money—and perhaps because they were games.

Finally, the McCarthy and Carty cases exemplify how the Irish, as well as all other non-English residents in England, had legal rights under the English poor law, a fact that surely encouraged an influx of sojourners into the country, who could hope—even if they gained no settlement—that the cost and trouble of removing them would be judged greater than the cost and trouble of relieving them.

*   *   *

5 March 1822

Margaret Morris, blind, aged twenty-seven years, came passed from St. Saviour. Her father kept the Swan, corner of College Hill, about eighteen months, and died there; this woman, being blind and in the workhouse, and maintained by the father. The mother-in-law would not maintain, therefore [the daughter] was passed to this parish as her father's [place of] settlement. Continued her at [K]ey's workhouse, Rockingham, Newington.

Her father left her a legacy, £60, which the parish received, paying the trustee, her uncle's expenses, £3.8.

Margaret Morris died at Mr. Deacon's, Stepney Green Union House, aged forty-six years on 23 March 1839.

It seems likely Margaret Morris was given something better at Key's than she would have received at Showel's, thanks to her father's legacy, but it does not appear to have spared her placement in a union workhouse, one of a species of generally impersonal and unpleasant institutions formed by the union of many parishes to provide institutional relief in accordance with the Malthusian and Benthamite elements contained in the Poor Law Amendment Act of 1834.

* * *

30 November 1816

Thomas Morris, and Ann, his wife, both near forty years of age, have seven children, five of whom are at home—resides (in half a cottage) at Pye Corner in the parish of Sawbridgeworth in the County of Hertfordshire, about twenty-four miles from London, and three from Harlow in Essex—pays £5 per annum rent. He gained a settlement here by living footboy with Mr. John Wardell at Golden Heart Wharf two years, 1797 and 1798, or thereabout, and has not gained any legal settlement since, as appears by an affidavit annexed.

Applied personally this day for relief to be enabled to pay his rent, about £5.16, due at Michaelmas, 1816, which if not paid before Xmas, 1816, his landlord, Michael Hankin, Esq., would distrain [Morris's goods], and then [Morris] and his family would be passed to here, and the parish where he lives and earns his bread by daily labor would forbid him living there again.

Sunday, 8 December 1816, J. Fisher and William Archer, two overseers, hired a one-horse chaise, and went to Pye Corner, and found the above account literally true, that his being so distressed this year was on account of a severe fit of illness he had in this last summer, and the badness of the season, which has thrown so many on the parish where he lives, that they [the settled poor] have the preference in the labor, and he has consequently been out of employ at times. Found him, his wife, and five children, and his mother, all sat down to a decent but homely dinner in a poor cottage, but comfortable.

The overseers agreed to settle his rent to Michaelmas last, on his sending an affidavit to the truth of the above, which he sent the 10 December, by John Dean, the Hunsdon carrier, to the Vine Inn—and paid him £5.12, as per receipt.

1818: The names of the seven children and how disposed of: Thomas, aged 16 years, apprenticed to John Farline, shoemaker at Harlow—been five years; Frances, aged 14 years, servant to Samuel Rice, 12 Wall Street, Cripplegate—been one year; Elizabeth, aged 12 years, at home; Charles, aged 11 years, at home; John, aged 9 years, at home; Sarah, aged 6 years, at home; Ann, aged 2 years, at home.

* * *

20 November 1815

John Peacock, thirty-eight years of age, a wife, thirty-four years (Olivia), have four children, viz: a girl, aged 7, a boy 5, a girl 2¼, and an infant girl 11 weeks old.

Gained settlement by servitude with his brother, Beadlom Peacock, who lodged at Mr. Atkins, White Horse, Queen Street; was passed from Lambeth about six or seven years ago, and [their] last relief was in February 1815—been married about fifteen years—had a ready furnished lodging in the Boro' [of Southwark], the first two or three years at 3/6 per week, until they had children, which they did not like to have in that house.

Lived seven years in Queen Street, Hammersmith, opposite the Ship, paid 2/10½ per week, being about £7 per annum—removed from thence to Swaby's Court, Fore Street, Lambeth, where they have lived the last five years past.

He works as a sculler, in a very bad boat (that will hardly swim) at Lambeth—he is short and slender—gave her present relief, 6/—she wanted a weekly allowance, which the churchwarden declined.

NB: Not a trusty man.

December 1816: Came again in great distress, his boat stove to pieces in a gale of wind—gave him a petition with which he was enabled to purchase a new boat, and allowed them 6/ per week during pleasure.

1822: 5/ per week.

A marginal note, perhaps reflective of a lack of trust in Peacock, read: "Married at Christchurch, Middlesex, August 11, 1801—J. F. see certificate."

* * *

[no date] 1815

Margaret Phillips, a widow, age seventy-four years, resides Kent Road —sells fruit in the streets, and sweeps crossings of streets, and is lame.

Her husband lived coachman with Mr. Decures, Queen Street (late Hawksworths). Pensioner at 4/ per week.

1822: Order to Bear Lane Poor House.

1823: Discharged by own wish, and put on pension list at 2/6 per week.

1828: Several times in and out of farm house.

1829: In at Showels.

She was "in" at age 88 on the final entry to the variously named facility in Bear Lane. The names given to the house St. Martin, Vintry, used to farm its refractory and impotent poor suggest how difficult it is to distinguish between "workhouse" and "poorhouse," for here the same clerk used whatever name apparently came first to his mind.

* * *

[no date] 1815

Thomas Pine, single man, age about sixty years, served his apprenticeship to William Clark, a dyer in Vine Court—was impressed—has a bad leg—in the workhouse.

31 May: Mr. Proud, the churchwarden, gave 30/ to Pixley [presumably an employee of the workhouse] to provide clothes for Pine, but [Pine] threatened and abused Pixley in so gross a manner that he was obliged to give Pine the money, which he did not lay out in clothes, and has since absented himself from the workhouse. The churchwarden ordered that he should not be readmitted without a special order from him. He absented himself about 5 June.

NB: It appears he is able to carry a sack of coals; if so, an unfit object to be maintained by the parish.

Was passed from St. Mary, Stratford, Bow, 28 June 1816, he being lame. J. F. procured a carriage for him to Showel's Poor House, Bear Lane.

1827: Deceased.

The picture of an old salt intimidating a timorous functionary to part with money intended for clothes is attractive, and one can imagine a visit to a public house followed shortly thereafter. But the laconic end to the story was over ten years of poorhouse regimen before Pine's death in 1827. Presumably Pixley or his successors had ample opportunity to restore the flow of intimidation to its normal course.

* * *

13 May 1818

Mary Savage, widow, and two children, Mary aged seven and John aged five years—came passed from the Holy Trinity Parish. Her late husband was a soldier; in Mr. John Man's service weekly, and lodged at the Fox and Goose, Brickhill Lane, where they gained a settlement by paying (as they say) 4/ per week—is now distressed for the means of obtaining the certificate of her marriage from Sheerness in order to get her children in the Military Asylum, Chelsea.

On the 27, we received the certificate by post, which cost us with the temporary relief we gave her, about £1.

NB: We are doubtful she ever paid above 3/6 per week in this parish [insufficient to establish settlement by £10 annual rental, whereas 4/ a week brought a settlement].

1821: Her eldest daughter, Margaret, came passed to us from Queenhithe, with a child she had by John Kirk, born in Grub Street. Being illegitimate, the parish officers of St. Giles, Cripplegate, allowed her 2/ per week (J. Kirk having deserted her), and we gave her 2/6 per week during pleasure.

30 September: He married [Margaret] at Shoreditch, and in October we gave her £3 to furnish a room.

1824: Pension, 2/6 per week, for boy John. The mother is married, or ought to be.

1827: The daughter, Mary, apprenticed with Sir John Fellowes' Charity.

29 October 1829: Mary Savage attended at a vestry meeting, and proposed if the parish would give her a portion of £5, the man, John Rain, whom she had been living with about eight years would marry her. The vestry gave her £1 to buy clothes and for the present, and when she produced the certificate of her marriage they would see what they could do for her, but held out no promise or conditions.

18 November, Monday: They produced the certificate, having been married at St. Leonard, Shoreditch, that morning (signed [by] A. P. Kelly).

19 [November]: Gave them £4, and bound the boy John apprentice to John Rain with Sir John Fellowes' Charity money—gave them £10.[7]

Even though the parish suspected the Savage claim to a settlement by rental, they did not dispute it, no doubt for lack of evidence, and even though the writer of this report thought she ought to have been married to Rain, the parish did not investigate, but waited until the couple approached them with a proposition and then used parish funds and a private benefaction to buy themselves out of any future obligation toward this family, for Rain was settled elsewhere. Why this particular family was treated so generously, compared to Elizabeth Lancaster at the time of her marriage to Leonard Allingford twelve years before, who only received 25s., is unknown and somewhat puzzling, if there was any reason to doubt the legitimacy of Mary Savage's settlement. Perhaps her first husband had been a hero in the wars or the parish officers found her unusually beguiling, or—what is most likely—the perceived value of a marriage to someone settled elsewhere was appreciated better in 1829 than in 1817. Whatever the reason, the difference exemplifies the wide latitude the authorities had in distributing welfare—one reason why Pine's intimidating treatment of Pixley in the previous case was uncommon.

*　*　*

25 March 1817

John William Smith and Sophia, age about forty years, and Mary, his wife, age about thirty years, passed this day from St. Bennets, Paul's Wharf; has no children alive. Obtained his settlement by being born in Sugar Loaf Court, Little Elbow Lane, where his father and mother lived, and removed to the Fox and Goose, Brickhill Lane, where they died in 1797 while he was at sea—was never apprenticed or lived yearly servant; has been at sea until 1815, when he was discharged from the *Aboukir*, 74 [guns], at Chatham—has been jobbing ever since, driving carts for Clark, Day, and Press; he broke a blood vessel about a month ago, unloading a load of coffee at Brewers Quay; has not been able to go to work, but is an outpatient of Bartholomew's Hospital—his wife goes charing, etc., but has nothing to do at present.

NB: Gave them temporary relief.

They lodge at No. 3, Helmet Court, near Bennets Hill, Upper Thames Street, two pairs of stairs, room at [blank space] per week; landlord's name, Blockett.

We are informed by his sister [Sophia?] that this woman [with] whom he cohabits is not his wife, and that he does not belong to us. About two years since he paid 7/ a week for unfurnished lodging (some months) in Chapel Court, [Southwark] Boro', under a feigned name—at present he is confined for debt (July 1817); the woman pressed so very much for relief, but we refused on the above account.

13 March 1818: Came passed again, and produced a certificate of

her marriage at Shoreditch in November last. I gave them an order to
Showells, but they would not go.

A disgruntled or guileless relative's story could alter lives, as
this sister's account did for her brother and his companion, or
as John Truck's father did for him and the parish officers of
East Budleigh. In Smith's case, there was clearly fraud, since he
claimed to be married in March 1817, but the certificate of marriage was dated in November of that year. The settlement Smith's
sister said he had earned in Southwark by rental payment would
be a second case of fraud, if true, but because that might have
been more difficult to prove, they were at least granted entry
to the workhouse. It is possible that the use of a feigned name
may have been an attempt to guard his settlement in St. Martin,
Vintry, but he may also have been avoiding his creditors, which
is more likely in the circumstances. In any case, the parish was
sufficiently suspicious to confine their offer to the minimal one
of the "workhouse test" (relief only there), an oft-used way of
punishing recipients thought guilty of laziness or dishonesty.

*   *   *

8 October 1816

Charlotte Stevenson, twenty-two years of age, born at Chertsey, Surrey—gained settlement by living servant about sixteen months with Mr.
Jonathan Sills, corner of Little Cheapside, Hambro' Wharf—applied for
relief, being with child by Henry Diplock, about twenty-four or twenty-
five years old, a journeyman linen draper, whom she has known for this
seven years past, and has visited her at Mr. Sills, and promised to marry
[her]. But when she informed him of her situation about four months
since, [he] absconded, and she has not heard of or seen him since. He
said he was going to Southampton, and would return in a few days.
He lodged then in Camomile Street. His brother kept a linen draper's
shop in Great Hermitage Street, where he failed, then went into lodgings in Jane Street, Commercial Road. Removed from thence about two
months since to somewhere in Sussex. His father [is] a shopkeeper, etc.,
at Westerham in Kent. Her mother [is] married to a second husband,
Thomas George (which surname she generally goes by); was an excise-
man, but now a laborer in husbandry at Chertsey. She has lodged the
last four months with Diplock's sister, a Mrs. Gower, a dressmaker and
milliner, 178 Strand, and intends going to lodge with Mrs. Powell, a

green grocer, No. 24, North Street, Manchester Square—expects to be put to bed in about a month.

Agreed to allow her 6/ per week for the present.

14 November: Put to bed of a boy in North Street, Mary le Bow Lane —kept on her allowance one month after her confinement on account of her being very ill—took cold through the imprudence of the nurse, when we continued a temporary relief until she was quite recovered, when she applied to the officers of Mary le Bow parish, who took Diplock and settled with him, so the child does not become chargeable here.

NB: When she recovered, we withheld the allowance—consequently [she] was obliged to apply to Mary le Bow parish officers.

St. Martin's earlier solicitude toward Charlotte Stevenson appears to have been motivated less by sympathy with her at Diplock's betrayal than her willingness to have the baby at a greengrocer's shop some 250 yards outside of St. Martin, Vintry, in the parish of St. Mary le Bow, the latter being given the task of finding the putative father and relieving the illegitimate child. Parking unmarried, pregnant paupers outside the parish of settlement was one way a parish could ease future relief burdens, for the illegitimate child was generally held to be a charge on the parish of its birth, but of course a parish ran the risk of retaliatory action in kind. It is not clear in this case why St. Martin, Vintry, withheld her allowance in the end—perhaps because Mary le Bow's previous actions suggested the parish could be put upon, or perhaps what is meant here is that she was applying only for the child's allowance. She herself was legally still a charge on St. Martin, Vintry.

*   *   *

[no date] 1815

Mary Swinney, a widow, age thirty-six years, has four children to maintain; resides Broadwall, Christchurch [Surrey]. Her husband lived with Mr. Hawksworth, 49 Queen Street. Sells meat and butter in the streets, and goes out washing and charing.

A pensioner at 8/ per week.

March 1817: The oldest of the above children (a boy, about seventeen years of age) is employed at Mr. Hawes, soap manufacturer, at 8/ per week.

The second child, Peter, about fifteen, is employed by Carter, a butcher at Broadwall, who gives him 1/ per week and victuals.

The other two are at home with the mother, No. 3, Hope Alley, Broadwall.

5 [March?]: Mrs. Swinney was this day delivered of a girl in Hope Alley, by a charity midwife, and Mrs. Winfred, a neighbor who attended her out of charity. A Mr. Reilly, a deal porter at Nicholson's Timber Yard, said he was the father of the child, and that he was ready and willing to marry her, but *she* would not, so he said he would take care of her and her children while he had work. Child died.

NB: We agreed to continue the 8/ per week for the present to take care of the two youngest children of Swinney.

April 1818: Reduced her pension to 5/ per week.

1 March 1819: Have found that Mrs. Swinney had rented and lived in a house in Broadwall in the parish of Christchurch, for which she paid 5/ per week before she was passed to this parish (in April 1814), but at that time there was an Act of Parliament in force (called a local act) which exempted Christchurch and [some] other parishes from persons gaining settlements under £20 per year; consequently, [she] was passed here, as her husband's prior settlement.

There was another Act passed since (54 George III, *cap.* 170), which repealed so much of the aforesaid act as related to settlement by rent, the same as if the aforesaid local act had never passed. Therefore J. F. (after giving her notice) ceased giving her any more relief, and referred her to the parish officers of Christchurch, where she lived.

They would not relieve her, but committed her to Horsemanger Lane Gaol as a vagrant!, confining her there seven days!! Then [they] sent her to this parish by a vagrant pass, to which there is no appeal. J. F. then applied to the sitting alderman [of London], and obtained an order for removal to Christchurch Parish Officers, where J. F. removed her and children on 4 March 1819, at their Committee Room in the workhouse, Charlotte Street, Surrey.

The underlining and exclamation marks in the above excerpt suggest that in the view of the recordkeeper the other parish had behaved very badly indeed. Doubtless there was more to the story than is recorded here—a judgment on the woman's character, some heated altercation between her and the officers of Christchurch (her refusal to marry Mr. Reilly suggests she had an independent mind). Whatever the details, confining her to gaol as a vagrant does appear exceedingly high-handed. Parking pregnant, unmarried paupers across a parish border was one thing—evasive, but not necessarily inhumane. The same could not be said of this affair.

On the other hand, Christchurch was undoubtedly upset at being the victim of ex post facto legislation. The £10 annual rental worked in the cities as a kind of haphazard rent control system in which resident landlords were under pressure by parish officers to keep rents below that amount. Christchurch thought its local act lifted this control, and rents would naturally have risen. Now they were caught by the later act. This was unfair, and a fundamental principle of English jurisprudence had been violated.

Christchurch could not punish Parliament or the other parish, but it could victimize Mary Swinney and her two young children. It must be assumed that interparochial disputes over settlement often had comparable consequences.

*   *   *

8 March 1817

Samuel Thorne, single man, about thirty-four years of age, came this day passed from St. Luke, Old Street; gained settlement here by apprenticeship to Harvey, basket maker, in the late Delights Tenements, Queen Street (now Muggeridge's Warehouse) about twelve years ago; has been to sea ever since, until about seven months ago, when he was discharged from the *Montague*, 74 [guns]—has been selling fruit, and trying to get work, but owing to the exigencies of the times, cannot get work to do.

NB: Allowed him 2/ per week for the present to pay his rent.

Sent him to Showell's, Bear Lane, where he stayed a few weeks, when he was discharged at his own request.

19 December: Came again, and gave him an order for Showell's, and whilst he was there, went out and married Margaret, 12 January, who came passed to us in February, 1818. He went to sea in February [1818?], so we sent her to Showells, where she stayed until 29 March, when her husband fetched her away!

December 1818: Came again, per vagrant pass from the Lord Mayor; gave her an order to Willis's, Mint St., Southwark, where she remained until 12 May 1819, when she was discharged, saying she was going to cut pens for Jacobs at Canterbury.

22 February 1820: Came passed again, and put her in Showells, Bear

Lane. Rather think she is, or ought to be, married to a man who occasionally visits her, whom J. F. forbade to be admitted.

June 1820: Married at Bishopsgate Church, having run away from workhouse; ceased relief.

Presumably Samuel Thorne had been lost at sea, given the change of focus in the report and his wife's remarriage. It is somewhat unusual to find a young, ablebodied single man, such as Thorne, passed to his parish of settlement, but the years after Waterloo were desperate for many of the British poor. St. Martin, Vintry, in league with St. Michael, Royal, sent a petition to Parliament on 25 April 1817 complaining of the "want of Trade and the means of employment, and the scenes of misery which present themselves from these causes."[8] These were, of course, national problems.

Another representative element in Thorne's history was the fate of his former dwelling, Delights Tenements, which had once been multiple residences for the poor (Elizabeth Lancaster and her mother had lived there also), but which had since become a warehouse. Such changes were profoundly altering the character of the City. Its population was still dense in the early nineteenth century, with about 100,000 living within the square mile, but it was declining as people sought more room and lower rents outside the walls, and as the City was increasingly given over to businesses, warehouses, and transportation routes.[9]

*　　*　　*

[no date] 1815

Susannah Young, married eighteen years, her husband at sea. She is thirty-eight years of age, and has two boys to maintain, ten and seven years old, in a school at Whitechapel. Works at her needle, making slops, etc.—resides No. 10, Nightingale Lane. Gained settlement by lodging, corner of Little Elbow Lane, Thames Street, about eight years since. Not heard from her husband for twelve months; he was carman to Gubbins and Cork.

A pensioner on 4/ per week.

1816: James Young returned from sea—bad leg, ruptured, etc.—in St. Thomas Hospital—supplied him with money to purchase truss, and relief several times.

May 1818: The pension being stopped, they were all four passed to us again from Whitechapel, and upon his promise never to come chargeable any more, we gave him and his two sons £3 to clothe them, and take them to his brother, William Young, Hunnington, Devon.

1819: Susannah Young died.

James Young's promise to St. Martin, Vintry, was not legally binding, of course, but a parish might risk such an outlay in hope of placing sufficient miles between the parish and the pauper that the authorities in his new home would prefer to give casual relief to the sojourner than be at the expense of removing him to his parish of settlement. Under just such an arrangement Harriet Williams may well have made her journey to Devon.

The author of these reports is unknown. Whoever he was, he had a fine, flowing hand and kept up his reports between 1815 and 1829. Later entries in another hand round out some of the reports he had begun. The writing was somewhat more cryptic and abbreviated than rendered here, but I have attempted to preserve the flavor of the original, even at the price of some irregularities in composition.

The facts this unknown writer noted were the sort of information a good vestry clerk or overseer of a small parish might keep in his head, and so one wonders why he thought it necessary to write it all down. Was he an extraordinarily conscientious clerk, who liked to write? Very likely, but there is an additional explanation. These reports would have made an excellent reference for the parish officers, those who were either new to the job or not in close touch with one another on a day-to-day basis. We know from the reports that this parish contained at least two active overseers, John Fisher and William Archer, and that the churchwardens were also employed in poor law matters. St. Martin, Vintry, was too small to afford a full-time professional officer, and the amateurs were too scattered in their urban employments for frequent interchanges; the reports were therefore a means of encouraging some consistency in decision making. Legal information and details on how the law actually worked would be especially useful for the inexperienced officers in weighing the merits of a claim and then deciding on the amount and method of relief, but all officers could benefit by consulting the records.

The number of poor handled by the larger metropolitan parishes, such as St. Pancras or St. Leonard, Shoreditch, required a professional officer, usually with the title of assistant overseer. Such an individual could not know the peculiar circumstances of each case and would be sufficiently familiar with the law to keep the records brief. Relief in the larger parishes was necessarily standardized, and there was less likelihood of major differences in the quantity or quality of relief than in smaller parishes, where officers could make judgments not only on the worth of a claim but on their perception of the worth of the pauper.

The scribe at St. Martin, Vintry, was most likely a highly efficient parish clerk, paid for his services, who had to deal tactfully with those empowered to make decisions in poor law matters. It is interesting to note that between 1813 and 1815 the parish spent four times as much on settlement matters and other overseers' and churchwardens' expenses, in proportion to its costs of poor relief, than the national average.[10] That was to some extent a reflection of the parish's size, which at its widest point measured only 200 yards across. It simply was not possible for the metropolitan poor to live and work from birth to death within parochial boundaries, especially in a parish as small as this one. Naturally, settlement questions would figure heavily in the administration of relief.

The keeping of reports, and the reports themselves, suggest a parish keen not to be put upon, either by sojourners or by other parishes. They do not reflect great generosity of spirit, either on the part of the anonymous writer or of the parochial administration he served, yet it was an administration that seems to have been competent and, within limits, caring.

Informal inventories such as this seldom survive and have been lost along with the equally ephemeral pauper petitions and examinations, yet there is certainly much in these reports that was characteristic of poor relief in other metropolitan parishes, most particularly in what they reveal of the physical mobility of the poor. Clearly, few of the metropolitan poor who survived infancy could have lived within the bounds of a single parish. Virtually all were at one or another time in their lives sojourners.

St. Martin, Vintry, made no attempt to keep its paupers home, and indeed preferred to give outparish relief so that their settled poor could find employment in some other parish. This meant that parish allowances could be kept to a minimum, as a supplement to whatever the pauper might be able to earn elsewhere. There was another major advantage in outparish relief: a pauper sojourner might earn a new settlement through renting, or his children might do so through hiring or apprenticeship. Even paupers who were entirely dependent on the parish, or whose characters were judged unfavorably, were sent away, to sojourn at the workhouse in Bear Lane across the river in Southwark.

SEVEN

A Westmorland Township:
Kirkby Lonsdale

WESTMORLAND IS PARTIALLY described in its name—west moorland. "A region of lofty mountains, naked hills, and black barren moors," it was called in 1795,[1] although later writers were more impressed by the grandeur of its hills, forests, and lakes. Kirkby Lonsdale is of a different character. Located in the south-eastern corner of the county, the township is less dramatically scenic than the Lake District to the west and the Yorkshire Dales to the east, but there is beauty in its gentle hills, patchworked with farms and woods, as Wordsworth, Turner, and Ruskin found. In the early nineteenth century the town of Kirkby Lonsdale was a thriving market center, bordered on the east by the deep-banked River Lune. Some 1,500 people lived there, making it the third-largest town in Westmorland (after Kendal and Ulverston) and the commercial center of the upper Lune Valley.[2] In consequence, Kirkby Lonsdale supported a variety of tradesmen, artisans, and small industries, but often had a problem employing its poorer inhabitants.

For the poor who stayed in the township there was work as laborer or servant in good times, and a weekly pension of two to three shillings from the overseers in bad, accompanied by additional financial help in the form of grants for house rents, clothing, shoes, medical emergencies, and funerals. For those who could not make do with these forms of outdoor relief, there was the "extensive" workhouse, erected in Kirkby Lonsdale in 1811 and incorporated for this purpose by a private act of Parliament. It came to serve seventeen townships. Eight of them were in Westmorland, but seven of them were in Lancashire, and two in Yorkshire. Geography was the determining factor, as it was for the migratory routes followed by most of the Kirkby

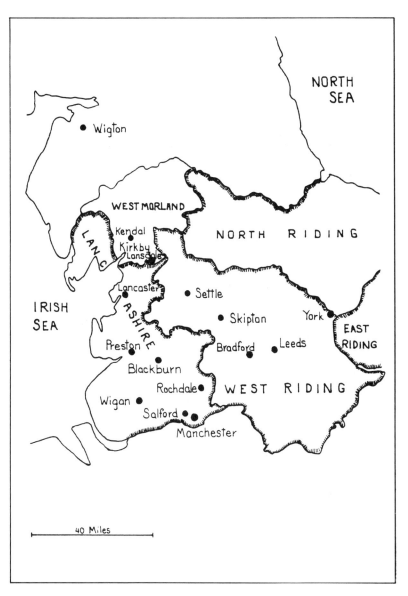

Kirkby Lonsdale and Beyond

Lonsdale poor who were willing to venture forth. West, north, and east of home lay hills, moors, and fells, but to the south the roads led invitingly into Lancashire and the West Riding, where new industries were developing, and it was in that direction that most of the poor who sought to better their fortunes naturally went.

Far from impeding the movement of their poor, the township's authorities actually encouraged it. Woolcombers, weavers, shoe-makers, and common laborers were most likely to leave. Not many of them were actually subsidized to go, although a few were so helped. George Goad was even given £3.8 "to assist him in going to the West Indies,"[4] but that was exceptional. The poor usually left on their own for other communities in northeastern England, yet they had the assurance that should they experience hardship in their new location their home township of Kirkby Lonsdale would assist them in the same way it did the poor who stayed home. Since there were jobs, and rumors of jobs, in the heartland of the Industrial Revolution, it is not surprising that many of the ablebodied and adventurous poor left, taking their children with them, for the young could sometimes find work in the new factories more easily than could their parents. About a third of the township's migrants went to three towns —Kendal, Lancaster, and Preston. Another third went to places within a rough pentagon defined by Blackburn, Wigan, Man-chester, Bradford, and Skipton. The remaining third scattered, with a few going as far as Edinburgh and London.

Kirkby Lonsdale's practice of relieving its nonresident poor was common in other parts of England, St. Martin, Vintry, being an example, but it was especially widespread in northeastern England. Pauper removals were relatively rare events, for so-journers in need simply wrote home, or had a landlord, a local overseer, a friend, or a hired pen write for them. There were even standard printed forms one township could send to another in which the guest township billed the home township for the so-journers' expenses. Consequently, large numbers of sojourners moved in the industrial North, seeking and finding work, en-couraged in their migration by the expectation that they would be relieved by their home township should they have need.

The system was feasible because the sojourning poor usually

did not move far away, and when settled in their new location, they tended to stay there, thus becoming known to the local authorities. The North, in fact, created an informal Law of Settlement of its own, in which settlement examinations, removal orders, suspended orders of removal, and other forms of magisterial intervention were only used as a last resort. To some extent that was true everywhere in matters of casual relief, meaning occasional relief given for a specific purpose, such as the purchase of new shoes. However, the system in the North involved regular pay, meaning an ongoing weekly dole and other benefits regularly bestowed. Overseers there tended to rely on their counterparts in other townships, and sometimes on the poor themselves, to make accurate assessments of need. There were, of course, controls. Relief was scaled to family size, for example, and based on what overseers considered an appropriate cost for a requested item. And there was also an informal system of investigation to catch welfare cheats and to identify overseers who were being too generous with other townships' money.

Nonresident relief was ideally suited to the industrial North and provided a cushion in times of cyclical unemployment, allowing the poor to seek jobs where they might find them.[5] That it has escaped the attention it deserves is largely owing to the few records the system produced and the poor survival rate of those that were.

Kirkby Lonsdale is an exception. Some 1,300 letters, bills, and petitions survive, dating from 1809 to 1836, and they reveal not only how the system worked for this particular township but also the expectations and practices of overseers and other authorities throughout the West Riding and Lancashire. That this collection survives at all is a historical accident, but that the material was collected in the first place is the work of one man, Stephen Garnett (1769–1840). Garnett assumed different titles at different times, but he was continuously involved with the township's relief of its poor from 1809 to 1836 and kept a fair portion of his correspondence. Little is known about him, although he was clearly a man of some energy and resolution. When he was in his mid-twenties, he married a woman in her mid-thirties, and they had four children. He pursued concurrently the occupations of grocer, seedsman, auctioneer, and overseer. There is some evidence he loved his two daughters and enjoyed gardening, but there is much clearer evidence that he disliked writing letters and parting with the township's money. The latter trait no doubt favorably impressed the township's vestry and must have been a factor in Garnett's long tenure as overseer, but it did not please the desperate paupers and exasperated overseers from other townships who sent him letter after letter, pleading with him to fulfill Kirkby Lonsdale's obligations. Most of the letters would never have been written had Garnett remitted funds promptly.

Garnett was apparently a hard case, quick to suspect and slow to trust, and the letters he received suggest that he was largely insensitive to the pleadings of others. When he filled out the questionnaire from the commissioners gathering evidence for the famous 1834 *Report* "for inquiring into the Administration and Practical Operation of the Poor Laws," he expressed satisfaction with the current order of things, but it is doubtful if the outparish poor of his township would have provided so rosy an assessment. Garnett could always argue that those who were dissatisfied could return to Kirkby Lonsdale, and some did. A few were returned by removal orders when other parish officers lost all patience. The option of returning was, however, cold comfort to those who had put down roots in a new community and whose hope of finding employment was there, not in the township through which the lovely River Lune ran.[6]

Yet Garnett deserves a defense. Correspondents had a natural interest in magnifying needs, and it was not always easy for Garnett to know the truth of the matter. Since there was always the option of returning to Kirkby Lonsdale, Garnett could take comfort in the thought that a pauper in dire need could adopt that recourse. Moreover, the collection consists of letters *to* Garnett; only a few copies of his outgoing correspondence survive. Those copies do not suggest a monster in human frame, and many of the incoming letters, as will be seen, imply a certain measure of trust, even cordiality, between the sender and Garnett. Finally, his long service as an overseer suggests that he was to some extent efficient, and that included the avoidance of scandalous neglect, except perhaps in the case of Mary Dixon, as will be seen.

The sixteen cases presented in this chapter represent the range of circumstances recorded, reflect the importance of nonresident relief in the North, and indicate something about the man to whom the letters were sent.

* * *

29 October 1809

I hope you will excuse this trouble that I give you, but my reason for doing so is that days is short and weather so very bad and the journey long, and I so weak at this time, and fear that if I went so far in the state of health I am in at present that I should stop with you. If you will be so good to send me my pay, and something more, as my rent is near due, you will much oblige your humble servant,

Sara Poole
Standingstone, near Wigton, Cumberland

And in a postscript she added: "Sir, please let me have your answer by the post." She was writing from a place approximately fifty miles north of Kirkby Lonsdale, for not all sojourners took southern roads. Although she was married to an Irishman, Dennis O'Hara, that did not affect her English settlement, for he "belongs where I belong."[7] O'Hara was an industrious weaver, in the opinion of his employer, a judgment Thomas Irving, the local overseer, thought worthwhile conveying to Garnett. Garnett's predecessor as overseer responded favorably to Sara Poole's letter (note her use of her maiden name in this context), and she actually wrote him a thank-you note, the only one extant in the township letters, but Garnett later proved so dilatory in making payment that Irving got a suspended removal order for Poole, requiring Garnett to pay. She never returned to Kirkby Lonsdale, the last entry for her being the bill for her funeral expenses five years later.

* * *

26 August 1812

I received yours of June 29, and it will hurt me very much if you still refuse to pay my rent, which was £4 last midsummer, and my landlord is determined to make a distress of my few things if I do not pay him, which is impossible for me to do without your assistance.

A gentleman of the law took my examination respecting my settlement, and is clearly of opinion that it is at Kirkby Lonsdale, so that if you still object to pay my rent my landlord will distrain, and the overseers must remove me and family thither. I have likewise paid into the club at Skipton many years, and am almost one year in arrears there, which if I do not discharge in a fortnight, shall be excluded, so that look which way I will I am quite lost without your kind assistance, which I hope you will have the goodness to consider, and assist me at this time, which will be ever gratefully acknowledged by, Sir, your most obedient, humble servant,

    Christopher Johnson
    Embsay, near Skipton, Yorkshire

Johnson somehow managed to avoid removal back to Kirkby Lonsdale, but his problems with Garnett continued. Embsay was about 27 miles southwest of the township. By 1818 Johnson had moved his family about 13 miles further away, to Wilsden, near Bingley, Yorkshire. Five years later the overseers of Wilsden wrote Kirkby Lonsdale a long letter in which they discussed not only the Johnson family but the system of nonresident relief in general.

16 October 1823

Gentlemen, we are the overseers of the poor of Wilsden, and we are applied unto for relief, and we have examined a pauper whose name is Christopher Johnson, and by his examination he clearly appears to belong to you. His wife, says Dr. Cooper of Bingley, is the most afflicted with the Scrofula or King's Evil that he ever saw a person. She has eight or nine places that discharge a great quantity of matter. For the last year she has gone to bed and from, with two crutches, but for some time she has been confined to bed, and it is impossible for her to be removed. They have a girl about sixteen years old [who] has always been afflicted and now she has some ulcers, and can do but very little in the house. A boy about eight years is much the same. They have two children who are not arrived at the age the others were when the above symptoms broke out.

Christopher Johnson is a very quiet, industrious, sober workingman, but he is only a common day laborer, at times at the road and at driving a one-horse for coals, or working on the land. He has been in our town five or six years, and we should have removed him long since, if it had not been for the above good qualities, and a majority at our vestry meeting were in favor of letting the poor man and his family alone. They

Samuel Bough, "View of a Manufacturing Town," mid-nineteenth century (The Trustees of the British Museum)

have a woman about one half of every day to get the job done for the family and his wife.

Now we will give you our best advice in this case. We think the woman will not live many weeks, by the Dr.'s account. Now if you will send us £2 we will make it go as far in relief as we possibly can, and if she be removed [dies] soon we will send you what remains. You may smile at that, and say you would give but little for what we should send you— but we do assure you if there were a shilling to show, you should have it. We have done so by other towns before, and for our frugal management of their paupers we have had the thanks of their vestry meetings. What money you send us you may send by the guard of the Leeds and Kendal Union Coach, seated up, and order the guard, Thomas, to put it into the post office at Bingley, directed to Tweedy and Anderson, Wilsden, Bingley. You must pay the guard a trifle, and you might get the guard to inquire in Bingley of our character and responsibility.

We have said what we think is sufficient, and were we applied unto for a like case in a similar manner we should send as we advise above; if you do not send or write to us in one day after you receive this, we will immediately apply to our magistrates at Bingley for a suspended order, but we think your good sense will not let us do so—but you know we must act for our own safety. And remain your sincere friends,

Tweedy and Anderson
Overseers of the Poor at Wilsden, near Bingley, Yorkshire

A marginal postscript noted that Johnson had earned his settlement in Kirkby Lonsdale as a hired servant, five or six years before he was married, with a Mr. Hall, who kept a public house, and that "the poor man had seven children, some time since, but three are dead."

The overseers of Wilsden clearly regarded Johnson as both wretched and deserving, and doubtless the family had already received some local charity, but no relief was given in response to this letter. Garnett usually responded to threats, and Johnson's need was clear, but Garnett appears to have counted on local concern for the family being sufficient to prevent removal, and perhaps it was, for there is no record of a removal order, suspended or otherwise, and no further correspondence either concerning the Johnson family or by these pedagogic correspondents.

*   *   *

23 February 1813

Sir I am oblidgd trouble you again as I have been so bad for this mounth past that I have not been able to do any thing but thank god I am a rather better my Disorder is the Rupter and if it do not return I shall be able to do something in a week or tow my wife still contiies very bad she was as ill last week as she has been since she began she has not been Twenty yeards from Door since Martinmas we should have been very trouble some but for my friends at Kirkby they have been very kind money gos but a very little way when two old folkes is both Bad and cannot help themselves but has to hire so please to return something by the bearer it will very much oblige yours,

Jas. Hall
Kendal, Westmorland

This letter from James Hall is given without editorial intervention, for it is clearer in content than most. Yet it is representative in form; its absence of punctuation and idiosyncratic spelling and capitalization are all characteristic of pauper petitions and overseers' letters.

The Halls were weekly pensioners, receiving two to four shillings, depending on circumstances, and a bit more for special needs. Living only twelve miles from their township, the Halls received visits from friends in Kirkby Lonsdale, who could help them directly, and indirectly by returning home to pressure Garnett to action. Moreover, Garnett's correspondents and acquaintances were more likely to be able to give him firsthand information about paupers living near by; that generally meant a more open purse. The greater the distance, the less relief amounts were likely to be, and the same was true for week-to-week dependability of payment. This was natural, and it naturally restrained most sojourners from moving very far from their settlements.

*   *   *

28 November 1816

After repeating my grateful thanks to you, and through you to the principal inhabitants of your township for the assistance you afforded me last February, I feel myself rather hurt when I again address you on the same subject. One of my daughters being married, I am obliged to keep my eldest daughter at home to take care of my five younger children. By the different people from your neighborhood, you will have been informed of the situation in which they found my family, all in clean and sweet apparel, but thin, patched, and nearly worn out. As times are very bad and hard here, may I beg you will remit me something towards putting my infants into warmer clothing during this inclement season? With the most perfect respect to you and all the good inhabitants, I am, Sir, your very humble servant,

John Loftus
No. 31, Queen Street, Preston, Lancashire

Loftus's wife had died in childbirth the previous year, but the child had lived, leaving him six children to support. He did not request a weekly allowance, only casual relief, and the township acceded on this and other occasions. Granting casual relief was inexpensive, his need was unequivocal and verifiable, and he knew how to write an ingratiating letter. Although Preston was thirty miles from Kirkby Lonsdale, so many of the township's outparish poor settled there that Garnett could keep a check on them, as the Loftus letter indicates. Loftus later remarried, lived three-score year and ten, and only occasionally approached his township for aid.

* * *

1 February 1817

I am sorry to trouble you, but necessity forces me to it, as you have not answered Mr. Darr [inkblot] letter, and they have sent [inkblot] baillifs today to my house, but they have given me until Tuesday to pay the poor tax. I have had the misfortune to cut myself today, for I am past sawyering, and am hewing shears. I have three miles to go backward and forward every day for about 7/ per week, and cannot make more, so I hope the gentlemen will send £1, and I will endeavor to make up the rest. So I remain your humble servant,

William Addison
Lancaster, Lancashire

He was granted only 10s. Even an outparish pauper might have to pay local poor rates, once the 1795 act abolished ratepaying as a means of acquiring a settlement. Another expense was writing letters to overseers, if one hired an amanuensis—and *re-*

ceiving letters from overseers, for letters were usually paid for on receipt. The cost of hearing from home was 6d in Lancaster, 7d in Preston and 9d in Bradford. These were not trifling amounts when a pauper earned as little as Addison. Garnett often entrusted messages and funds to carriers he knew, but this was not always possible. Alternatively, a pauper might be able to entrust the whole process to a charitable third party, as in the next example.

*　*　*

3 July 1817

I am appointed by the committee of the benevolent society to look into the distress of the poor. I found John Resonel belonging to your parish in bed, very poorly. He cannot work. We have got him under the care of the dispensary. He has a wife and two little children, the oldest only four years old.

Now let me and you put ourselves in his situation. You know we should want help for our daily bread. It is not the wish of our heavenly Father that we should famish for want of bread. May God of his tender mercy give you a soft heart to do what you can for his family while he is confined. When he is better, I will inform you. As I am a stranger to you, if you will refer to our overseer you will find it no imposition. I remain respectfully,

John Goodell, Woolen Draper
Preston, Lancashire

This is the only letter about Resonel, and the only one from this woolen draper and his society, but it is likely that Garnett was not very cooperative. Perhaps Resonel did not belong to Kirkby Lonsdale. Apart from that, the letters in this collection suggest that a sojourning pauper had better luck working through the overseers where he was resident than through well-meaning third parties, and naturally so. Goodell's letter could be safely ignored, but an overseer could issue a removal order and thus bring expense to Kirkby Lonsdale. Garnett was a businessman who rarely deviated from the least expensive and least troublesome course of action.

*　*　*

5 September 1817

I hope you will pardon the liberty I take in troubling you with this to inform you that my mother is yet living, but from every human appearance she may depart any hour. For the last month I have never had the candle out by night. I have done everything in my power for her. I have passed my word with Caleb Metcalf, grocer in French Lane, for 11/6 in necessaries, unknown to my husband. He is wanting his money, and it is not in my power to pay it. I beg the favor of you and the other gentlemen, whom it may concern, to be so kind as to discharge it. You would greatly oblige me if you would have the goodness to give an order to Mr. Jackson for that purpose. You will greatly oblige your most obedient, humble servant,

Margaret Redhead
Kendal, Westmorland

Jackson, a Kendal overseer, appended a note confirming Redhead's story, but Garnett was apparently unpersuaded. "Not Granted" is written in a firm hand at the bottom of this letter.

* * *

[ca. 1820]

Being informed that one Christopher Bracewell of Hornby is coming to Kirkby Lonsdale, and he will very likely become a burden to the town, as he went to live at Lancaster once, and they would not let him stop on account of his large family, he having a wife and eight children, and he having failed once, I think it my duty to let you know he is coming this Martinmas, as being a friend and well-wisher to Kirkby Lonsdale.

Anonymous
Addressless

Although this unpleasant little note is unsigned, the writer may have hoped to benefit, either because he believed Garnett would know his identity or because he planned to meet Garnett later and reveal his good service to the township. Garnett may not have paid informers directly, but there are several instances in the collection of persons giving him negative information about others, even members of their own family. Jealousy among relief recipients and the hope of currying favor were doubtless incentives.

Not every township provided nonresident relief, and Hornby, presumably the township of that name in Lancashire, may have given up on this large family, as Kirkby Lonsdale did in the case of Elizabeth Longhorn, as will be seen. In the circumstances, it is pleasant to record that a Christopher Bracewell had established himself as a linen and woolen draper in Kirkby Lonsdale, according to Parson and White's 1829 *History, Directory and Gazetteer of . . . Cumberland and Westmorland.*

*   *   *

27 June 1822

I wish to know the reason you did not send the money last Tuesday, as me and my children are suffering in the house. I cannot get a day's work in this country as there are so many out of work. It will much oblige me if you send the money as soon as you possibly can, and pay the carrier, as I am not able.

Sir, I am sorry to trouble you for favor, but if possible can you help me to new shifts for me and two children, as we are quite naked. I should like you never to miss sending the money any more, for I cannot get one penny of trust, as I am not known in this town. So no more from

Mary Dixon
Preston, Lancashire

She had the misfortune to be the wife of a poacher who was then in the house of correction. Even before her husband was caught poaching, the family had been on poor relief, although the Kendal overseer had expressed to Garnett his reluctance to advance Dixon relief, "owing to his being so young a man." To the family of a lawbreaker Garnett showed little pity. Perhaps some element of old Germanic tribal law survived to influence social welfare in this and other cases where the family was made to suffer for the sins of one member.

On a visit to Preston, William Carus Wilson, a well-known member of the gentry who lived near Kirkby Lonsdale, was invited by another gentleman to visit Mary Dixon. Carus Wilson found her situation to be "one of the most deplorable cases of distress I ever witnessed," he later informed Garnett. "She is lying in a wretched hovel. . . . Her two children appeared weak and poorly, and are wholly dependent on the neighbors for everything. The miserable woman told me that she had again and again made application to the overseers of Kirkby Lonsdale for help, to which no attention was paid."

She had been given a weekly pension of 3*s.*, which was not unusually low for Kirkby Lonsdale, but her letter indicates how much reliance she could place on regular payment. Even if payments had been on time, 3*s.* a week was not enough to maintain a family of three; 5*s.* would have been barely sufficient, if the family were in good health and the rent paid. However, it was lack of casual relief to supplement the pension, as well as Mary Dixon's lack of friends in Preston that made her case desperate. The dispensing surgeon of Preston, who had written on her behalf to Kirkby Lonsdale, reported "that her illness was occasioned by want of necessary sustenance!" (his exclamation mark). Garnett dared not ignore such criticism and responded by allowing the local authorities to make whatever arrangements were necessary for the Dixons. A nurse was accordingly hired to look after the mother and two children, both of whom were suffering from dysentery, and the house they occupied was given a thorough cleaning, since it was "lost in filth and vermin."

Carus Wilson's second letter to Garnett contains the harshest criticism of Garnett found in the township letters.

I wish I could feel satisfied that you were as free from blame in this sad case as you represent, but I candidly confess that I am prevented by the many concurring testimonies in this place. It seems they went over to you three months ago for a pair of clogs and some other articles, all of which she was denied. She came home weary and dispirited, and has been worsening ever since. She assured me yesterday that she had sent repeated messages to you since her illness by the carrier, besides what the dispensing surgeon mentioned, and at all events it might have been taken, I think, for granted that where the husband was in prison the wife and two children could not be expected to live on 3/ a week.

Overseers, I am aware, are often grossly imposed upon, but that does not excuse such neglect as in the present instance has been attended with such wretched consequences; and happy will it be if an awful account has not to be rendered hereafter in the case of Mary Dixon, as well as of poor Swan of Whittington.

Mary Dixon died, apparently of starvation or a disease that feeds on the starving; expenditures were 15*s.* for the coffin, 6/1 for funeral dues, and 14s. to the Widow Seed for attendance. The Dixon children were then put out to nurse at the same allowance that had formerly been accorded mother and children together.

This is perhaps the worst case of neglect in the township letters, yet there are few cases where one senses that relief was anything but grudgingly given in an atmosphere of suspicion and parsimony. Garnett did not have to wait for the Poor Law commissioners to discover the doctrine of "less eligibility" (that dependence on relief should be the least eligible alternative to any other means of support) or "the workhouse test" (full relief given only there). It is doubtful that Garnett ever read Malthus —he was a man more comfortable with numbers than letters— but he behaved in a manner consistent with the dismal doctrine that to help the poor encouraged their propagation and thus augmented the problem.

On the other hand, petitioners, and those who wrote on their behalf, were naturally disposed to color the circumstances darkly, and it was not always easy to single out the worthy claim from the spurious, especially for paupers sojourning elsewhere. Garnett relied on the reputation of the person or family requesting relief, and that knowledge doubtless influenced his decisions, sometimes wisely and sometimes as in the case of Mary Dixon. Garnett also expected other townships to provide occasional relief to sojourners, even as his own township did. Yet it remains true that Garnett's angle of vision was quite different from Carus Wilson's, perhaps in part because Garnett was answerable to a vestry and to ratepayers, whereas Carus Wilson, who was a man unusually gifted in extracting moral lessons from personal experiences, as his many publications attest,[8] could give free play to his sense of charity.

*   *   *

22 May 1822

Gentlemen, I wonder you should object paying my rent, as the winter [?], and my family being so very large, for I am sure that I can not pay it myself, and the rent day was on Saturday. But I have begged to be excused until your vestry meeting, and if it be not settled at your meeting we must be sold up and come to you by a removing order. Gentlemen, if you think proper that it will be any better for us to come to you, and throw me and my children out of work, we are very willing to come.

Christopher Grime
Settle, Yorkshire

And a postscript read: "Please to send it by return of post." There was often an implied threat in pauper petitions of returning home, either willingly or through a removal order, for a return held promise of higher expense for the township. Even with the trouble and cost of correspondence, the nonresident poor were a bargain; otherwise they would never have received subsidies. Grime had, in fact, been removed to Kirkby Lonsdale, together with his family, almost ten years earlier, but had left again for Settle, about fifteen miles to the southeast. The largest number of letters in the collection relate to this one nuclear family (60 items between 1827 and 1835). Most of them are quite short, reminding Garnett that the house rent was due, requesting casual relief, or castigating the township for "negligence" and for being "very inconsiderate." Grime was one of the most independent-minded of the township's nonresident poor, and there was nothing ingratiating in his approach—a reason why he may have had to write so often and why he found it useful to get testimonials from overseers, landlords, and former employers regarding his character and industry.

There are indications that he may not have excelled in either respect. On two occasions he deserted his wife (1818 and 1835), and in 1823 one of Garnett's correspondents checked on the Grime family, only to find that four of the children were then employed at Mr. Clayton's mill at a combined weekly income of £1.3.6 and that Grime himself, also employed by Clayton, received 15s. a week. The family thus was receiving nearly £2 a week, a comfortable income and far beyond a pauper's mite. The informant was Thomas Grundy, perhaps a relative of Samuel Grundy, a carpet manufacturer of Kirkby Lonsdale who had served with Garnett as overseer of the poor. In the opinion of Thomas Grundy, "this fellow deserves punishing for such a rascally application to his parish."

Such a letter fed Garnett's suspicion that the township's funds were being squandered through spurious claims, yet few other instances in the township letters hint at fraud, and none so blatantly. Whether one attributes this mainly to the honesty of most of the petitioners or to Garnett's informants must depend more on preconceptions than on the evidence. As for Grime, he may have been imperfect, but his vigorous independence shines through in his letters, refreshing amid the pathetic supplications of others.

* * *

1 February 1824

This is to inform you that my apprentice, Matthew Cockin, has this day broke open my box, stole his indentures out of my pocket book, and run away from his apprenticeship. I have every reason to believe that his father is privy to the above transactions, as frequent conversations have passed between them lately. However that may be, I have scarce a doubt but he is at his father's house now. You will no doubt be surprised that I should trouble you with this account, but I was induced to do so from the knowledge of your late kindness to my family, and not knowing any other person about Kirkby who ever discovered the slightest interest for our welfare, my request is that you (without injuring yourself) would give a look out for this boy, as I am now, after a vast deal of trouble and expense, set down in a large manufacturing town with the prospect of a favorable [residence] before me; his services may become as valuable as they have hitherto been the reverse.

The boy has lately renewed his acquaintance with another boy of the name of Driver, a plumber and glazier, formerly of Kirkby, but now working somewhere in this neighborhood. It was after one of his rambles with this fellow, and coming home drunk and late in the night, that he, in answer to my reproaches, told me that he would leave me, telling me at the same time that his father had advised him to run away last autumn when my wife and he were shearing at Mr. Gibson's. These and many other circumstances confirm me in the belief that his father is at the bottom of this wicked [conspiracy].

I wrote this day to his father, and also to a nephew of mine in Preston, with orders to take a constable to secure him if they should find him lurking at his brother William's. I have also written Liverpool, giving the same directions to a brother of mine who resides there. I may add that he has taken a great part of my work tools and other things which he has no business with. With my sincere wishes for your welfare, I am yours,

George Salkeld
Manchester

Salkeld, formerly a pauper in Kirkby Lonsdale, had attempted
to better his fortunes elsewhere, as other members of his family
had done. A shoemaker confronting the common problem of a
runaway apprentice, he also needed to ingratiate himself with
Garnett, whose good offices may have meant more than any
assistance Garnett might give in finding Cockin. Only the month
before Salkeld had written Garnett of the difficulty in finding
work in Manchester after leaving Kirkby Lonsdale for want of
work there. But he had obtained, he wrote, a "Sunday's musical
situation in the established church, after very close scrutiny, and
in the face of very powerful opponents. The salary is £12 a year,
a small sum, no doubt, but with the respectable connections it
may lead to may become invaluable to me. I tell you I had no
small difficulty in procuring a decent shirt to be present at the
examination."

He had a family of eight, which was visited at different times
by smallpox and dysentery. The township sent them casual relief from time to time in response to Salkeld's letters or to the
more urgent ones written by his wife, Ann. The last letter from
Salkeld was from Lancaster Castle, where he had been imprisoned for debt, unjustly so in his opinion. That was seven years
later when he was attempting to become Manchester's responsibility by virtue of paying a rent of £15 per annum; he needed
a final subsidy from his township to establish a new settlement.
"Granted 2.0.0" appeared in Garnett's hand at the bottom of the
last letter the Salkelds wrote Kirkby Lonsdale. Presumably, the
final subsidy freed the township from this large, impoverished
family.

*   *   *

10 May 1826

Mr. Garnett, Sir, if you would have the kindness to send me £1.10
by William Fawcett to the children, I would be much obliged to you. I
make no doubt but you have had the shocking account of this town and
neighborhood, which has made all into confusion, for trade is totally at
a stand. There has been a good many killed and wounded at different
places—seven men and one woman at Chadderton, three men at Has-
lington, two wounded at this town severely, and many slightly hurt.
A regiment of soldiers arrived yesterday from Ireland. It's believed by

many the work of destruction will be at an end, for every day they are taking men up for the late riot. Up to this time all is peaceable and quiet, and the Manchester Market coaches came in unmolested last night, which has so long caused a great tumult every Tuesday night. The last weekly account here is 2,233 families relieved every week by public subscription, which is allowed to be above 14,000 individuals. But I hope things will come 'round in a few weeks. It is not pleasant to hear so much of a warlike sound among a starving people. I am yours, &c.

William Lowry
Blackburn, Lancashire

In the same month a correspondent from Preston wrote: "There never was such times in Preston in our times nor in the times of our fathers." A "handsome subscription" from the townspeople had been raised, for "work is so scarce that nothing can be earned."[9]

Lowry of Blackburn was a Scot, whose only claim on the township was through two children from his deceased wife's previous marriage. This may have given him somewhat greater independence of pen, and certainly his news-filled letters are a literary cut above the usual Kirkby Lonsdale pensioner's plea. The following month he wrote again of the situation in Blackburn—his stepchildren were starving, there was no work, and he found it difficult to write of "the famine and destruction of the pressure of the times that has befallen upon all the working class of people." He was granted a weekly allowance of 1s. for the children.

In February 1827 a special rate was levied to compensate Blackburn employers for the power looms destroyed in the riots. Late that spring Lowry wrote to request the overdue payment for his house rent, to complain that the pension was irregularly paid by William Fawcett, Garnett's agent, and to grumble at the expense of his correspondence with Garnett. But he also had some local news.

I hear as a great many families [have] gone from this town to America within the two months past, and more are going; nothing but emigration is talked of here, for all that can get away.

In the Bills of Mortality there have been above one hundred children dead in the workhouse in the past six weeks; many families have lost all their children, four or five in number; some call it the Black Fever.

The troubles Lowry related—noted in the *Annual Register* as "Disturbances in Lancashire"—have been passed over by historians, presumably because they were local, mainly apolitical, and lacked articulate leaders. Yet thousands took to the streets of first Blackburn and then Manchester, an estimated thousand power looms were destroyed, and handloom weavers battled dragoons. Lowry, at any rate, thought it newsworthy that men armed with knives, homemade spears, scythes, sledgehammers, and even a few pistols and guns trooped around the environs of Blackburn destroying every power loom they could lay their hands on and pelting with rocks the soldiers that attempted to stand in their way.[10]

Cyclical unemployment in the North and the new technology had devastating effects on handloom weavers, the largest single industrial occupation in England in the early nineteenth century, and the power loom was naturally identified as the tangible cause of their distress. The poor law was ill-equipped to cope with massive industrial unemployment. Nonresident allowances from agrarian townships to their poor sojourning in the mill towns may have helped, as Lowry was helped by Kirkby Lonsdale, but it was not enough. It is hard to exaggerate the suffering occasioned by early industrialism or to understand why intelligent men accepted a worldview that permitted it to happen. The Law of Settlement eased the process somewhat by moderating migration and by providing de facto unemployment benefits from agrarian England to sojourners in industrial England, yet the law was not part of the new ideology and was, in fact, identified by proponents of the new economic views as a mercantilist contrivance restraining the free movement of labor. And so it was. But that law had as its premise that each person had a right to sustenance in the parish or township where he had inherited or earned a settlement. Lowry's paltry allowances from Kirkby Lonsdale, which lasted until 1832, would no doubt have displeased some political economists, although Malthus himself questioned the wisdom of dismantling the settlement laws.[11]

* * *

10 June 1826

I, Samuel Parkinson, beg to inform you that I taught Agnes Wilkinson to weave myself, for we both lived with my mother until her disease. 1/6 per week is all I [request] at present. It greatly depends on my health. If I should not be able to work as I have done I could not support her with it. Handweaving is in a shocking distressed state at this time, and not the least hope that it is going to mend, as power weaving is getting on so rapidly. I hope, sir, you will have the goodness to send an answer back immediately, for distress among cotton weavers is every week worse. I remain yours truly,

Samuel Parkinson
Waddington, Yorkshire

Agnes was then 60 and living with her half-brother, Samuel, according to the chapel warden and overseer of Waddington. They were given an allowance to pay the rent on their miserable home, but not until two years after Samuel wrote. Agnes died in 1834, and the cost of her coffin was duly communicated to Garnett, but over a year later Waddington was still requesting reimbursement.

* * *

Between 1813 and 1835, the various branches of the Nelson family cost Kirkby Lonsdale a total of £422.18.9 in poor relief, nearly half of which went to an aged woolcomber, Joseph, his wife, Grace, and their three children. Joseph had established his settlement in Kirkby Lonsdale as an apprentice in the 1760s, but he had spent most of his adult life working in the West Riding, apparently without receiving poor relief until an account was established in 1807 with the overseer of Clayton Heights, a bleak and hilly town in the outskirts of Bradford. In the spring of 1809, Garnett was told that Joseph was then between 60 and 70 years of age and in poor health. Compounding the situation, he had "a young wife that hath little management in her," and they had one child, with another on the way. "His situation is so pitiful it is enough to break the hardest heart," the overseer told Garnett, with little obvious effect on the heart he was trying to influence.

But Joseph himself took matters into his own hands by threatening the local overseer with a summons if his family were not given relief. Since the costs of any magistrate's order would fall on Kirkby Lonsdale, Garnett responded to this news with some financial assistance. When Joseph fell ill in 1813, his wife summoned the local overseer before the magistrate, who ordered that the family be paid 8s. a week during the illness, not deeming the 2s. in emergency relief allowed by the overseer to be sufficient. That did not prevent Joseph's household goods from being sold up in partial payment of his overdue rent, but all the forced sale brought was £1.7.6. The family then moved back to Kirkby, but perhaps Garnett did not care to have such resourceful claimants close by. In any event, the family soon returned to Yorkshire, this time settling in Great Horton, another town on the outskirts of Bradford and just a short distance from Clayton Heights, living "at a place called 'parradice.'" There they were befriended by John Haley, a neighboring farmer. Horton was a rapidly growing town with an economy built on coal and cloth, but the Nelsons had little to offer. Joseph entered his last illness, with Haley reporting that "old Joseph" is "really very short of breath and spits a great deal" and that Grace was expecting yet again. Joseph died in 1814, leaving a wife and three daughters. "I never saw a poorer family," Haley wrote. Joseph had belonged to an Old Combers Club, and they had paid him a small pension in his illness as well as something toward his burial, but it was not nearly enough to make the family independent of their township.

Haley then took widow and children under his wing. "I write free of favor to anyone," he told Garnett, and it seems likely. He was not an overseer, nor is it likely he was the Nelsons' landlord —landlords naturally had an interest in supporting their tenants' petitions for relief. Haley's letters focused not on rents or finances but on the family's well-being. Never in a long correspondence is there any hint of a pecuniary interest on Haley's part beyond payment for money he had advanced. It was well the Nelsons had a good neighbor, for misfortune dogged them. In 1815 the oldest daughter burned herself badly, and two years later was reported still to look "like a ghost." Nevertheless, she could earn her meat through childcare; the second daughter also began to help the family finances in like manner. Grace herself could earn only about 2s. a week through spinning worsted. In

1819 the family was sold up once again, preparatory to removal back to their township, but Haley negotiated a settlement with Garnett that allowed them to stay.

Over the years Garnett was persistently delinquent in meeting the Nelsons' expenses, and at times as much as £20 was due. Haley advanced the Nelsons money and charity-in-kind beyond anything he could ever have expected Kirkby Lonsdale to repay. By 1821 he was calling the widow "old Grace," although she had been a "young wife" to the Clayton Heights overseer twelve years before. She died in 1824, and since her relatives would have nothing to do with her, £2 was needed from her township to see her decently buried.

By that time her two older daughters had places, but Betty, the youngest child, proved difficult for all concerned. She was boarded with Ruth Nelson, a member of another pauperized branch of the Nelson family,[12] but Haley reported that Ruth was "hurt" with Betty, so the girl was taken in by Haley's daughter, who "pities Bett," and with reason, for Betty was "very deficient in memory and sense, and can not see well in one eye. A very simple, foolish creature, and cannot learn anything," Haley wrote. Still later he called her "an idle, nasty, slovenly girl, but always forward at meat, and will eat as much as three girls of her age." She obtained some of her food by stealing. Haley concluded that she belonged in Kirkby Lonsdale's workhouse, but Garnett replied that she would have to walk to get there, something Haley thought she was incapable of doing. Then Betty "cried and promised to be a better girl," and Haley allowed her to stay on.

Her next delinquency was abandoning a baby she had been charged to tend and running off to Ruth Nelson's home, which was "a very disorderly house," Haley had by now concluded, filled with "idle and naughty" children. Betty returned once again to the Haleys, much against John Haley's inclination. The final incident occurred in 1829 when Betty broke a bowl, and although nothing was said to her about it, she ran away to Kirkby Lonsdale. Haley was uneasy about her welfare and wrote, "We wish her well at the far end." That ended Haley's close relationship with the Nelsons, but not the township's; in the 1830s Kirkby Lonsdale was compelled to pay child support to Great

Horton for two illegitimate children born to other daughters in the Nelson family. A third generation of Nelson paupers had entered the world.

It is impossible to read this lengthy correspondence and not conclude that Great Horton's officers and one good neighbor, John Haley, were humane and responsible in their treatment of the Nelsons. Efforts were made to place the children carefully in order to break the cycle of poverty. Garnett, however, was characteristically parsimonious and delinquent in making payments. Yet the root cause of the Nelsons' difficulties was not Garnett or the shortcomings of nonresident relief or character deficiencies in the Nelsons themselves. Unemployment and industrial dislocation in northern England were the underlying cause of the family's plight, which was causally related to the central issue in the letters—poor health, occasioned by accidents, respiratory disease, typhus, and almost certainly in Betty Nelson's case, mental retardation (Haley thought she bordered on "Idiotism").

The Nelsons represent the horrible epitome of all that could go wrong for sojourners, with the significant exception that they had a helpful neighbor and conscientious overseers. No family on nonresident relief involved for Kirkby Lonsdale so much of the dreaded "trouble and expense." [13]

*   *   *

Most of the township's nonresident poor went to a particular town and settled there. Of the over 200 sojourners who petitioned Garnett at some point in his 27 years in office, only 26 can be identified with certainty as having moved at least twice, and only 7 of that number had sampled three or more towns. [14] The widow Elizabeth Longhorn was in a class by herself. She traveled back and forth between Preston, Lancaster, Manchester, Salford, Bradford, and Rochdale in the decade after Waterloo, seldom resting long in any one place and frequently in need of a pension, rent money, or casual relief. There is an urgency to the scrawled and barely decipherable letters she had written on her behalf. William, her husband, who died in 1816, had also been skillful in conveying his family's urgent needs, although not with absolute honesty in the opinion of another township's overseer. Arrears in rent subsidies and various illnesses, especially of her young daughters, Ellen and Bessy, were Elizabeth's most persistent reasons for writing, and she demanded that her needs be addressed.

Thomas Darwen, acting overseer of Lancaster, wrote Garnett in 1818 that he would not act as intermediary between her and her township any longer—"any other person I have no objection to pay, and should be glad to serve you in anything but this." Two years later Darwen's successor, Stephen Stockdale, declined to have "anything more to do in this business. I hope you will order some other person to pay her in my stead—she is so very clamorous." Her letters reflect the overseers' experiences. "If you do not let me have [relief]," she wrote on one occasion, "I shall be obliged to go to some justice." Another time she wrote, "I cannot nor will not be quite lost while I have a parish to flee to." She once told Garnett, "I cannot bear to see my children punished, as they have been." At times the township lost patience with her; in 1819, for example, the vestry ruled that "if she cannot do, she may come to the workhouse." She did indeed return to the township, but soon she was off again to Preston, where a few months later she was complaining of an overdue rent subsidy and a sick child.

In 1820 she decided to move from Preston to Manchester, but William Davis, a Preston overseer, wrote Garnett that he had refused her request for moving expenses. "Her little girl has been dismissed from our mill on account (as I understand from the manager) of her refusing to do the work assigned to her by her taskmaster." Davis was uncertain of the Longhorns' prospects in Manchester, but thought if Elizabeth "were less disposed to travel," she might find something for her daughter in Preston. Davis also warned Garnett not to "continue to encourage her claims," but she may have had friends in Kirkby, for she was frequently granted relief by order of the vestry (which was usually more forthcoming than Garnett). She did indeed move to Manchester and was able to find work there, but she still needed money for clothes and "to buy a bed and some necessary things." She was in service to "a very good lady," but toward the end of the year Elizabeth had moved across the River Irwell to Salford, and was getting her living by washing. The family still lacked a bed, and the children needed clothes. The washing business went well for a time, but in 1821 she reported that £5 worth of clothing had been stolen from her and that her youngest child's eyes were quite bad. Then Elizabeth herself fell ill. While recuperating, she had an opportunity to buy an £8 mangle, with only £2 needed as a down payment. Kirkby Lonsdale gave her nothing.

In 1823 Elizabeth was given 15s. to return to her township. She returned, but left soon after. At this point Kirkby Lonsdale apparently abandoned her. Later that same year, one of her grown daughters brought Elizabeth to Bradford, lame in one leg and with breast cancer, so it was claimed. The daughter and her husband, a woolcomber by trade, demanded relief from Kirkby Lonsdale, but received nothing.

In late December Elizabeth wrote her township of the depressed state of affairs in Bradford, with "scarcely a woolcomber in work at this time in this town," and her son-in-law "on tramp ever since he fell out of work." Her two young daughters had work in the mills three days a week, and she herself was making something, but had hope of better employment in Rochdale, where "I think by the blessing of the Almighty we should be able to do very well if we could once get there." She needed her township to help her with her arrears in rent, but Kirkby Lonsdale refused. She moved anyway, in January 1824, but was forced to sell all her goods to pay the rent. She wrote from Rochdale, very ill, in need of everything, and her daughter wrote six months later, threatening to "throw her [mother] on the town" if relief were not forthcoming, but nothing was given. In 1826 Elizabeth's grown daughter and son-in-law wrote, referring only to Elizabeth's dependent daughters, who had been out of work for twelve months, were without clothes, and in danger of being thrown into the street.

Elizabeth herself lived on, returned for a time to the workhouse in Kirkby Lonsdale, and ended her association with her township with an unusually troublesome and expensive settlement case (total cost: £40.15.7) in which it was decided she had acquired a new settlement in Yorkshire.[15] She may indeed have been "clamorous" and not altogether truthful, but there is something admirable in her refusal to settle in Kirkby Lonsdale's workhouse or to stay in one place to receive a pitiful pension and in her restless efforts to better her fortunes. Her needs and hopes wearied relieving overseers, Garnett, and the township's vestry, but her aspirations for herself and children represented a triumph of the human spirit.

Kirkby Lonsdale's township letters provide a revealing window on the unstable lives of workers in industrial north Britain and in heartbreaking detail reveal a society that made little provision for those only a week's wages away from pauperism.[16] Yet there was *some* provision, as the letters show, through an informal system of settlement that encouraged mobility in a way that could only have benefited burgeoning centers of industry.

Conclusion

THE PRE-1834 POOR LAW was like a brick wall, each brick a separate parochial entity, all held in place by the mortar of settlement laws. Without the mortar, the wall could not stand, but historians have generally seen only the specific bricks and imagined patterns in their ordering or in anything that lends itself to being counted. In consequence, no part of the Old Poor Law has been so repeatedly misunderstood, and not only on minor points of law.

T. S. Ashton wrote: "If a man left the parish in which he was domiciled, and remained in another for a full year, he lost his right to relief in the first and established a claim to it in the second." It was not so. According to Pauline Gregg, the "settlement laws prevented an English worker from leaving the village where he was settled, unless provided with a certificate," and that in factory towns "when trade slumped [the sojourner] was promptly passed back to the parish where he was 'settled.'" Neither statement is correct. Asa Briggs held that "the settlement laws of 1662 (modified in 1685 and 1693 [sic]) made birth or residence a necessary qualification for parish relief." That is misleadingly inadequate. Peter Laslett wrote: "Everyone knows that Elizabeth made each parish responsible for its own indigent persons, and that, when a pauper could be identified as from another community, he or she was sent along the highway from place to place until the place of settlement was reached."[1] That is not an accurate representation of the laws at any period of their history. But the assumption that "everyone knows" about the settlement laws has led to a woeful underestimation of their importance in shaping lives and influencing the economy.[2] All of these quotations come from excellent works, but all have the same lacunae. Part of the problem arises from overdependence on articulate critics of settlement living at the time, such as the 1834 Poor Law commissioners; more fundamental is a widespread unfamiliarity with settlement documents. The low survival rate of these documents is certainly a major reason for this, for settlement materials were usually in the form of loose sheets, gathered into bundles—ephemera easily consigned to the flames or the dustbin, lacking the durability and the patina of parish registers and overseers' account books. Those that escaped periodic housecleanings to find a refuge in an archive are but fragments of the whole, insulated by deadening legalisms, and made the more difficult to study because of the dispersal of these fragments in so many different depositories. Like the historian of still more distant times, students of the poor law must take what little exists and extrapolate.

It may be helpful to imagine something like the pre–1834 Law of Settlement from a hypothetical perspective. Suppose Peter Poorman holds no secure income, property, or office and has neither insurance nor savings. Suppose his only possessions are some clothes, pieces of furniture, and tools. Henceforth, his earnings must meet all expenses, whatever the illness, however long the bout of unemployment, unless he receives public relief or charity. Suppose, too, he lives in a world of rampant contagions, unsafe work conditions, and profound job insecurity. There are no retirement plans for such as he, except perhaps the hope that his similarly situated children might give him some assistance. Beyond family, his only hope in time of need lies in the compassion of wealthier neighbors, as from time to time they may see fit to display it, and in public relief, dispensed by the authorities in the neighborhood in which he is "settled." In this construct, *neighborhood* is quite arbitrarily defined as whatever ground he may reach in a ten-minute walk from his front door.

To this neighborhood Peter may look for help in time of need, yet some neighborhoods have greater resources than others, and some contain wiser, more generous, and more efficient neighbors than others. But suppose also that he is free to move to a new neighborhood and possibly earn a new settlement, or, if he chooses, to preserve his welfare link with the old.

In such a world Peter, if possessed of any prudence, would

give thought to how settlements are earned and lost. He would feel little restraint in moving short distances, but would think twice about long-distance movement, for fear of a painful removal some day to his home neighborhood or inadequate care in his new neighborhood. With youth's perennial hope of future opportunities to plan for hard times, he might be less attentive when young to settlement questions, but as the years went by, he would be increasingly concerned to find or retain a safe haven. Doubtless, he would rail against such a system, and all the more so if his settlement hinged on where he had slept on a particular night or how much rent he had paid in a transient lodging twenty years before. Nor is it likely he would be entirely scrupulous in remembering such details if by doing so his health and happiness would be immeasurably affected for the worse.

Any intelligent person subjected to this system would be unable to act as if this law of neighborhood did not exist or constituted only a minor inconvenience to his life, even though, like the modern income-tax payer, he might not understand all the law's complexities. No matter how vast the recordkeeping of welfare providers, those records could not begin to measure the millions of calculations people so circumstanced would make in plotting their futures. And if most of those records were destroyed, how easy it would be for historians a century or two later to pass over the system to focus on aspects of relief more clearly seen and more easily measured—expenditures, numbers relieved, buildings employed, and the like.

To return to the reality, those who lived in pre-1834 England were aware of the impact of the Law of Settlement on individual lives. Adam Smith wrote in 1776: "There is scarce a poor man in England of forty years of age, I will venture to say, who has not in some part of his life felt himself most cruelly oppressed by this ill-contrived law of settlements."[3]

William Blackstone also did not underestimate the Law of Settlement, which he believed contrary to the theory behind Common Law. Under "Rights of Persons," he included personal liberty, which "consists in the power of locomotion, of changing situation, or removing one's person to whatsoever place one's own inclination may direct." The Law of Settlement infringed on such liberty, and had also "given birth to the intricacy of our poor laws, by multiplying and rendering more easy the methods of gaining settlements; and, in consequence, has created an infinity of expensive lawsuits between contending neighbourhoods, concerning those settlements and removals."[4] One might argue, to hoist Blackstone on his own petard, that easy methods of gaining settlement and the reasonable certainty of relief the system made possible greatly *increased* personal liberty. Apart from that, both Smith and Blackstone were surely correct—the Law of Settlement *was* pervasive, oppressive, intricate, and expensive to administer. Moreover, the law's restrictions fell most heavily on those least able to help themselves and on those parishes already heavily burdened with the costs of poor relief.

Yet there is another way to view the law. However inhumane and inequitable it undoubtedly was, it rested on the principle that each person had a *right* to relief, not merely in an abstract sense but *from* a specific agency and *at* a particular place, with the concomitant right to appeal if relief were not forthcoming or was inadequate in amount. All this did not prevent horror stories, but by assigning responsibility the law necessarily promoted it.

Beyond contributing to the development of a more substantive poor law and affecting physical mobility, with consequences for employment and economic development, the Law of Settlement may have inhibited population growth. E. A. Wrigley has argued that the key to British population growth in the eighteenth century lies in the timing and incidence of marriage, which in turn was "responsive to long-term variations in economic conditions." More people married, and at an earlier age, thus increasing the birthrate, and in the late eighteenth century "the country slipped its shadow in a manner which contemporaries such as Adam Smith, Malthus or Ricardo found hard to believe possible."[5] The relationship of the poor laws to marriage and population growth is extraordinarily complex. On the surface one might assume that the greater availability of welfare would encourage earlier marriages and larger families, and this was undoubtedly so in certain times and places, but as Malthus himself suggested in a letter of 21 July 1822 to Thomas Chalmers, the poor laws, through the power of pauper removal, could check population increase by giving parochial authorities some control over the sojourning poor, as so many of the young were. Sojourners were probation-ers, who were most secure in their residence when single, and, if married, more secure when childless. No surer route to removal existed than for a poor couple to have a child that required expenditures from the host parish. "I think that anything like an abolition of the present laws of settlement," Malthus wrote Chalmers, "would be accompanied by more evil than good."[6]

It is possible the Law of Settlement acted as a moderating agent, contributing something to prudent marriages and family planning, at least among the youthful poor who left home, as most of them did. If this was a check, it was admittedly a modest one, since young sojourners could often make do without relief and the prevalence of nonresident allowances reduced fear of removal.

To advance to still larger speculation, how did Britain escape social and political revolution in the late eighteenth century, in the wake of France's experiences, and while itself undergoing the profound economic dislocation caused by nascent industrialism? And how did this smaller, less populous country win its wars with France in the Age of Revolution? Surely the combination of martial vigor and domestic torpor the British common people displayed in an era in which their country assumed leadership in the development of industry and the acquisition of empire owed something to the social security they possessed, however inadequate it was in any absolute sense or relative to later provisions. It may well have been the comparative sophistication of its social welfare system, as well as of its financial and political institutions, that gave Britain an edge in an age of great change. Only those who view British history *in vacuo* can remain blinkered critics of that welfare system and the Law of Settlement—the mortar without which a parochially based relief system could not have worked.[7]

Catherine Lis and Hugo Soly believe that it was no accident that England, "where nascent industrial capitalism was entering a new phase," was also the country where "a 'total' system of public support was instituted for the first time." In their view, social-welfare reform was the consequence of a blending of religious and moral motivations with "the real or imagined interests of employers and authorities," and it was economic and political arguments that, in fact, triggered reform. With regard to the settlement laws, they aver: "Nowhere else in early modern Europe was the mobility of the rural population led down the 'correct' paths by legislation."[8] Change is complex, and motivation especially difficult to determine. I prefer the eighteenth-century social mercantilist's perspective, which sees change resulting from a combination of factors—political, moral, economic—no one of which in itself would be sufficient to effect change. Multi-causation is not the historian's way of weaseling; it is simply how things generally happen.

However one views a causative relationship between capitalism and poor relief, economic development in the eighteenth and early nineteenth centuries in England could not help but be promoted by the way the Law of Settlement was administered. The law, be it remembered, generally did not restrict the young, healthy, ablebodied, and unmarried person from migrating toward whatever place offered economic opportunity, but it did restrict the less employable poor, especially those burdened with dependents. Whether one was removed or permitted to sojourn was influenced by the costs of both options and by the needs of employers. The system of nonresident relief was ideally designed to cushion cyclical unemployment and temporary disability. The parish in which poor persons sojourned was given a flexible work force, available as needed and at times subsidized by other parishes that derived little or no benefit from their poor parishioners' labor.

This was extraordinarily unfair, and, in the opinion of a contemporary pamphleteer, the manufacturing regions "ought to bear the inconvenience of [unemployment] themselves, for the same reason upon which their mills and engines are obliged to eat up their smoke,"[9] but fairness and capitalist advantage are separate things. Of course, the Law of Settlement could on occasion restrict migration in economically damaging ways, and Adam Smith saw the law as a mercantilistic device that inhibited economic growth. But was it? The effect of the law was to subsidize areas with improving industry at the expense of depressed areas. In this process, local officials exhibited, alternatively, brightness and benevolence, stupidity and cruelty, but their guiding goals were to avoid unnecessary trouble and cost, goals most easily achieved by a prudently selective resort to the

Law of Settlement and at least some minimal concern for the so-journer's welfare. Studies of modernization might benefit from a deeper understanding of how social-welfare practices in the first industrial state moderated migration,[10] for the way that legislation was enforced was a contributing factor to the Industrial Revolution.

But what did the Law of Settlement do *between* rural parishes? Here we come to the distinction between "open" and "close" parishes (in close parishes, one to three owners controlled land and accommodation, whereas in open parishes this restriction did not apply). It has been suggested that in the close parishes cottages were destroyed, depriving workers of the means to acquire settlements. Open parishes were thus placed in the invidious position of housing, and maintaining in time of need, the poor who worked in nearby close parishes. This is what many contemporary commentators believed, and it may have been true to some limited extent, although insofar as it was so landowners in close parishes enjoyed subsidies that could be plowed back into agricultural improvements. Yet there is no real evidence that close parishes were at all numerous, or that their relief costs were significantly less than those of open parishes, or that anything like a system of preventing acquisition of a settlement by cottage destruction existed. This is perhaps one of the semi-myths of the Old Poor Law, like Speenhamland. Of course, there were parishes in which the domiciles of the poor were destroyed, and perhaps in some cases a motive was to deny settlements, but there was no system of destruction.[11]

"In this age the poorer sort of men are straight inclined to marrie without any respect howe to live; hereof it is that the world growes so populous and poore; for commonly the poore do most of all multiply children." Those words were written in 1601, the year the Elizabethan Poor Law was consolidated.[12] There is nothing new under the sun, at least where attitudes toward the poor are concerned. Certainly later reformers were to echo this Elizabethan, especially in the time of Malthus. Indeed, the 1834 Poor Law Commissioners' *Report* draws more heavily on a current of Malthusian opinion, reflected in pamphlet literature, than on the evidence they had collected to support their conclusions.[13] Yet Anthony Brundage may be correct in seeing the 1834 Poor Law Amendment Act as less an effort to impose an ideology as an effort to restore control of local government's most important function, care of the poor, to those who, in the eyes of Parliament, were best equipped to govern locally—the magistrates.[14] To that end, it was easier for the commissioners to rail against the semi-mythical Speenhamland system than to tackle head on the enormously complex Law of Settlement, where local interests diverged and no clear path beckoned.[15]

Nevertheless, the 1834 act did entail important changes in settlement, and through successive legislation the whole complex structure was gradually dismantled until, in 1876, three-years' residence became the simple key to settlement. By then, Britain had weathered the earliest phases of industrialism and pioneered the development of the railway; it was surely time for parochial settlements based on moral presumptions and legally defined merit to end.

Yet without the parochially based settlement system in the century and a half before 1834 there could not have been an effective poor law, and without the Law of Settlement, much would have been different. We can never rerun historical experience to measure cause and effect in any exact sense, but it is difficult to think that the coming of the Industrial Revolution would have been less disruptive without an effective poor law—and it was extraordinarily disruptive even so. Like a vast kaleidoscope, the pattern was dramatically altered, and it is hard to exaggerate the pain this entailed for ordinary people, as some of the stories in this collection exemplify. Even though the Law of Settlement acted as a moderating agent in this era of change, on the individual level it could exacerbate tragedies arising from broken families, unemployment, and poor health.

How representative is this collection of cases? In some respects, it is quite unrepresentative, for in making the selection I favored troubled families, interesting occupations, long-distance migration, and exceptional settlement problems. Yet each case has within it elements that were ordinary at the time. And it is well to remember that variations as well as norms help define the workings of any law or institution.

This book has attempted to show how the pre-1834 poor law worked on the level of the individual who was suddenly confronted with need or with the attentions of parish authorities fearful of that individual's potential need. The conclusions sketched here result from an attempt to see the system from the pauper's perspective and extrapolate probable consequences therefrom, for there is enormous condescension in the view that the poor were wholly passive to their lot, acted on but not acting. The most active petitioner of all those in this collection was Elizabeth Longhorn, who aspired to better things and struggled to achieve them. She was independent, willful, and combative, but it is hard not to admire those qualities in a person whose life was so very much under the control of others.

Yet the very nature of the records biases one toward the record-keepers, the givers of relief. In Harriet Williams's case, for example, one glimpses less the individual herself than those who responded in varying ways to her need—the implicit concern of the Kenton clerk who transcribed her story; the inhumane efficiency of Mr. Bidwill, the professional welfare officer of St. Thomas, Exeter, who had her dumped out of his parish; the parochial mentality of Farmer Pooke of adjoining Exminster, who helped her walk out of his parish; the aversion to unpleasantness of the gentleman in the gig who gave her a ride through Powderham parish, until he realized she was troublesomely ill; and the two laboring men who found her in the road, and instead of passing by took the trouble to borrow a chair in order to bring her to the Dolphin Inn. Perhaps they had heard in Kenton's fine fifteenth-century church the enduring parable of Luke 10: 30–37, but just as likely they were inspired, like the Good Samaritan himself, by a compassion that transcends time, culture, and ideology.

Appendix: Cases Cited

The cases are listed alphabetically according to the principal person concerned (not always the deponent), with the place generally being where the person was at the time, excepting that all parishioners of St. Martin, Vintry, are recorded in that parish.

The abbreviations used below are explained at the start of the Notes.

Addison, William   Lancaster, Lancs., 1817
    CRO/K (KL), WPR/19
Baker, William   Southampton, Hants., 1773
    DRO, 269A/PO46
Barker, Ann   St. Martin-in-the-Fields, Westminster, 1791
    Westminster City Libraries Archives Section, F5074
Bell, Thomas   Reading, Berks., 1826
    GL, MS9047
Bignall, John   Great Stanmore, Mx, 1823
    GLRO (MR), DRO. 14/F2/1
Bracewell, Christopher   Place unknown, ca. 1820
    CRO/K (KL), WPR/19
Bridcutt, Ruth   Bethnal Green Road, L, 1827
    GL, MS4243A
Brooks, Sofia   St. Martin, Ludgate, L, 1775
    GL, MS1331/1
Busby, Simon   Totnes, D, 1830
    DRO, 1579A/B/(7)
Calvin, Ann   Warkleigh, D, 1795
    DRO, 1710A/PO10
Carr, John   GL/SMV, 1820–23
    GL, MS2847
Clarke, Thomas   Great Stanmore, Mx, 1823
    GLRO (MR), DRO. 14/F2/1
Cleghorn, John   GL/SMV, 1815–27
    GL, MS2847
Craddock, Ann   St. Mildred, Poultry, L, 1826
    GL, MS4437
Davey, Josiah   Southampton, Hants., 1856
    DRO, 814A/PO122

Davies, Elizabeth   GL/SMV, 1815–21
    GL, MS2847
Dawe, James   East Budleigh, D, 1818
    DRO, 1180A/PO319
Denty, Thomas   Modbury, D, 1786
    DRO, 269A/PO97
Dixon, Mary   Preston, Lancs., 1822–24
    CRO/K (KL), WPR/19
Dodds, James   Georgenympton, D, 1819
    DRO, 1469A/PO132
East, Samuel   Kenton, D, 1821
    DRO, 70A/PO6004
Edmunds, Rebecca   Kenton, D, 1773
    DRO, 70A/PO6074
Fewings, James   Sampford Courtenay, D, 1822
    DRO, 1232A/PO60
Fewins, James   Exeter, D, 1830
    DRO, 132A/PO157
Fishley, Mary   Shebbear, D, 1800
    DRO, 1097A/PO50
Gillingham, Esther   St. Luke, Chelsea, L, 1793
    GLRO (LR), P74/LUK/15
Godfrey, Ann   Exeter, D, 1784
    DRO, Quarter Sessions Order Bk., 1777–91
Grime, Christopher   Settle, Yorks., 1822
    CRO/K (KL), WPR/19
Hall, James   Kendal, Westmor., 1813
    CRO/K (KL), WPR/19
Hartley, Reuben   GL/SMV, 1815–17
    GL, MS2847
Hathaway, Henry   Harrow-on-the-Hill, Mx, 1790
    GLRO (MR), DRO. 3/F3/2/219
Higgins, Mary   Friern Barnet, Mx, 1810
    GLRO (MR), DRO. 12/1/D2/1
Hutchins, Elizabeth   GL/SMV, 1817–33
    GL, MS2847
James, Frederick   Kenton, D, 1834
    DRO, 70A/PO6299
Johnson, Christopher   Embsay, Yorks., 1812
    CRO/K (KL), WPR/19
Johnstone, William   Great Stanmore, Mx, 1832
    GLRO (MR), DRO. 14/F2/1
Jones, Ann   Friern Barnet, Mx, 1806
    GLRO (MR), DRO. 12/1/D2/1
Jones, Sarah   St. Mildred, Poultry, L, 1825
    GL, MS4437

Keate, John   Chardstock, Dorset, 1709
    DRO, Membury PO2
Kidson, Robert   Place unknown, 1833
    GL, MS8892
Kingston, Francis   Blackawton and Diptford, D, 1790
    DRO, 818A/PO74
Lancaster, Elizabeth   GL/SMV, 1815–17
    GL, MS2847
Lively, Elizabeth   GL/SMV, 1818–22
    GL, MS2847
Loftus, John   Preston, Lancs., 1816
    CRO/K (KL), WPR/19
Longhorn, Elizabeth   Preston, Lancaster, Manchester, Salford, and
    Rochdale, Lancs.; Bradford, Yorks., 1816–24
    CRO/K (KL), WPR/19
Lowry, William   Blackburn, Lancs., 1826
    CRO/K (KL), WPR/19
McCarthy, Daniel   GL/SMV, 1816
    GL, MS2847
Morey, William   Charles, Plymouth, D, 1843
    DRO, 995A/PO247
Morris, Margaret   GL/SMV, 1822–39
    GL, MS2847
Morris, Thomas   GL/SMV, 1816–18
    GL, MS2847
Morton, William   St. Helen, Bishopsgate, L; Dublin, 1740–45
    GL, MS6886
Murray, Michael Frederick   Exeter, D, 1777
    DRO, Quarter Sessions Order Bk., 1777–91
Neek, Sarah   Greenwich Road Academy, L, 1822
    GL, MS9047
The Nelsons   Clayton Heights and Great Horton, Yorks., 1813–35
    CRO/K (KL), WPR/19
Northway, John   Ilsington, D, 1831
    DRO, 122A/PO165–67
Oldfield, John   Sidmouth, D, 1789
    DRO, 1855A/PO28
Peacock, John   GL/SMV, 1815–22
    GL, MS2847
Phillips, Margaret   GL/SMV, 1815–29
    GL, MS2847
Phillips, Phoebe   Liberty of Saffron Hill, Hatton Garden, and Ely
    Rents, Mx, 1797
        Holborn Central Library, Liberty of . . . , Examination Bk., 1793–99
Pine, Thomas   GL/SMV, 1815–27
    GL, MS2847

Pissey, Margaret   Manchester, Lancs., 1828
    GLRO (MR), DRO. 3/F10/1/12
Polyblank, Joseph   West Alvington, D, 1775
    DRO, 818A/PO54
Poole, Sara   Standingstone, Cumbr., 1809
    CRO/K (KL), WPR/19
Radford, James   Tavistock, D, 1826
    DRO, 1579A/B(7)
Randle, John   St. Ethelburga, L, ca. 1821
    GL, MS4243A
Redhead, Margaret   Kendal, Westmor., 1817
    CRO/K (KL), WPR/19
Renur, Richard   Totnes, D, 1828
    DRO, 1579A/B(7)
Resonel, John   Preston, Lancs., 1817
    CRO/K (KL), WPR/19
Rowe, Elizabeth   Marystow, D, 1786
    DRO, Plymouth Branch, P.890/143
Rowe, Samuel   Modbury, D, ca. 1816
    DRO, 269A/PO110
Ryde, Denny   Ashburton, D, 1832
    DRO, 1518A, add 2–3/PO55
Salked, George   Manchester, Lancs., 1824
    CRO/K (KL), WPR/19
Sanders, Alexander   St. George the Martyr, Southwark, L, 1806–27
    GLRO (LR), P92/GEO/23
Savage, Mary   GL/SMV, 1818–29
    GL, MS2847
Shaw, William   South Molton, D, 1829
    DRO, 1262M/Z16
Smith, John William   GL/SMV, 1817–18
    GL, MS2847
Smith, William   Lombard Street, L, 1822–25
    GL, MS9047
Stevenson, Charlotte   GL/SMV, 1816
    GL, MS2847
Swinney, Mary   GL/SMV, 1815–19
    GL, MS2847
Taylor, Sarah Ann   St. Leonard, Shoreditch, L, 1832
    GLRO (LR), P91/LEN/1250
Thomas, Thomas   East Budleigh, D, 1793
    DRO, 1180A/PO247
Thompson, Mary   St. Leonard, Shoreditch, L, 1805
    GLRO (LR), P91/LEN/1217
Thorne, Samuel   GL/SMV, 1817–20
    GL, MS2847

Toms, Margaret   St. Leonard, Shoreditch, L, 1800
  GLRO (LR), P91/LEN/1216
Tooke, Elizabeth   St. Mary le Strand, Mx, and Westminster, 1799
  Westminster City Library Archives Section, G1017
Tooley, Jonathan   St. Leonard, Shoreditch, L, 1784
  GLRO (LR), P91/LEN/1208
Torr, Jane   Kenton, D, 1798
  DRO, 70A/PO6167
Truck, John   Bodmin, Cornwall, 1817
  DRO, 1180A/PO315
Tucker, Charles   Kenton, D, 1825
  DRO, 70A/PO6254
Wadland, Joseph   Sampford Peverell, D, 1762
  DRO, 1198a A/PO88
Wallbank, Martha   St. Ethelburga, Bishopsgate, L, 1857
  GL, MS4243A
Warren, William   Kenton, D, 1827
  DRO, 70A/PO6263
Welch, Sarah   Harrow-on-the-Hill, Mx, 1783
  GLRO (MR), DRO. 3/F3/2/199
Wilkinson, Agnes   Waddington, Yorks., 1826
  CRO/K (KL), WPR/19
Williams, Harriet   Kenton, D, 1829
  DRO, 70A/PO6283
Williams, Mary   Sidmouth, D, 1834
  DRO, 1855A/PO28
Young, Susannah   GL/SMV, 1815–19
  GL, MS2847

Notes

The following abbreviations are used for documents:

CRO/K (KL)   Cumbria County Record Office, Kendal, Kirkby Lonsdale
D   Devon
DRO   Devon Record Office
GL   Guildhall Library, London
GL/SMV   Guildhall Library, London, St. Martin, Vintry
GLRO (LR)   Greater London Record Office (London Records)
GLRO (MR)   Greater London Record Office (Middlesex records)
L   London
Mx   Middlesex

Books listed in the bibliography are cited in shortened form below.

Chapter 1

1. Bodkin, *Brief Observations*, pp. 35–36.

2. Blackstone, *Commentaries*, 1:127; see 39 Elizabeth, *cap.* 3 (1598); and 43 Elizabeth, *cap.* 2 (1601).

3. The civil parish was the usual unit of poor law administration, but in northern England townships exercised this function, recognized by 13 & 14 Charles II, *cap.* 12 (1662), and there were at different times and places various unions and divisions of local government entities for poor law purposes. Whatever the arrangement, the word generally used to define the basic unit of poor law administration was *parish*.

4. I am very grateful to Joan Sinar for bringing Kenton's exceptional collection to my attention in 1962; she was at that time the County Archivist of Devon. All examinees, deponents, and petitioners in this and subsequent chapters are listed alphabetically, with provenance, in the Appendix.

5. Samuel Banfill, *Report of an Attempt Made in the Parish of St. Thomas . . . for the Better Relief and Employment of the Poor . . .* (Exeter, 1828).

6. Gamlingay Poor Book, Cambridge County Record Office (no specific reference when viewed in 1967). E. M. Hampson noted a "spontaneous increase in kindliness," especially in settlement matters, as the century progressed (*The Treatment of Poverty in Cambridgeshire*, Cambridge, Eng., 1934, p. 102). Such assessments are necessarily impressionistic.

7. DRO, Farway, Overseers' Account Book, 1826–36, 25 Mar. 1827, 67A/PO18.

8. Clark, "Migration," pp. 72 and 77, respectively. Robert W. Malcolmson writes: "For most people mobility was a normal expectation" (*Life and Labour in England, 1700–1780*, New York, 1981, p. 74). This was certainly no less true of the early nineteenth century.

9. Charles Tilly, "Migration in Modern European History," in *Human Migration: Patterns and Policies*, ed. William H. McNeill and Ruth S. Adams (Bloomington, Ind., 1978), p. 68.

10. A statute of 1743 provided that if the mother of a child born in a state of vagrancy had been detained and conveyed to a justice of the peace, the child would take its mother's settlement (17 George II, *cap.* 5).

11. See the dooms of Hlothaere and Eadric (685–86), Wihtraed (695), and Ine (688–95). Vagrants in Fewings's time could be imprisoned and whipped and even transported for multiple offenses. For further discussion, see Chapter 4.

12. Bott, *Laws Relating to the Poor*, 2:482.

13. 8 & 9 William III, *cap.* 30 (1697). For Charles Wilson's discussion of social mercantilism, see "The Other Face of Mercantilism," *Transactions of the Royal Historical Society*, 5th ser., 9 (1959): 81–101. The key settlement statutes were 12 Richard II, *cap.* 3 and *cap.* 7 (1388) for the earliest statutory provisions; 13 & 14 Charles II, *cap.* 12 (1662) for the explicit power of parish officers to remove sojourners even on suspicion of future chargeability; 4 William & Mary, *cap.* 11 (1691) for settlements by merit; 35 George III, *cap.* 101 (1795) for restricting removal to those in health and actually chargeable; and 4 & 5 William IV, *cap.* 76 (1834), which simplified settlement, complicated removal, and pointed the way toward determining settlement on the basis of residence. A fuller analysis of them may be found in my article, "Impact of Pauper Settlement," pp. 47–54.

14. Smith, *Wealth of Nations*, pp. 69–76; Jeremy Bentham, "Fragment on Settlement," 1786, University College, London, Bentham MS, box cli/16.

15. Marshall, *English Poor*, p. 248.

16. David Ashforth, Michael Rose, and others have argued that the 1834 act did not significantly change settlement law. The difference in view may be principally one of perspective. A focus on the years immediately before and after 1834, with an eye to practice and to legislation still to come, could lead one to question the 1834 act's significance; for such a view, see Michael E. Rose, ed., *The Poor and the City: The English Poor Law in Its Urban Context, 1834–1914* (New York, 1985), pp. 8, 61–62. However, if one looks at the long history of settlement law and practice, the 1834 act's changes are more likely to seem like a significant turning point.

17. 19 Henry VII, *cap.* 12 (1503–4); 39 & 40 Victoria, *cap.* 61 (1876). The first act differed in making birth coequal with residence in determining settlement. See also *Poor Laws*, Sel. Cttee. Rep.; 1817 (462), vi, 26–27.

Chapter 2

1. GLRO (LR), St. Luke, Chelsea, Minutes of Committee, 1793–96, 26 Aug. 1794, P74/LUK/15; DRO, Merton, Settlement Examinations, 1779–1850, entry for 26 July 1802, 2044A/PO351.

2. GLRO (LR), St. Leonard, Shoreditch, Settlement and Bastardy Examinations, 1813–32, P91/LEN/1250.

3. *London Parishes . . . within the Bills of Mortality* (London, 1824), pp. 128–31.

4. There is no doubt that marriage often triggered the interest of parish officers in sojourners' settlements, although John Bartlett's parish diplomatically examined him on the day *following* his marriage (Wiltshire Record Office, Purton, Settlement Examinations, 1785–1813, entry for 21 Mar. 1809, 336/44–32).

5. The Caledonia School may have been the "Caledonian Asylum for Educating and Supporting such Children of Soldiers, Sailors, and Marines, natives of Scotland, as cannot be admitted into the Royal Institutions of Chelsea and Greenwich." Johnstone's child does not appear to have met the requirements of the institution, but I can find no reference to another Caledonia School in London at that time. There were, however, many blue-coat schools, here and elsewhere in England, so called from the almoner's blue coat. The particular one meant in this instance is not clear; possibly it was at Christ's Hospital. Blue-coat schools were for charity children.

6. At the time, the Great House, later known as Hill House, was caught up in a complicated estate settlement that went to Chancery, and it was available for renting. I owe this information to Ann Crawford, assistant archivist at the GLRO (MR) in 1972, when I came across the Johnstone case.

7. DRO, Ilsington, Settlement Papers, 1775–1848, entry for 28 Apr. 1812, 122A/PO74.

8. London settlement examinations often contain references to a wedding "in the liberty of the Fleet," a favorite resort of the bigamist since marriages could be entered upon easily there. 35 George III, *cap.* 67 (1795) reduced the crime of bigamy from a felony, as established by 1 James I, *cap.* 11 (1603), to larceny because the harsher penalty had led to poor enforcement.

9. GLRO (LR), St. Leonard, Shoreditch, Settlement and Bastardy Examinations, 1783–88, entry for 3 Nov. 1784, P91/LEN/1208.

10. GLRO (MR), Harrow-on-the-Hill, Settlement Papers, 1697–1849, entry for 11 May 1789, DRO3/F3/2/215.

11. GL, St. Mary, Aldermary, Miscellaneous Papers, 1728–1833, entries for 13 Nov.–13 Dec. 1823, MS9047.

12. GL, St. Mildred, Poultry, Paupers' Examination Book, 1812–58, MS4437.

13. GLRO (MR), Harrow-on-the-Hill, Miscellaneous Poor Law Records, entries for 25 Aug. 1829 and 5 Sept. 1829, DRO3/F10/1/13.

14. See Snell, *Annals*, pp. 78–79.

15. This was true even for foreigners. As Chief Justice Ellenborough said in *King* vs. *Eastbourne* (1803): "The law of humanity, which is anterior to all positive laws, obliges us to afford [foreigners] relief, to save them from starving; and [settlement] laws were only passed to fix the obligation more certainly, and point out distinctly in what manner it should be borne" (Burn, *Justice of the Peace and Parish Officer*, 3:546). Needless to say, theory did not always accord with practice.

16. Sidney and Beatrice Webb defined the Old Poor Law as the "relief of the poor within a framework of repression" (*Old Poor Law*, p. 396). That is a distortion. "Paternalism," not "repression," is the *mot juste*. Of course, paternalism can be repressive or benevolent, or both at the same time, and so indeed it was with the Old Poor Law, whose implementation varied with time, locality, and circumstance.

Chapter 3

1. DRO, West Alvington, In-house Poor Account Books, 1765–93, 818A/PO1-3. Like Kenton, this parish has an exceptionally full collection of records relating to poor law administration, and like Kenton, it was first brought to my attention by Joan Sinar.

2. Out of 985 settlement examinations sampled for this purpose, taken from twenty parishes in six counties, 679 had either a hiring and service or an apprenticeship as the basis of the settlement. Specially printed forms were used by some parishes specifically for hiring and service settlements. E. M. Hampson found in a sample from early eighteenth-century Cambridge that 221 out of 499 cases involved a hiring and service ("Settlement and Removal," p. 279). In 1828 the Select Committee on the Law of Parochial Settlements found annual hirings "the most prominent and frequent cause of litigation" (*Poor Laws*, Sel. Cttee. Rep.; 1828 [406], iv, 201). Almost every knowledgeable contemporary singled out hiring and service settlements as giving "rise to the most numerous and complicated questions of law and fact"; the words are Michael Nolan's, perhaps the leading early nineteenth-century authority on settlement (*Speech*, p. 59). Little wonder that this form of settlement was abolished by the 1834 Poor Law Amendment Act. L. Bradley discovered from a sample of 3,200 removal orders between 1720 and 1834 that married men were especially vulnerable, particularly when they had families to support ("Derbyshire Quarter Sessions Rolls, Poor Law Removal Orders," *Derbyshire Miscellany* 6, pt. 4 [1972]: 106). See also my article, "Impact of Pauper Settlement," for a discussion of the grounds for settlement and removal.

3. Renting was undoubtedly the easiest way to arrange a settlement (except perhaps settlement by marriage), for all manner of tenements qualified, and multiple rentings in more than one parish could be combined to reach the £10 rental, settlement being in the parish where one rented and also resided. Although parish authorities and landlords did

exercise prudence (and doubtless this settlement provision often kept rents lower than they otherwise might have been), it was still possible for the canny sojourner to achieve settlement before overseers and other ratepayers were aware of what had happened. 59 George III, *cap.* 50 (1819) tightened up many of the conditions, however, and in particular required a full year's residence in the parish in which one rented.

4. A trial period was a standard precaution. George Rixon was bound apprentice in 1798 by St. Luke, Chelsea, to Mr. James Pierson, captain of the *Eagle*, a collier, with a fee of £4, but only "after having had a trial voyage & approves of his situation." Joseph Carter, ribbon weaver in the same parish, acquired James Sheffield, aged about ten, as his apprentice in 1795 because the boy "wants to go and Carter likes him." Even so, there was to be a month's trial. GLRO (LR), St. Luke, Chelsea, Minutes of Committee, entries for 1 Sept. 1795 and 26 June 1798, respectively, P74/LUK/15. Quite apart from humane considerations, if any, it was simply common sense to arrange apprenticeships that had some chance of succeeding in order to lessen the likelihood of future dependency.

5. See Jonas Hanway, *The State of Chimney-Sweepers' Young Apprentices* (London, 1773); and idem, *Sentimental History of Chimney Sweepers in London and Westminster* (London, 1785); see also David Porter, *Considerations on the Present State of Chimney Sweepers* (London, 1792). Hanway and Porter inspired a 1788 statute to regulate such apprenticeships; Shaftesbury's Act of 1875 abolished them. The subject is explored in my biography, *Jonas Hanway* (London, 1985), pp. 118–22, 169–70.

6. Bott, *Laws Relating to the Poor*, 2:197.

7. GLRO (LR), St. Luke, Chelsea, Minutes of Committee, entry for 19 Aug. 1794, P74/LUK/15.

8. DRO, Totnes, Settlement Examinations, 1821–38, entry for 28 June 1826, 1579A/B(7).

9. GLRO (LR), St. Leonard, Shoreditch, Settlement and Bastardy Examinations, 1797–1802, entry for 18 Aug. 1798, P91/LEN/1216.

10. DRO, Kenton, Settlement Examinations, 1731–1834, entry for 1833 [day and month left blank], 70A/PO6286.

11. DRO, Chagford, Settlement Papers, 1798–1848, PO143.

12. The relevant excerpt may be found in Carl Stephenson and Frederick George Marcham, eds., *Sources of English Constitutional History* (New York, 1937), p. 710.

13. The most prolific eighteenth-century writer on the problems of domestic servants was Jonas Hanway, in such works as *Eight Letters to His Grace, Duke of [Newcastle]* (London, 1760); *The Sentiments and Advice of Thomas Trueman, a Virtuous and Understanding Footman* (London, 1760); and *Virtue in Humble Life* (London, 1774). Hanway specifically railed against the impediments to marriage for domestic servants, partly because this contributed to immorality and partly because it checked population growth. For a history of domestic service, see J. Jean Hecht,

The Domestic Servant Class in Eighteenth-Century England (London, 1956).
No one, to my knowledge, has assessed the special problems domestic
servants encountered with the Law of Settlement.

14. A young male or female servant might be more highly rewarded
at the outset of service than in later years, judging by the declining value
of contracts found in some examinations. This could reflect a servant's
references or a truer appreciation of his abilities, but it could also reflect
the demand for handsome young male and female servants. Not all
domestic servants became old retainers, and, of course, many of them
viewed service as a transition between youth and the real business of
life, which involved marriage and family.

Chapter 4

1. Cholwich served as sheriff of Devon in 1781 and mayor of Tiver-
ton in 1800 and was a good example of the Georgian gentry. See W. G.
Hoskins, "Three Studies in Family History," in *Devonshire Studies*, ed.
W. G. Hoskins and H. P. R. Finberg (London, 1952), pp. 78–94.

2. The right of irremovability until chargeable was accorded cer-
tificated persons in 1697; mariners and soldiers exercising a trade in
1757; gatekeepers on turnpike roads in 1773; all members of the armed
services and their families, including militiamen, in 1784; members of
benefit societies in 1793; and everyone else in 1795. In this case veterans
merely enjoyed a right a few years in advance of the majority of the
poor.

3. *An Analytical Digest of All the Reported Cases Determined by the High
Court of Admiralty of England, the Lords Commissioners of Appeal in Prize
Cases* (Harrisburg, Pa., 1848), pp. 454–55. There is no record of the brig
Speedwell in Public Record Office, *High Court of Admiralty: Index to Prize
Papers, 1739–1748* (London, 1973).

4. GL, St. Helen, Bishopsgate, Vestry Book, 1720–65, MS 6846/2.

5. GL, St. Michael, Crooked Lane, Settlement Examinations, entry
for 22 Nov. 1818, MS2776.

6. The same ship on which Elizabeth Terry's uncommunicative husband had served; see Chapter 2.

7. Thomas Walter Williams, *A Compendious and Comprehensive Law
Dictionary* (London, 1816), unpaginated, under "Impressment."

8. DRO, Northam, Settlement Papers, 1771–1835, entry for 1834 [day
and month not given], 1843A/PO28. 2 & 3 Anne, *cap.* 6 (1705) protected
parish apprentices from impressment until age eighteen; by the same
act a voluntary binding to sea service brought a three-year exemption
from impressment. This was amended by Anne, *cap.* 19 (1705), since the
earlier exemption was "manifestly abused," by making all exemptions
end at age eighteen. But then 13 George II, *cap.* 17 (1740) gave landsmen
serving on merchant ships exemption for three years, and 2 George III,
cap. 15 (1761) protected apprentices in fishing vessels to age twenty

(with some limitations regarding the number of apprentices and the size of vessel). The maze of regulations was doubtless ignored on countless occasions, but the legal protection of youthful sea apprentices appears to have been sufficiently respected by impressment officers to make sea apprenticeships attractive insurance for masters and apprentices.

9. DRO, Kenton, Settlement Examinations, 1731–1834, entry for 8 July 1834, 70A/PO6294.

10. Slack, "Vagrants and Vagrancy," pp. 364, 368.

11. DRO, Quarter Sessions, Book of Sessions Orders, 1777–1835. The cost and difficulty of conveying vagrants to Exeter from Plymouth meant that only a fraction of those apprehended were ever tried; a problem discussed by J. J. Chapman, in *Poor Laws*, R. Com. Rep.; 1834 (44), xxviii, 457.

12. The passing of Irish sojourners was made legal only in 1819, and it was generally as vagrants that the Irish were returned to their native island. There was, indeed, a well-developed system for sending them back, with considerable evidence of collusion on the part of those Irish migratory laborers who wanted free passage home. See Mark Neuman, *The Speenhamland County: Poverty and the Poor Laws in Berkshire* (New York, 1982), pp. 45–46, for a discussion of Irish migratory labor (Berkshire was a principal route of passage). For interesting testimony on deporting the Irish to Ireland, see *On the Laws Relative to the Passing of Poor Persons Born in Ireland to Their Own Country*, Sel. Cttee. Rep.; 1833 (394), xvi.

Chapter 5

1. DRO, Plymouth Branch, Marystow, Settlement Papers, P890/143.

2. 17 George II, *cap.* 5 (1744). Requiring the poor to wear a special badge, known as "badging" (8 & 9 William III, *cap.* 30 [1697]), is another example of legislation that local authorities widely ignored.

3. After 35 George III, *cap.* 101 (1795), no person could be removed unless actually chargeable and in sufficient health to travel, except those judged to be persons of ill-repute (by one or more witnesses before two or more magistrates) and pregnant, unmarried women.

4. DRO, Kenton, Overseers' Accounts, 1816–22, 70A/PO7.

5. The legal responsibility of grandparents, parents, and children was assigned by 43 Eliz., *cap.* 2 (1601) and complemented by 59 George III, *cap.* 12 (1819), which gave overseers the right to seize goods belonging to the deserting parent or spouse and to apply the same to the family's benefit.

6. DRO, Cheriton Bishop, Overseers' Accounts and Rates, and Settlement Papers, 1738–1917, entry for 1 Oct. 1833, 132A/PO160.

7. GL, St. Mary, Aldermary, Miscellaneous Papers, 1728–1833, entry dated 5 June 1827, MS9047.

8. See note 3 to this chapter.

9. The parish vestry got around to deciding only in 1830 that any occupier taking an apprentice from *outside* the parish would be penalized by forthwith having to take an additional parish apprentice, that is, a pauper's child, from within the parish. DRO, Cheriton Bishop, Vestry Minutes, 1822–46, entry for 25 Mar. 1830, PO1. This was a common policy elsewhere to discourage masters from providing settlements by apprenticeship to sojourners. The masters' incentives to do so, if not humanitarian or familial, were the subsidies that parishes were willing to pay in order to have their poor children earn settlements in other parishes.

10. As in the case of Chagford. DRO, Chagford, Vestry Minutes, 1825–39, entry for 18 Nov. 1830, PP1.

11. Of the 1,399 patients discharged between 1787 and 1788, 1,013 were listed as cured, 168 as "benefited," 26 as incapable of further relief, and 30 as having died; the remainder were released for various reasons (e.g., discharged for irregular conduct or at their own request). See DRO, Devon and Exeter Hospital, "Patients' Journals," 1753–1860 (with gaps), 1260F/HR 1–10. Admittedly, this was a good period for the hospital. Even so, and allowing for judicious admissions and discharges, the record suggests success. The figures given here are from Lady Day (Mar. 25) to Lady Day, a traditional end and beginning in English local records of the time. Medical relief under the pre-1834 poor law is an important subject deserving more research. For additional information on the Devon and Exeter Hospital, see John Caldwell, "Notes on the History of Dean Clarke's Hospital, 1741–1948," *Transactions of the Devonshire Association* 104 (1972): 175–92.

12. The Court of King's Bench was quicker to act in cases of apparent fraud in the early eighteenth century, but became increasingly reluctant to enter the thickets of conflicting testimony. Bott wrote in 1800: "When a case is pregnant with circumstances of fraud the Court has repeatedly said they cannot infer fraud; that fraud is a fact to be expressly stated" (*Laws Relating to the Poor*, 2:149). But cf. *Cases and Resolutions of Cases*, p. 2.

13. DRO, Ilsington, Settlement Papers, 122A/PO165–67.

Chapter 6

1. Several paupers were displaced in consequence of "the Southwark Bridge Act of Parliament driving the people out of the houses and tenements authorized to be taken down" (GL, St. Martin, Vintry, "Examination of the Poor," 1815–29, entry for Ann Plinth's report, 1816, MS2847; all cases included in this chapter are taken from this source). According to a survey conducted by the Company of Parish Clerks in 1732, the parish at that time had 140 houses; 90 years later only 60 houses remained. Between 1801 and 1831 the population of the parish was halved. See *New Remarks of London* (London, 1732), pp. 94–96;

and *Population*, Accounts and Papers; 1831 (348), xviii: 164, respectively. These statistics give a clear illustration of the depopulation generally occurring within London's walls and in this particular case the consequences of anchoring a large bridge in a small parish.

2. Bear Lane was the location of Showel's (also spelled Showell's) Workhouse, in an area of Southwark once noted for blood sports and theaters. Showel's was apparently a private workhouse and was used by other City parishes as well. In 1742 St. Martin, Vintry, had possessed its own workhouse, as well as thirteen almshouses, the latter reputed to be the benefactions of Sir Richard Whittington, better known for his cat. However, by 1777 the parish had taken to contracting (farming) the care of its poor to an establishment at Mile End. By 1815 the parish had instituted a new arrangement, relying on outdoor relief (i.e., relief given outside of the workhouse), most of it alloted to persons living outside the parish, with the workhouse in Bear Lane being used for those who could not care for themselves and for the ablebodied poor the parish wished to discipline. For earlier information on the care of the poor of St. Martin, Vintry, see *New Remarks of London* (London, 1732), pp. 94–96; and *Poor Laws*, Cttee. Rep.; 1777 (34), iv, 48–49.

3. Founded by Thomas White and chartered in 1626, Sion College had two principal purposes: to bring the London clergy together (a library was one aspect of the association) and to assist the poor through the provision of almshouses.

4. GL, St. Michael, Royal, Vestry Minutes, 1774–1827, entry for 26 July 1816, 601/2. St. Martin, Vintry, held occasional united vestry meetings with its neighbor to the north, whose church it had shared, since the church of St. Martin, Vintry, had burned in the Great Fire of 1666 and had not been rebuilt. The memorial was originally addressed to "the Gentlemen of the Inquest of the Wards of Vintry and Dowgate," but this designation was crossed out in the document, and it appears to have been sent to all landholders, leaseholders, and inhabitants of both wards.

5. GL/SMV, "Examination of Poor," entry for Mary "Carty," 13 Sept. 1816. Until 59 George III (1819), *cap.* 12, Irish and Scottish sojourners could not be removed unless they were convicted of vagrancy. This usually meant they had been caught begging. The 1819 act gave magistrates discretionary power to remove those who were chargeable, whether or not they were adjudged to be vagrants. In fact, local authorities had always had considerable discretion in determining who was to be removed, but the removal of ablebodied Irish and Scottish sojourners who were willing to work was not generally considered the cheapest and least troublesome alternative.

6. Bodkin, *Brief Observations*, p. 6.

7. Sir John Fellowes, Bt. (ca. 1671–1724), subgovernor of the South Sea Company, was disgraced in the 1720 Bubble scandal in which ill-founded faith in the company's future created a mania of specula-

tion. Important people were implicated in corrupt practices, losing both money and reputation. Sir Robert Walpole came to power by riding out the crisis and protecting some of those who were involved, but Fellowes was thrown to the wolves; the House of Commons forced him to forfeit £240,000 of his personal estate, leaving him with only £10,000. Even so, he managed to establish a small endowed charity to provide £10 a year for the purpose of apprenticing poor boys. In this case, both Mary and John Savage appear to have been beneficiaries of this charity. I am indebted to James Tyler, Rare Books Assistant at Cornell University, for guidance in discovering this obscure charity.

8. GL, St. Michael, Royal, Vestry Minutes, 1774–1827, MS601/2.

9. Francis Sheppard, *London, 1808–1870: The Infernal Wen* (Berkeley, Calif., 1971), pp. 19–22.

10. GL/SMV, Vestry Minutes, 1743–1829, entries for 1813, 1814, and 1815, MS606/1; *Poor Laws*, Accounts and Papers; 1818 (82), xix, 636. It is possible, of course, that if figures were available for both the parish and the nation in earlier or later years, the relative costs of settlement in this comparison might be substantially different. Indeed, the reports, which begin in 1815, may have been an attempt to curb administrative costs. Nevertheless, it is highly probable that small urban parishes generally faced exceptional problems in coping with the complex Law of Settlement and that this was reflected in disproportionately higher expenditures for visiting the poor outside the parish, removal expenses, and litigation.

Chapter 7

1. "An Account of Westmorland," *New Universal Magazine* 97 (Nov. 1795): 337.

2. Joseph Nicolson and Richard Burn, *The History and Antiquities of the Counties of Westmorland and Cumberland* (London, 1777): 1:224. Kirkby Lonsdale continued to grow in the early nineteenth century, from 1,283 in 1801 to 1,686 in 1831 (*Population*, Accounts and Papers; 1831 [348], xviii, 276).

3. CRO/K (KL), Agreement re union of parishes and use of Kirkby Lonsdale workhouse, 1814, and other related papers, 1810–30, WPR/19.

4. CRO/K (KL), Overseers' Accounts, 1813–22, entry for 29 Sept. 1819, WD/Cr. I am particularly grateful to Sheila MacPherson, Cumbria County Archivist, for her assistance in using the multifarious records of this township.

5. An anonymous justice of the peace for Westmorland and Lancashire called it "that most desirable object, the extension of parochial relief to persons residing *out of* their townships, who are often employed more profitably, and enabled to live more comfortably than if they were removed" (*The Names of Parishes and Other Divisions Maintaining Their Poor Separately in the County of Westmorland*, Kendal, 1802, p. iv). Michael

Nolan commented on the general frequency of the practice, based as it was on "principles of humanity" and "mutual advantage," and wanted to make it "legal to a limited extent" (*Speech*, p. 60). (It was not *illegal*, of course, but there was no legal recognition of the practice.) There were, however, those who criticized "the great and constant demand, every town, and manufactury makes upon the neighbouring villages for labourers and servants; who are therefore reared by the latter for the use and enjoyment of the former" (Weyland, *Short Inquiry*, p. 201). Nonresident relief was especially common in the North. Between 1801 and 1831, Westmorland lost 12,491 persons, and the West Riding gained 37,222, and Lancashire, 183,534 (Deane and Cole, *British Economic Growth*, pp. 108–9). There are no figures on the number who migrated in youth and returned to Westmorland later in life. Michael Rose noted the frequency and importance of nonresident relief in the West Riding, concluding that it worked well for all concerned ("The Administration of the Poor Law in the West Riding of Yorkshire [1820–1855]," Ph.D. diss., Oxford, 1965, p. 282). Overseers' letter books for Lancaster, 1809–19 (Lancashire Record Office, ref. PR866), and churchwardens' accounts for Manchester, 1809–48 (City of Manchester, Archives Department, M3/3/4/6A & B), indicate the prevalence of relief to nonresidents.

6. The social composition of the township is profiled in William Parson and William White, *History, Directory, and Gazetteer of the Counties of Cumberland and Westmorland* (Leeds, 1828), pp. 694–95; and its treatment of the poor in Eden, *State of the Poor*, 3:771–76; and *Poor Laws*, R. Comm. Rep.; 1834 (44), xxxv–xxxvi (Appendix B2, "Answers to Town Queries"), 243ff. Apart from material on Garnett in the township's records, there is some information in Edward Bellasis, *Westmorland Church Notes* (Kendal, 1888), 1:92–93; Garnett's will in the Lancashire Record Office (proved 2 Sept. 1840); and the Garnett family tombstone, the best-preserved and most informative one in St. Mary's churchyard, Kirkby Lonsdale.

7. A woman married to a Scot or an Irishman retained her premarital settlement. See Bott, *Laws Relating to the Poor*, 2:82, 84; and Robert Foley, *Laws Relating to the Poor*, 3d ed. (London, 1751), pp. 249–57. An apocryphal case gave rise to a famous catch:

> A woman having a settlement
> Married a man with none;
> The Question was, He being dead,
> If that she had, was gone?
> Quoth Sir *John Pratt*—Her settlement
> Suspended did remain,
> Living the husband: But, him dead,
> It doth revive again.
> *Chorus of Puisne Judges*—
> Living the husband: But him dead,
> It doth revive again.

Pratt was made Lord Chief Justice in 1718. Burn discusses the matter in

Justice of the Peace and Parish Officer, 3:766–67. In fact, one could legally lose a settlement only by acquiring a new one.

8. William Carus Wilson (1792–1859) was a member of one of Westmorland's most distinguished families. His father lived at Casterton Hall, an estate less than a mile northeast of Kirkby Lonsdale, and in 1825 was MP for Cockermouth, in the Lowther interest. The son, who held a B.A. and M.A. from Cambridge, became rector of Whittington in 1825, the north Lancashire location from whence the allusive Swan came. Carus Wilson became a well-known writer and editor; see his monthly publication, *The Friendly Visitor*, and his lachrymose *Memoir of a Beloved and Long-afflicted Sister* (Kirkby Lonsdale, 1831).

9. CRO/K (KL), Township Letters, 1809–36, letter from Abraham Sedgwick, 25 May 1826, WPR/19.

10. *Annual Register* (1826), pp. 63–65. "At the heart of the class struggle were the handloom weavers," Paul Richards writes ("The State and Early Industrial Capitalism: The Case of the Handloom Weavers," *Past & Present*, no. 83 [May 1979]: 92).

11. See the Conclusion.

12. According to Mr. Brett Harrison, Leeds District Archives, Ruth was the widow of John Nelson, Joseph's son by an earlier marriage, and sister-in-law to Betty. Harrison has made a detailed study of the Nelsons and of Kirkby Lonsdale's records.

13. The sketch of the Nelsons is based on 103 letters in the collection relating to the various branches of this family, supplemented by the overseers' accounts and settlement papers of Kirkby Lonsdale.

14. Some of the items in the collection are anonymous or otherwise obscure, making a precise tally of the township's sojourners impossible.

15. The settlement case was found in an uncatalogued box of miscellaneous records, CRO/K (KL), WPR/19, supplemented by otherwise uninterpretable entries in the overseers' accounts.

16. I am currently editing a more extensive collection of the exceptionally full records of this township.

Conclusion

1. T. S. Ashton, *The Industrial Revolution* (London, 1948), p. 110; Pauline Gregg, *A Social and Economic History of Britain, 1760–1972*, 7th ed. (London, 1973), p. 31; Asa Briggs, *The Age of Improvement* (New York, 1959), p. 59; Peter Laslett, *The World We Have Lost*, 3d ed. (London, 1984), p. 34.

2. E. P. Thompson, in *The Making of the English Working Class* (New York, 1963), scarcely mentioned settlement, except in a passing reference to the edge it gave the Irish in the industrial labor market by inhibiting the mobility of English laborers (p. 223). Probably the more important contribution of the settlement system was to provide relief to the Irish resident in England of a casual, yet extensive, nature and

to give them the opportunity to acquire settlements, most importantly through renting and through marriage. Hobsbawm has seen the settlement laws in conjunction with Speenhamland as pauperizing, demoralizing, and immobilizing, but gives settlement peripheral attention in *Industry and Empire* (London, 1968), p. 84.

3. Smith, *Wealth of Nations*, p. 176.

4. Blackstone, *Commentaries*, 1:130, 362.

5. E. A. Wrigley, "The Growth of Population in Eighteenth-Century England: A Conundrum Resolved," *Past & Present*, no. 98 (Feb. 1983): 136, 148.

6. As quoted in Patricia James, *Population Malthus: His Life and Times* (London, 1979), p. 450. James P. Huzel has argued that the poor law did not promote population growth, and he may be correct, but the subject requires further study. Huzel's are perceptive studies, but he relies too heavily on the impact of the allowance system, builds on an unrepresentative parish (Barham, which Jonas Hanway considered a model parish), neglects recent literature relevant to the subject, and concludes too much; see his "Malthus, the Poor Law and Population in Early Nineteenth-Century England," *Economic History Review*, 2d ser., 22 (1969): 430–52; and "The Demographic Impact of the Old Poor Law: More Reflections on Malthus," *Economic History Review*, 2d ser., 23 (1980): 367–81.

7. The idea that the poor law aided political stability is old and is to be found in writings of the time, such as Jonas Hanway's *Letters on the Importance of the Rising Generation* (London, 1767), 1:172; and in later studies, such as E. M. Leonard's *Early History of English Poor Relief*, pp. vii–viii. The many fruitful studies of French social-welfare history by Olwen Hufton, Cissie C. Fairchilds, Colin Jones, and others help place British welfare history in clearer perspective. Of course, "the poor law as antidote to revolution" is, of its nature, an unprovable view and runs counter to some powerfully held convictions about the social effects of industrialism. One might argue that the pre-1834 poor law ought not to have been parochially based, so that settlement could have been greatly simplified in a regional or national context, but that is anachronistic and takes no account of what was possible for that time and society.

8. Lis and Soly, *Poverty and Capitalism*, pp. 221–22.

9. Davison, *Considerations on the Poor Laws*, p. 85.

10. Barrington Moore, Jr., in *Social Origins of Dictatorship and Democracy* (Boston, 1966), notes the sorts of persons who migrated from rural to urban England (p. 27), but not the role of the welfare system in the process. Surely the Third World gives ample evidence of the frightful problems accompanying an urban revolution that is out of pace not only with economic growth but with provisions for social welfare.

11. See B. A. Holderness, " 'Open' and 'Close' Parishes in England in the Eighteenth and Nineteenth Centuries," *Agricultural History Review* 20 (1972): 126–39. This excellent article provides evidence undermining

the importance of the distinction between the two sorts of parishes, but suggests that the problem was most common in Lincolnshire and neighboring counties. It may indeed have been a factor with some regional significance.

12. *An Ease for Overseers of the Poor* (Cambridge, Eng., 1601), p. 26.

13. A compelling instance of the commissioners' neglect of evidence lies in the lack of interest their respondents to "Rural Queries" and "Town Queries" showed in creating larger units of poor law administration, which was the principal direction of the New Poor Law. Of 1,470 returns to "Rural Queries," only 16 percent favored *any* change in units of poor law administration. There was more interest in the towns, but even there, only a quarter of the 581 respondents favored a change. See *Poor Laws*, R. Comm. Rep.; 1834 (44), xxxiv–v, queries 52 and 14 respectively.

14. Anthony Brundage, *The Making of the New Poor Law* (New Brunswick, N.J., 1978), p. 182.

15. Outdoor relief (relief given outside of workhouses) and family allowances were common under the pre-1834 poor law, but "Speenhamland" implies a systematic subsidization of laborers according to a scale adjusted to the size of their families and the price of bread. For further discussion, see Mark Blaug, "The Myth of the Old Poor Law and the Making of the New," *Journal of Economic History* 23 (1963): 151–84; my critique, "The Mythology of the Old Poor Law," *Journal of Economic History* 29 (1969): 292–97; and D. A. Baugh, "The Cost of Poor Relief in South-East England, 1790–1834," *Economic History Review*, 2d ser., 28 (1975): 50–68.

Bibliography

The first section of this Bibliography lists a few contemporary pamphlets and some of the most important legal treatises, casebooks, and parliamentary papers. The edition cited is the one used in the Notes, but much can be learned from using various editions of a Bott or a Burn. Unless otherwise noted, the place of publication for these works is London.

The second section is a highly selective list of twentieth-century works, most of which have direct bearing on settlement law and practice. The Appendix and the Notes give further indication of the research, particularly in archival materials. The Industrial Revolution and the poor laws have inspired a large literature, but no useful purpose would be served by weighting this slender study with a comprehensive guide.

Contemporary Works

Archbold, John Frederick. *The Act for the Amendment of the Poor Laws, with a Practical Introduction, Notes and Forms.* 3d ed. 1835.
———. *The Law Relative to Examinations and Grounds of Appeal in Cases of Orders of Removal, with Forms in All Cases Which Occur in Practice.* 1847.
Blackstone, William. *Commentaries on the Laws of England.* 4 vols. 1765–69.
Bleamire, William. *Remarks on the Poor Laws, and the Maintenance of the Poor . . . .* 1800.
Bodkin, William Henry. *Brief Observations on the Bill Now Pending in Parliament to Amend the Laws Relative to the Relief of the Poor.* 1821.
Bott, Edmund. *The Laws Relating to the Poor, Including the Collections Originally Made by E. Bott, Esq., and Afterwards Edited by F. Const, Esq.* Revised by John Tidd Pratt. 2 vols. 6th ed. 1827. [First published in 1771, with many revisions thereafter, this is a thorough guide to the working of settlement law before 1834.]
Brydges, Sir Egerton. *Letters on the Poor Laws . . . .* 1813.
Burn, Richard. *The History of the Poor Laws, with Observations.* 1764.
———. *The Justice of the Peace and Parish Officer.* 4 vols. 20th ed. 1805. [First published in 1755, this was the guide most widely used by the

poor law authorities of the time, running through 30 editions, the last in 1869. It is extremely helpful for the law and practices, but less so for the history of settlement laws.]

Burrow, James. *A Series of the Decisions of the Court of King's Bench upon Settlement Cases from the Death of Lord Raymond in March 1732.* 2 vols. 1768.

Cases and Resolutions of Cases, Adjudg'd in the Court of King's Bench Concerning Settlements and Removals . . . . 4th ed. 1742.

Colquhoun, Patrick. *A Treatise on Indigence* . . . . 1806.

Dalton, Michael. *The Country Justice.* 5th ed. 1635. [First pub. in 1618.]

Davison, John. *Considerations on the Poor Laws.* 2d ed. 1818.

Eden, Sir Frederic Morton. *The State of the Poor.* 3 vols. 1797.

Great Britain, Parliamentary Papers (in chronological order):

Report from the Committee Appointed to Review and Consider the Several Laws Which Concern the Relief and Settlement of the Poor . . . . 1775 (31), iv. *Second Report* . . . . 1775 (32), iv.

Report from the Select Committee on the Poor Laws. 1817 (462), vi.

Report from the Select Committee on the Law of Parochial Settlements. 1828 (406), iv.

Report from His Majesty's Commissioners for Inquiring into the Administration and Practical Operation of the Poor Laws. 1834 (44), xxvii–xxxviii. [There are interesting differences between the slender 1834 *Report* (xxvii) and the many volumes of evidence that accompanied it; the first is useful for opinion, and the second for practices and the views of local administrators of the poor law.]

Report of George Coode, Esq. to the Poor Law Board, on the Law of Settlement and Removal of the Poor . . . . 1851 (675), xxvi. [A thorough study, Coode's assessment is radically different from the one presented in this book. Coode established the modern interpretation of the Law of Settlement, used by the Webbs and most later students of the poor law.]

Howlett, the Rev. John. *The Insufficiency of the Causes to Which the Increase of Our Poor and of the Poor's Rates Have Been Commonly Ascribed* . . . . 1788.

Mangin, Edward. *Parish Settlements and Pauperism.* 1828.

Moggridge, J. H. *Remarks on the Report of the Select Committee of the House of Commons on the Poor Laws* . . . . Bristol, 1818.

Nicoll, S. W. *A Summary View of the Report and Evidence Relative to the Poor Laws* . . . . York, 1818.

Nolan, Michael. *The Speech of* . . . , *Delivered in the House of Commons 10 July, 1822.* 1822.

———. *A Treatise of the Laws for the Relief and Settlement of the Poor.* 3 vols. 4th ed. 1825. [First published in 1805, this is perhaps the best guide to settlement laws.]

Phillpotts, the Rev. Henry. *A Letter to the Rt. Hon. William Sturges Bourne,*

M.P., on a Bill Introduced by Him into Parliament . . . . 2d ed. Durham, 1819.

A Plea for the Poor. 1759.

Reasons Humbly Submitted to the Honourable Members of Both Houses of Parliament, for Introducing a Law, to Prevent Unnecessary and Vexatious Removals of the Poor . . . . Cambridge, Eng., 1774.

Smith, Adam. *An Inquiry into the Nature and Causes of the Wealth of Nations*. 1776.

Weyland, John. *A Short Inquiry into the Policy, Humanity, and Past Effects of the Poor Laws*. 1807.

Whitbread, Samuel. *Substance of a Speech on the Poor Laws* . . . . 1807.

White, John Meadows. *Parochial Settlements, an Obstruction to Poor Law Reform*. 1835.

Modern Works

Burnett, John, ed. *Useful Toil: Autobiographies of Working People from the 1820s to the 1920s*. London, 1974.

———. *Destiny Obscure: Autobiographies of Childhood, Education and Family from the 1820s to the 1920s*. London, 1982.

Clark, Peter. "Migration in England During the Late Seventeenth and Early Eighteenth Centuries." *Past & Present*, no. 83 (May 1979): 57–90.

Davey, Herbert. *Poor Law Settlement and Removal*. London, 1908.

Deane, Phyllis, and Cole, W. A. *British Economic Growth*. Cambridge, Eng., 1962.

Fraser, Derek. *The Evolution of the British Welfare State: A History of Social Policy Since the Industrial Revolution*. New York, 1973.

Hampson, Ethel M. "Settlement and Removal in Cambridgeshire, 1662–1834." *Cambridge Historical Journal* 2 (1928): 273–89.

Himmelfarb, Gertrude. *The Idea of Poverty: England in the Early Industrial Age*. New York, 1984.

Holdsworth, W. S. *A History of English Law*. Vols. 4, 6, 10, and 13. London, 1924–52.

Jackson, J. T. "Long-Distance Migrant Workers in Nineteenth-Century Britain: A Case Study of St. Helens' Glassmakers." *Historic Society of Lancashire and Cheshire Transactions* 131 (1981): 113–37.

Landau, Norma. *Justices of the Peace, 1679–1760*. Berkeley, Calif., 1984.

Leonard, E. M. *The Early History of English Poor Relief*. Cambridge, Eng., 1900.

Lis, Catherine, and Soly, Hugo. *Poverty and Capitalism in Pre-Industrial Europe*. Atlantic Highlands, N.J., 1979.

Long, Moira, and Maltby, Betty. "Personal Mobility in Three West Riding Parishes, 1777–1812: Skipton, Addington and Bolton Abbey." *Local Population Studies*, no. 24 (Spring 1980): 13–25.

Marshall, Dorothy. *The English Poor in the Eighteenth Century: A Study in Social and Administrative History*. London, 1926.

Mills, D. R. "Francis Howell's Report on the Operation of the Laws of Settlement in Nottinghamshire, 1848." *Transactions of the Thoroton Society* 76 (1972): 46–52.

———. "The Poor Laws and the Distribution of Population, c. 1600–1860." *Institute of British Geographers Transactions and Papers* 26 (1959): 185–95.

Oxley, Geoffrey W. *Poor Relief in England and Wales, 1601–1834*. Newton Abbot, 1974.

Patten, John. "Rural-Urban Migration in Pre-Industrial England." *Research Papers, School of Geography, University of Oxford*, no. 6 (May 1973).

Pelham, R. A. "The Immigrant Population of Birmingham, 1686–1726." *Transactions of the Birmingham Archaeological Society* 61 (1940): 45–80.

Perkin, Harold. *The Origins of Modern English Society, 1780–1880*. London, 1969.

Poynter, J. R. *Society and Pauperism: English Ideas on Poor Relief, 1795–1834*. London, 1969.

Redford, Arthur. *Labour Migration in England, 1800–50*. 2d ed. Edited and revised by W. H. Chaloner. Manchester, 1964.

Rose, Michael. *The English Poor Law, 1780–1930*. Newton Abbot, 1971.

———. "Settlement, Removal and the New Poor Law." In *The New Poor Law in the Nineteenth Century*. Edited by Derek Fraser. New York, 1976, pp. 25–43.

Slack, Paul A. "Vagrants and Vagrancy in England, 1598–1664." *Economic History Review*, 2d ser. 27 (Aug. 1974): 360–79.

Snell, K.D.M. *Annals of the Labouring Poor: Social Change and Agrarian England, 1660–1900*. Cambridge Studies in Population, Economy and Society in Past Time, vol. 2. London, 1985.

Styles, Philip. "The Evolution of the Law of Settlement." *University of Birmingham Historical Journal* 9 (1963): 33–63.

Taylor, James Stephen. "The Impact of Pauper Settlement, 1691–1834." *Past & Present*, no. 73 (Nov. 1976): 42–74.

Thomas, E. G. "The Poor Law Migrant to Oxford, 1700–1795." *Oxoniensia* 45 (1980): 300–305.

Webb, Sidney, and Beatrice Webb. *English Poor Law History*, Part I, *The Old Poor Law*. English Local Government Series, vol. 7. London, 1927.

Index